Social History of Africa

LIBERATING THE FAMILY?

Social History of Africa Series
Series Editors: Allen Isaacman and Jean Allman

LIBERATING THE FAMILY?

Gender and British Slave Emancipation in the Rural Western Cape, South Africa, 1823–1853

Pamela Scully

HEINEMANN
Portsmouth, NH

JAMES CURREY
Oxford

DAVID PHILIP
Cape Town

Heinemann
A division of Reed Elsevier Inc.
361 Hanover Street
Portsmouth, NH 03801-3912

James Currey Ltd.
73 Botley Road
Oxford OX2 0BS
United Kingdom

David Philip Publishers (Pty) Ltd
PO Box 23408
Claremont 7735
Cape Town, South Africa

Offices and agents throughout the world

The author and publisher thank those who generously gave permission to reprint borrowed material:

Portions of Chapter 7 originally appeared as "Narratives of Infanticide in the Aftermath of Slave Emancipation in the Nineteenth-Century Cape Colony, South Africa" in the *Canadian Journal of African Studies* (30, 1, 1996).

Cover photo: "Genadendal" by George French Angas from the book *The Kafirs illustrated in a series of drawings taken among the Amazulu, Amapondo, and Amakosa tribes . . .* by George French Angas, London: J Hogarth 1849. Courtesy of MuseuMAfricA. Reference No. A131.

ISBN 0-435-07431-8 (Heinemann cloth)
ISBN 0-435-07427-X (Heinemann paper)
ISBN 0-85255-678-0 (James Currey cloth)
ISBN 0-85255-628-4 (James Currey paper)

British Library Cataloguing in Publication Data
Scully, Pamela
  Liberating the family? : gender and British slave
  emancipation in the rural Western Cape, South Africa,
  1823–1853.—(Social history of Africa)
  1. Family—South Africa 2. South Africa—Social conditions
  I. Title
  306.8'5'09687355

  ISBN   0-85255-628-4 paper
          0-85255-678-0 cloth

Library of Congress Cataloging-in-Publication Data
Scully, Pamela.
    Liberating the family? : gender and British slave emancipation in
  the rural Western Cape, South Africa, 1823–1853 / Pamela Scully.
      p.   cm.—(Social history of Africa)
  Includes bibliographical references and index.
    ISBN 0-435-07431-8 (cloth).—ISBN 0-435-07427-X (pbk.)
    1. Slavery—South Africa—Cape of Good Hope—History—19th
  century. 2. Slaves—Emancipation—South Africa—Cape of Good Hope—
  History—19th century. 3. Slaves—South Africa—Cape of Good Hope—
  Social conditions. 4. Cape of Good Hope (South Africa)—Social
  conditions. 5. Social change—South Africa—Cape of Good Hope—
  History—19th century. I. Title. II. Series.
  HT1394.C3S38 1997
  306.3'62'096873—dc21

                                           97-37305
                                              CIP

Cover design by Jenny Jensen Greenleaf
Cover photo: Drawing by George Angas of freed people at Genadendal mission station, c1840s.

Printed in the United States of America on acid-free paper
01 00 99 98 97 DA 1 2 3 4 5 6 7 8 9

To Clifton, and in celebration of Benjamin and Christine

CONTENTS

LIST OF FIGURES AND MAP

ABBREVIATIONS

AG	Attorney General
APS	Assistant Protector of Slaves
ASL	African Studies Library, University of Cape Town
ASMR	*Anti-Slavery Monthly Reporter*
ASR	*Anti-Slavery Reporter*
CA	Cape (Government) Archives, Cape Town
CAL	Caledon
CC	Civil Commissioner
CCP	Cape Colony Publications
CFS	The Children's Friend Society
CGH	Cape of Good Hope
CL	Cory Library, Rhodes University, Grahamstown
CO	Colonial Office
CP	Clerk of the Peace
CSC	Cape Supreme Court
CWM	Council for World Mission
DRC	Dutch Reformed Church
GB	Great Britain
GH	Government House
GL	Green Library, Stanford University
HA	Heideveld archives of the Moravian Church, Cape Town
JL	Jonsson Library, Stanford University
JP	Justice of the Peace
LCA	Clerk of the Legislative Council
LMS	London Missionary Society
PRO	Public Records Office, London
PA	Periodical Accounts
PS	Protector of Slaves
RM	Resident Magistrate
SACA	South African Commercial Advertiser
SAL	South African Library, Cape Town
SG	Secretary to Government
SJ	Special Justice
SM	Special Magistrate
SMS	Stellenbosch Missionary Society
SOAS	School of Oriental and African Studies, University of London
SSC	Secretary of State for Colonies
STB	Stellenbosch
SWM	Swellendam
UCT	University of Cape Town
USSC	Under Secretary of State for Colonies
VOC	Dutch East India Company
WOC	Worcester

ACKNOWLEDGMENTS

The University of Michigan helped change the way I view the world. If this book has anything to offer, it is owing to the stimulating intellectual environment provided by the Departments of History and Anthropology. Ann Stoler's seminars on the historical anthropology of race, sexuality, and colonialism remain a highlight of my years at Michigan and have greatly shaped this thesis. Keletso Atkins and Rebecca Scott introduced me to new ways of thinking about the past and inspired me to try to write a book worthy of their own work. I am grateful to Laura Downs for helping me get to grips with comparative work on gender and labor.

Fred Cooper deserves special mention. Fred was an outstanding advisor. I am most grateful for his ongoing support and friendship, trenchant criticisms, and most of all, for his intellectual curiosity and generosity which made studying with him such an exciting and enjoyable experience.

My undergraduate and early graduate years in the History Department at the University of Cape Town convinced me that I wanted to become an historian. Colin Bundy encouraged me to believe that it was possible. The late Marie Maud and the late Colin Webb made history come alive in ways which inspired my decision to do graduate work in history. Nigel Worden's support of younger scholars in the field of slave studies in South Africa is legendary. I have been inspired both by Nigel's work and by the stimulating courses I took with him in comparative colonialism and slavery.

Kenyon College has provided me with a most supportive environment over a number of years. I am grateful to Cindy Wallace and Carol Marshall of interlibrary loan in the Olin Library. The members of the history department welcomed me into their midst and have made me feel very at home. Thank you all. While I completed research in South Africa the history department at UCT gave me the opportunity to discuss my work. The book benefited greatly from the help of the librarians at the African Studies Library at the University of Cape Town, especially Laureen Rushby. The reading room staff of the Cape Archives were very helpful as were the staff of the South African Library and the Heideveld Theological Seminary. Thanks too to the staff of the Cory Library in Grahamstown for directing me to their holdings on the Methodist Missionary Society. Mr. Isaac Balie helped me locate information and made available early volumes of the *Periodical Accounts* at the wonderful museum he founded at Genadendal. The staff of the Jonsson Library of Government Documents at Stanford University also helped me find sources and provided an excellent working environment.

The research on which this book is based was assisted by a grant from the Joint Committee on African Studies of the Social Science Research Council and the American Council of Learned Societies with funds provided by the Rockefeller Foundation for the 1991–92 academic year. That year I also received funding from the Ford Foundation through the Center for African and Afro-American Studies at the University of Michigan, and from the Center for the Education of Women at Michigan which awarded me a Mary Malcomson Raphael Fellowship. The Rackham Graduate School provided me with funding for the year of writing up in 1992–93. A faculty grant from Kenyon College funded additional research at Stanford Library as did a fellowship from the National Endowment of the Humanities. This grant enabled me to do more research and to spend time turning the original thesis into a book.

I am very grateful for the help of colleagues and friends for their critiques of drafts and their support in helping me finish. Audiences at Carnegie-Mellon, Cincinnati, Emory, Tufts, and Stanford Universities helped me greatly in formulating my arguments. I am most grateful to Chris Schmidt-Nowara, Steve Soper, and Geoff Eley who invited me to participate in the conference on rethinking European liberalism at the University of Michigan in April 1995. The papers and the stimulating discussions greatly helped frame the terms of this book. Kali Israel's comments on the thesis helped me with the revisions for the book. Thanks also to Andrew Bank, Jean Blankenberg, Helen Bradford, Edna Bradlow, Sandra Burman, Wayne Dooling, Marijke du Toit, Madhavi Kale, Catherine Hall, Kirsten McKenzie, Meredith McKittrick, Clare Midgley, M. D. Nash, Sonya Rose, Elaine Unterhalter, Patricia van der Spuy, Elizabeth van Heyningen, and Tom Winslow for sharing their work and pointing me to sources. I am very grateful to Robert Ross who has encouraged me to try to think creatively about the history of the Western Cape and whose close reading of the manuscript helped me avoid some errors of fact and judgment. I am also greatly indebted to Elizabeth Eldredge for her report on the manuscript. She helped clarify some of my ideas and suggested new avenues I might pursue. I hasten to take responsibility for any errors that remain. I am also very grateful to John Mason who first suggested I look at the cases on infanticide.

In South Africa Amy Thornton provided a most congenial living environment, endless cups of tea, and wonderful friendship. Richard Roberts and Amy Roberts welcomed me to Stanford for the very happy year I spent at the Center for African Studies. Thom McClendon was a great colleague and made helpful suggestions on Chapter 8. He and Nancy also made sure that 1994–95 wasn't just filled with work. Sheryl McCurdy helped in all sorts of ways. I owe a great debt to Joan Cadden, Jane Rutkoff, and Peter Rutkoff for their support and interest over the years. I have come to rely on Ian Fletcher for his bibliographic knowledge of the literature on the British Empire and for his generosity and friendship. Melissa Dabakis and Ellen Furlough encouraged me to persevere. Robert Hinton shared his library. Clifton Crais read various drafts and listened to many more versions. Philippa Levine provided incisive comments on a draft of the chapter on infanticide.

Lunches with Vivian Bruce Conger sustained me through the year of writing up the thesis and provided an enjoyable forum to discuss my work. Darius Conger provided essential statistical information and expertise, as well as endless patience. Sita Ranchod Nilsson helped me survive the experience of writing up the thesis. The Kenyonites in Granville have been a wonderful support group as we all try to combine family and work. Thanks especially to Meg Grossman. Lucinda Matthews loves my children for which I am so grateful. Via e-mail, Lisa Lindsay has kept me sane. Dorothy Hodgson has been a great friend and critic since UM days. Kerry Ward has been there almost from the beginning and has seen the book evolve from early discussions in the Leslie building. My parents, Larry Scully and Christine Scully, continue to remind me that distance is indeed no hindrance to love and friendship. Anna von Veh really has been there from the very beginning and has enriched my life beyond measure. Thanks, Dearest A.

Clifton has helped nurture both this book as well as Benjamin and Christine. It is dedicated to him.

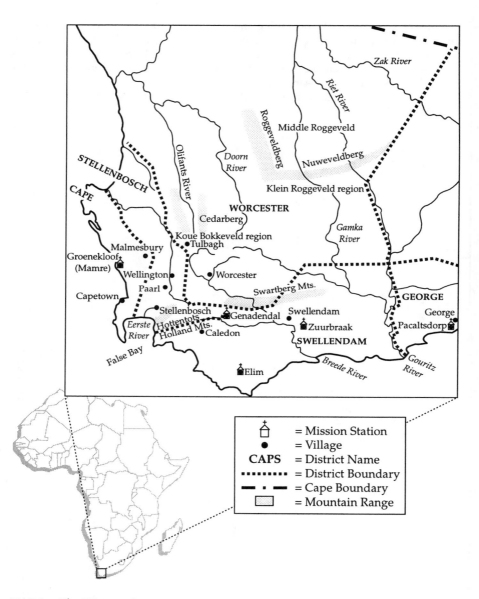

MAP 1. The Western Cape c. 1830

Introduction:
Family, Gender, and British Slave Emancipation

1 December 1838 brought the emancipation of slaves in the British Cape Colony. On that day the *South African Commercial Advertiser* welcomed the beginning of the new age with a column reflecting on the meaning of freedom. The *SACA* stated that emancipation returned Cape society to the "natural order" and "the practice of common justice between man and man." The use of the word man was not merely a linguistic convention. The *SACA* conceived of liberty as enabling slave men to embrace their legitimate masculinity:

> Freedom . . . offers something in addition to personal enjoyments. The Free-man becomes the Head of a Family. . . . The Father, however poor, however overlooked or despised by the world, is now an object, in one place at least, not only of love but *reverence*. There is now a circle where, if he chooses, he may reign as a King not only over the outward actions, but in the souls and hearts, in the thoughts and affections of his sincere and willing subjects and . . . he may perpetuate this his dominion, and strengthen it every day to the last of this life. . .[1]

In this understanding, the authority of men, and indeed their experience of freedom, depended upon the constraining of women's and children's liberty. But how widespread was the twinning of freedom and masculine authority, of freedom and feminine subordination, in the ideologies of abolition which led to the ending of Cape slavery? Did slave women and men share this gendered vision of freedom? And did significant disjunctures exist between freed peoples' experience of emancipation in the Cape Colony and the different ideologies of gender promoted by abolitionists, missionaries, and government officials?[2]

When the British abolished slavery in their Atlantic and Indian Ocean colonies in 1834 that infamous institution had been a central feature of economy and society at

---

1   SA, *SACA* Bound Volume, 1 December 1838, 196.

2   For a pioneering argument for the centrality of gender to historical analysis see Joan Scott, *Gender and the Politics of History* (New York: Columbia University Press, 1988), especially Ch. 1.

the Cape of Good Hope for nearly two hundred years. The Dutch East India Company introduced slavery shortly after its establishment of a supply station at the Cape in 1652. Slaves came from many different geographical regions and cultures including Indonesia, Macassar, Madagascar, and, increasingly from the late eighteenth century, from East Africa. By the period of amelioration in the 1820s some 52 percent of slaves had been born at the Cape.[3] By 1830 slaves numbered some 33,583 and settlers nearly 59,000. In addition, some 42,000 people, including people of indigenous descent, the Khoisan, and those of acknowledged mixed descent, worked in conditions approximating slavery.[4] In 1834 slavery was replaced by what became a four-year apprenticeship. Masters and slaves were supposed to learn how to operate within a wage labor economy. The ending of slavery dramatically altered the lives of ex-slaves and dependent laborers. Women and men, young and old, confronted the new possibilities and limits of freedom.

This book argues that the ending of slavery in the Cape Colony initiated an era of exceptional contestation about cultural categories and sensibilities. From the start of amelioration in 1823 through the ending of slavery in 1834 the world of people in the rural Western Cape increasingly floated adrift from the legal and social markers which had been established under slavery. Far more than simply abolishing bonded labor, British slave emancipation reconfigured the relations between men and women, and individual and society. It was precisely because emancipation implied, at least in theory, that slaves would be free to live as they pleased that claims regarding the legitimacy of specific family, labor, gender, and sexual relations became central to the struggle by various colonial groups to shape postemancipation society. For government officials the linkage of political economy to questions of cultural reproduction became a crucial component of the construction of colonial society in the mid-nineteenth century Cape colony.

The time of amelioration and emancipation from the 1820s through the 1840s marks an important period in the making of social and economic categories in South Africa.[5] The history of the ending of Cape slavery is inextricably entwined with a history of identity, or more accurately, with histories of identification.[6] The aftermath of

---

3   James C. Armstrong and Nigel Worden, "The Slaves," in Richard Elphick and Hermann Giliomee, eds., *The Shaping of South African Society 1652–1840*, 2d ed. (Cape Town: Maskew Miller Longman, 1989), 109–183, 132. On Cape slavery, see John Edwin Mason Jr., "'Fit for Freedom': The Slaves, Slavery, and Emancipation in the Cape Colony, South Africa, 1806–1842," 2 vols. (Ph.D. diss., Yale University, 1992); Mary Rayner, "Wine and Slaves: The Failure of an Export Economy and the Ending of Slavery in the Cape Colony, South Africa, 1806–1834" (Ph.D. diss., Duke University, 1986); Robert Ross, *The Cape of Torments: Slavery and Resistance in South Africa* (London: Routledge and Keegan Paul, 1983); Robert Shell, *Children of Bondage: A Social History of the Slave Society at the Cape of Good Hope, 1652–1838* (Hanover: Wesleyan University Press; University Press of New England, 1994); Nigel Worden, *Slavery in Dutch South Africa* (Cambridge: Cambridge University Press, 1985).

4   Richard Elphick and Hermann Giliomee, "The Origins and Entrenchment of European Dominance at the Cape, 1652–c. 1840, in Elphick and Giliomee, eds., *Shaping*, Table 11.1, 524.

5   On the importance of this period for the elaboration of racial ideologies see Andrew Bank, "Liberals and Their Enemies: Racial Ideology at the Cape of Good Hope, 1820–1850" (Ph.D. thesis, Cambridge University, 1995). Also Clifton C. Crais, *White Supremacy and Black Resistance in Pre-Industrial South Africa: The Making of the Colonial Order in the Eastern Cape* (Cambridge: Cambridge University Press, 1991).

6   Identification can be conceived of as a *process* used by both the powerful and the subaltern to establish claims to truth and power. The notion of identification is Fred Cooper's. Personal communication with author, November 1996.

slavery provided men and women, freed people, colonial officials, missionaries, and former slaveholders with new opportunities to try to situate themselves along multiple and sometimes antithetical axes in relation to one another. For example, when dealing with a former owner making claims on her labor, a freed woman might emphasize her married status and refuse to work for him or her, thus invoking an emerging idea that married women had a right and perhaps a duty not to work outside their own household or family. In another context, such as in social interactions with her male peers, that same woman might stress her status as a free woman, as independent.[7]

Yet this flexibility and nuance of identification came up against colonial regulations and practices which tended to try and force people into monochromatic social identities. For example, missionaries at the Cape sought to promote strict notions of gender distinctions which silenced, at least rhetorically, questioning of what it might mean to be a freed woman or man. I argue that ideas held by different participants about the capacities and roles of men and women crucially shaped the world of freedom into which ex-slave women and men were liberated in 1838. Gender relations, and ideas about gender identity, formed a central component of the political and social imagination of ex-slaves, abolitionists, and colonial officials. We also have to attend to the ways in which the ideas about family, gender identity, and labor were not necessarily reproduced uniformly in practice at the Cape. Even at the symbolic level, ideas about the gendered separation of spheres of activity, for example, were fraught with tension, always contested, and never stable. The economies of both England and its colonies always depended on working-class women's waged labor.[8]

Emancipation freed Cape slave women into an existing legal world which held a woman to be a minor, with her husband having control of her "person and her property."[9] Moreover, the very laws which ended and replaced slavery confirmed and enhanced the subordinate status of women both in the social sphere and in the world of wage labor. As we shall see, the theoretical impulses behind emancipation and the historical context of amelioration and abolition also emphasized women's and men's unequal access to power and placed sanctions on women's participation in the public sphere of contract. The program to ameliorate British slavery in the 1820s and 1830s, as well as legislation passed by the Colonial Office in the immediate postemancipation period, thus focused on the slave family, women's sexuality, and on the promotion of patriarchal familial structures and gender relations which officials believed conducive to the reproduction of a stable and industrious working class.

Contemporary beliefs, shared to different degrees by slaves and abolitionists, about the social and economic roles of men and women framed notions of labor in the era of emancipation. Ideas about men's and women's capacities were seen as derived from truths about the nature of the gendered body: that men were fit for the world of waged work outside the home and women were more suited to

---

7 See for example Chapter 5 and Chapter 8 following.

8 We know that the very process of industrialization in England, for example, entailed an enlargement of some categories of commodity production within the home itself. Louise Tilly and Joan Scott, *Women, Work, and Family*, 2d ed. (New York: Routledge, 1989).

9 However, it did permit antenuptial contracts which allowed a wife to dispose of her estate on her death. See S. B. Kitchin, "The British Colonies," Ch. 11, in *A History of Divorce* (London: Chapman Hall, 1912), 246–47; and Cape of Good Hope, "Report," Law of Inheritance Commission for the Western Districts G15-65 (Cape Town: Saul Solomon and Co., 1866), x.

domesticity. Cape slavery, unlike many other slave societies in both Africa and the British Caribbean, had also operated according to a gendered division of labor. Male slaves did mostly outside work and women predominantly did domestic work. Slaves thus brought to the experience of emancipation ideas about masculinity and femininity forged both under the regime of slavery and through discussions with peers about the meanings of freedom and family.[10]

Evidence suggests that after emancipation in 1838 ex-slaves reinforced a gendered division of labor which had been established under slavery, but also established their own criteria with regard to where married women would work for wages. After 1838 freed men did most of the agricultural labor, and women did domestic work. But freed people marked the break with slavery in part by ending women's domestic work for the former slaveholding community. They agreed that both women and girls would now try to avoid work within the settler household which had been one arena of sexual exploitation under slavery. Now women sought, where possible, to do domestic work for their own families rather than for others. This pattern of female domesticity was most marked on the mission stations which provided access to housing and promoted the notion of gendered separate spheres. It was less possible for people who had no alternative but to remain in permanent employment with former slaveholders.

Emancipation did mean a liberation, however limited, for freed women. For many women the gender subordination legally registered by emancipation was nonetheless a major improvement on their status and experience under slavery. And, as we shall see, even where women experienced domination by men in their families, the family seemed a sphere of liberation compared to the hostile environment of the "public sphere" of waged work in the postemancipation Cape.[11]

In addition, while freed men enjoyed significant legal powers over their wives and family this power often remained a fiction in a society stratified by race and class as well as by gender. The existence of nuclear patriarchal families within the freed community was tenuous at best in the first decade after 1838. The realities of the postemancipation economy meant that even on the mission stations, which actively championed masculine authority, women in fact enjoyed great power within the family since so many men had to live and work on the farms away from their families. And far from constructing nuclear families after emancipation where freed people were able to live with family members, their families often included extended family members as well as fictive kin. The living conditions for farm laborers and workers in the small villages of the rural Western Cape also did not easily facilitate the formation of discrete family units in which men could operate as spokespeople for their families.

Gender and Emancipation

The confluence of social and economic transformations in the colony and in Britain activated family, race, and gender as key components in the construction of knowl-

---

10 For a study on gender and Cape slavery see Patricia van der Spuy, "A Collection of Discrete Essays with the Common Theme of Gender and Slavery at the Cape of Good Hope with a Focus on the 1820s" (M.A. diss., University of Cape Town, 1993). See also Shell, *Children*.

11 Thanks to Elizabeth Eldredge for this point.

edge and society.[12] The British antislavery movement significantly shaped the process of Cape slave emancipation. This occurred in part because of the weakness of institutional antislavery sentiment at the Cape.[13] The relevance of British notions of antislavery for emancipation at the Cape also derived from the relative unimportance of the Cape within the British antislavery movement. Cape slavery was abolished in accordance with the legislation which reformed and abolished slavery in the West Indies, the major focus of British agitation against slavery. Indeed, it is difficult to find a mention of the Cape Colony in the campaigns or even much of the legislation ameliorating and finally ending slavery.

Cape antislavery arguments and perspectives surfaced only weakly in the metropole. Unlike their counterparts in England, evangelicals at the Cape directed their primary campaigns against bonded labor through championing of the rights of the indigenous Khoisan. The Cape thus was represented most forcefully in debates in Britain about labor and liberty through a discourse about the Khoi rather than one about formal slavery.[14] In the Cape itself, as Bank has shown, even liberals such as Thomas Fairbairn of the *SACA* who came to champion the abolition of slavery in the 1830s, nonetheless sided with slaveholders in 1826 in rejecting amelioration legislation. And Cape antislavery supporters' backing of slave abolition from 1832 also was very much propelled by developments within the British antislavery movement which moved from a promotion of gradual abolition to immediate abolition from the early 1830s.[15]

The timidity of the Philanthropic Society, founded in 1828 and the only society formed at the Cape to aid the amelioration of slavery, well represents the muted response of liberals in the Cape to the antislavery cause. The society failed as an abolitionist enterprise, helping to free only some 102 slaves in four years.[16] The society's philosophy nonetheless indicates the pervasiveness in both Cape as well as British metropolitan antislavery circles of a belief that appropriate gender roles would prepare slaves for freedom and secure the status quo in the postemancipation period. The society concentrated on the gradual abolition of slavery through the purchase of deserving female slaves. It did so partly because at the Cape children inherited their mother's status. The society also shared with its English antislavery peers a belief that women were the bearers of morality to the slave population as a whole, and that to free "deserving" women and train them to be good servants and dutiful wives would maintain social and economic stability once all slaves were freed.[17]

---

12   Intimate relations and women's experiences remain underexplored in the writing of South African history and neither race nor gender has been sufficiently problematized as a category with its own history. For a pioneering analysis of how one might conceptualize gender in South African history see Belinda Bozzoli, "Marxism, Feminism, and Southern African Studies," *Journal of Southern African Studies* 9, 2 (1983): 139–71. On rethinking race see Bank, "Liberals."

13   On the weakness of Cape antislavery sentiment, see Robert L. Watson, *The Slave Question: Liberty and Property in South Africa* (Hanover: University Press of New England, 1990).

14   On this history see Elizabeth Elbourne, "'To Colonize the Mind': Evangelicals in Britain and the Eastern Cape, 1790–1836" (Ph.D. diss., Oxford University, 1992), and "Freedom at Issue: Vagrancy Legislation and the Meaning of Freedom in Britain and the Cape Colony 1799–1842," *Slavery and Abolition* 15, 2 (August 1994): 114–50.

15   Bank, "Liberals," Ch. 2.

16   Watson, *Slave Question*, 85. Watson discusses the failure of Cape liberalism to develop a coherent antislavery agenda.

17   See Mason, "Fit for Freedom," 516–24.

British antislavery activists had long represented slavery through an iconography of the suffering mother rent from her children and of the man emasculated by slavery and unable to protect his family.[18] In the nineteenth century, contemporary concerns about family and gender relations within Britain itself amplified this older discourse about the links between slavery and masculine and feminine identities. The suppositions about male and female social roles contained in liberal political economy also helped solidify abolitionists' ideas about the gender relations appropriate to a society governed by contract.

Emancipation freed slave women into legal inequality in part because ideas about men's natural right to dominate women grounded the very concepts of freedom and free wage labor which guided the British abolitionist movement.[19] To many people in early-nineteenth-century Britain, slavery increasingly seemed anachronistic. Slavery made despots of masters by politicizing their domestic rule, and it crippled slaves by denying them the opportunity to be responsible individuals. Emancipation would incorporate both masters and slaves into a hierarchical political and social order. Free men would meet as free individuals who could contract freely with one another.[20]

Considerable tension existed within liberal political economy as to how to accommodate women into this world of contract and how to reconcile conflicting ideas about the family and the civil sphere. John Locke, for example, advanced the notion of a universal individualism which saw people as autonomous and engaged in relations of contract and competition. But he did not reconcile this belief in individual autonomy with his conception of a "transhistorical" family dictated by communal rather than individual obligations and governed by the husband who had ultimate decision-making power.[21] Indeed, Pateman has argued that the classic theorists of political economy "construct a patriarchal account of masculinity and femininity. . . . Only masculine beings are endowed with the attributes and capacities necessary to enter into contracts . . . only men, that is to say, are 'individuals.'"[22]

---

18 Moira Ferguson, *Subject to Others: British Women Writers and Colonial Slavery, 1670 1834* (New York: Routledge, 1992).

19 See Clare Midgley, "The Gender of Politics and the Gender Politics of History: Interpreting the Involvement of Women in the Anti-slavery Movement in Nineteenth Century Britain" (paper presented at University of California, Berkeley, April 1990), and *Women Against Slavery: The British Campaigns, 1780-1870* (London: Routledge, 1991). See also Catherine Hall, "White Visions, Black Lives: The Free Villages of Jamaica," *History Workshop*, Special Issue: Colonial and Post-Colonial History, 36 (Autumn 1993): 100–132, and *White, Male, and Middle Class: Explorations in Feminism and History* (New York: Routledge, 1992), Ch. 1.

20 Thomas C. Holt, *The Problem of Freedom: Race, Labor, and Politics in Jamaica and Britain, 1832–1938* (Baltimore: Johns Hopkins University Press, 1992), 32; David Brion Davis, *The Problem of Slavery in the Age of Revolution 1770–1823* (Ithaca: Cornell University Press, 1975), 380, and *Slavery and Human Progress* (New York: Oxford University Press, 1984). See *SACA*, 26 July 1837, for a Cape interpretation of the meaning of freedom in which Adam Smith is referred to constantly as the authority regarding the link between wage labor and the expansion of free markets.

21 Linda Nicholson, *Gender and History: The Limits of Theory in the Age of the Family* (New York: Columbia University Press, 1986), Ch. 5, 161.

22 Carole Pateman, *The Sexual Contract* (Stanford: Stanford University Press, 1988), 5–6. For another critique of conventional understanding of civil society and liberal political theory which have informed my thinking, see Joan Landes, *Women and the Public Sphere in the Age of the French Revolution* (Ithaca: Cornell University Press, 1988).

Social contract theorists accepted that women could enter into at least one kind of contract: marriage. But generally women's ability to engage in contracts was limited by their place as subalterns within a private sphere. In political theory women's position within both the political economy and the economy of free wage labor thus remained ambiguous. The position of women freed from slavery in particular exposed the contradictions inherent in the contemporary notions of contract. As individuals liberated from a state of slavery, women were now free to contract out their labor; however, the belief that they were minors within a patriarchal family undermined this freedom.[23] This tension helps explain why the era of slave emancipation at the Cape resonates with both sanctions upon and ongoing inconsistencies regarding freed women's relations to the workplace. Ambivalence about the position of the working wife, and especially of the black married freed woman pervaded antislavery discussions and Cape postemancipation labor legislation.

The patriarchal character of much amelioration and emancipation legislation also derived from political and economic discourse within Britain during this period which subjected gender relations to almost unprecedented scrutiny. Since the late eighteenth century, evangelicals (many of whom were abolitionists) had championed the notion of a separation of spheres. They offered the strict ordering of gender relations as a panacea to supposed moral and social ills produced by the Industrial Revolution and by claims to equality inspired by the French Revolution. By the 1820s the middle class increasingly supported the ideology of a patriarchal nuclear family with the man as head of household and the wife as the moral pillar of family and society.[24]

The decades of amelioration and apprenticeship coincided both with this assertion of a new moral order premised upon specific gender relations, but also with great anxiety by the British middle class regarding the effects of industrialization on women and children and on the working-class family. Reformers proposed a "restoration" of the proper gender order as the solution to the apparent collapse of the working-class family under pressures of urbanization and factory labor.[25] And a growing acceptance emerged in the mid-nineteenth century, at least within the middle class, of regular waged work as being a male activity, and of women's sexuality as being threatening to the stability of working-class society.[26]

In this context it is perhaps not surprising that abolitionists argued that free wage labor would work best if freed slaves adhered to specific gender roles. Abolitionists

23 See Amy Dru Stanley, "Conjugal Bonds and Wage Labor: Rights of Contract in the Age of Emancipation," *Journal of American History* 75, 2 (September 1988): 471–500.

24 See David Turley, *The Culture of Antislavery, 1780–1860* (London: Routledge, 1991), 44–45; Mary Poovey, *Uneven Developments: The Ideological Work of Gender in Mid-Victorian England* (Chicago: University of Chicago Press, 1988), Ch. 1; Leonore Davidoff and Catherine Hall, *Family Fortunes: Men and Women of the English Middle Class, 1780–1850* (London: Hutchinson, 1987); and Jeffrey Weeks, *Sex and Society: The Regulation of Sexuality Since 1800* (London: Longman, 1981).

25 F. M. L. Thompson, *The Rise of Respectable Society: A Social History of Victorian Britain, 1830–1900* (Cambridge: Harvard University Press, 1988), 85. See Mary Poovey, "Domesticity and Class Formation: Chadwick's 1842 *Sanitary Report*," in David Simpson, ed., *Subject to History: Ideology, Class, Gender* (Ithaca: Cornell University Press, 1991), 65–83. Chadwick's *Report on the Sanitary Condition of the Labouring Population of Great Britain* was started in 1839 and published in 1842.

26 On gender and labor in England see Barbara Taylor, *Eve and the New Jerusalem* (New York: Pantheon, 1983); and Harold Benenson, "Victorian Sexual Ideology and Marx's Theory of the Working Class," *International Labor and Working Class History* 25 (Spring 1984): 1–23.

were as concerned to initiate a new gender and moral order in the former slave colonies as they were to end slavery. Many British activists envisaged the abolition of slavery as the liberation of women into the protection of the patriarchal family, and the freeing of men into their rightful position as heads of households. Both men and women activists thus promoted and legitimated patriarchal nuclear families as the natural familial and gender organization appropriate to freedom.[27]

British slave emancipation in the 1830s thus freed male slaves at the Cape into a world which stressed, at least in theory, the equality of men before the law; although such equality coexisted with acceptance (at least on the part of the abolitionists) of social and economic hierarchies. Slave abolition offered the possibility that each male individual would be free to forge his own future, but that future was assumed to be one which echoed the beliefs of the British middle class. Indeed, the refusal of ex-slaves in the West Indies, and indeed the Cape, to conform to the visions of freedom of the abolitionists "became a crucial ingredient in the evolution of mid-Victorian racism."[28]

In the nineteenth century, race increasingly served to demarcate another limit upon liberalism's promotion of equal access to the civil sphere, and on the belief that power could be checked by neutral governmental institutions. Some of the major works of modern racial thought were born in the eighteenth century and clearly generated considerable popular interest by the first decade of the nineteenth.[29] Biological determinism located difference in race as well as gender. The classificatory discourse of nineteenth-century intellectual thought situated Europeans at the top of a pyramid of talent and birthright. Specifically, the male European exemplified this racial triumph of rationality and civilization, and the black woman symbolized rampant sexuality, depravity, and degradation.[30] This pairing of sexuality and race as categories which limited a person's experience of freedom had profound implications for freed women's lives in the postemancipation setting, as will be seen in the last part of this book.[31]

---

27 As Clare Midgley has stated, "antislavery ideology . . . was as concerned with proper gender and sexual relations as it was with proper work and class relations." Midgley, "Gender of Politics," 10. See also Catherine Hall, "In the Name of Which Father?" *International and Working Class History* 41 (Spring 1992), 25.

28 James Walvin, ed., *Slavery and British Society, 1776–1846* (Baton Rouge: Louisiana State University Press, 1982), 20.

29 See for example the works of Petrus Camper, *The Works of the Late Professor Camper, on the Connexion between the Science of Anatomy and the Arts of Drawing* . . . (London: Printed for C. Dilly, 1794); Johann F. Blumenbach, *On the Natural Varieties of Mankind* (1775; reprint, New York: Berfman Publishers, 1969); Jean Comaroff and John Comaroff, *Of Revelation and Revolution: Christianity, Colonialism, and Consciousness in South Africa*, Vol. 1 (Chicago: University of Chicago Press, 1991); and George Stocking, *Victorian Anthropology* (New York: Free Press, 1987).

30 This section has been inspired by Ann Stoler's seminar on Racial Thinking in Comparative Perspective at the University of Michigan, Winter 1990. See also Comaroff and Comaroff, *Revelation*, 105–108; and Sander L. Gilman, *Difference and Pathology: Stereotypes of Sexuality, Race, and Madness* (Ithaca: Cornell University Press, 1985).

31 For recent writings on meanings of race in the nineteenth-century Cape see Bank, "Liberals"; Vivian Bickford Smith, "Black Ethnicities, Communities, and Political Expression in Late Victorian Cape Town," *Journal of African History* 36, 3 (1995): 443–66; and Clifton C. Crais, "The Vacant Land: The Mythology of British Expansion in the Eastern Cape, South Africa," *Journal of Social History* 25 (Winter 1991): 255–74, and "Race, the State, and the Silence of History in the Making of Modern South Africa" (paper presented at the 1992 African Studies Association Meeting, Seattle, November 1992).

Cape Emancipation and Historiographies

The slaves who were freed at the Cape lived in one of the oldest settler societies on the African continent. The Cape experience of slavery and slave emancipation from the 1820s lay at the intersection of different "world systems" or historical experiences and geographies—those of Sub-Saharan Africa, early Dutch colonialism, and the British empire, particularly the British West Indies. This book has thus been informed by a number of regional and conceptual literatures and in turn hopes to contribute to the study of slave emancipation in Africa and the British West Indies. I analyze Cape slavery primarily through the views and actions of the slaves themselves.[32] This book incorporates the experience of bonded laborers of Khoisan and white descent into a study of slavery, thus drawing on recent work which argues against a legalistic definition of slavery in South Africa in favor of one which accounts for the significance of lived experience.[33]

Cape slavery was an African slavery most obviously because of its geographical location at the tip of that continent. The continental location helped create an ambiguous frontier between categories of slavery and freedom which was missing in most West Indian colonies. By the 1830s Cape slaveholders utilized, to different degrees depending on the district, various sorts of dependent labor. These included slaves, indigenous people such as the descendants of Khoisan (who while not geographically displaced, nonetheless were displaced into forms of dependent labor), and Africans taken by the British from other nations' slave ships and apprenticed to settlers in the Cape Colony. The overlapping of these categories created ambiguity not only in relation to labor but also to reproduction, as will be seen later in regard to the emergence of a "colouredcoloured" identity in the nineteenth century.

Yet in some aspects of slavery, and particularly in its experience of abolition, the Cape had more in common with the British West Indian emancipations than those in African colonial history. The Cape was a "West Indian" slavery in that the largest number of slaves came from distant areas and were placed in an economy geared towards export. And, as in the Caribbean, slavery at the Cape was marked by a racial divide. While taxonomies of race became much more rigid in the course of the nineteenth century in general, masters at the Cape were overwhelmingly regarded as white, while slaves were regarded as being of mixed, Asian or black descent, although some urban Free Blacks also owned slaves.

In addition, the ending of Cape slavery significantly predated most other emancipations in Africa. African slave emancipations happened mostly in the early twentieth century after the second wave of colonization of Africa in the late nineteenth century.[34] The Cape, in contrast, as the oldest British colony in Africa, was drawn into

---

32   For examples of this literature see Frederick Cooper, *Plantation Slavery on the East Coast of Africa* (New Haven: Yale University Press, 1977); Jonathon Glassman, *Feasts and Riot: Revelry, Rebellion, and Popular Consciousness on the Swahili Coast, 1856–1888* (Portsmouth, NH: Heinemann, 1995); and Mason, "Fit for Freedom." See also Claire Robertson and Martin Klein, eds., *Women and Slavery in Africa* (Madison: University of Wisconsin Press, 1983).

33   See Elizabeth A. Eldredge and Fred Morton, eds., *Slavery in South Africa: Captive Labor on the Dutch Frontier* (Boulder: Westview Press, 1994).

34   The big exception being the Gold Coast where slavery was abolished in 1874. See Gerald M. McSheffrey, "Slavery, Indentured Servitude, Legitimate Trade and the Impact of Abolition in the Gold Coast, 1874–1901: A Reappraisal," *Journal of African History* 24, 3 (1983): 349–68.

emancipation literally as part of the legislation which ameliorated and abolished slavery in the West Indies in the 1820s and 1830s.

Understandably, scholars of African emancipation have mainly concentrated on the emancipations of the late nineteenth and early twentieth centuries. They have also been especially attuned to the ways in which notions of class, culture, and labor shaped slave emancipation.[35] In contrast, this book analyzes an early-nineteenth-century emancipation in one of the oldest colonial cultures in Sub-Saharan Africa and makes gender a key category of analysis. *Liberating the Family?* examines a case in which colonialism predated slave emancipation. It argues that the political, juridical, and economic context of colonial slavery in the Western Cape as well as the class, racial, and gendered assumptions within antislavery thought helped to initiate new forms of control over black women's behavior and limited their participation in the waged labor force.[36]

An examination of labor and production must account for women's roles as producers of food and bearers of children, and, in many societies, as guardians of social values.[37] Chapter 5, which discusses labor and family, has been particularly informed by the writings on women and labor in African women's history. However, a weakness of this literature is that it has tended to rely on universal formulas about the relationship between production and reproduction which often break down when applied to discrete historical situations. In the case of the mid-nineteenth-century Cape, for example, no universal statement can be made about the relationship between women's roles as reproducers of children and as producers and workers within the colonial economy. Women's participation in the wage labor economy changed between 1838 and 1853, and arguments made by freed women and men, and by various colonial officials, about the connection between women's roles as mothers and their identities as workers invoked different associations between reproduction and labor at different periods.[38]

Capitalism, including the notions of wage labor which were at its center, came to South Africa not as an abstract system of productive relations, but as one continually threaded and rethreaded with historically shaped cultural constructs and assumptions. As Fred Cooper has argued, the colonialist debates over how to deal with and

35   Glassman, *Feasts and Riots*; Frederick Cooper, *From Slaves to Squatters: Plantation Agriculture and Labor in Zanzibar and Coastal Kenya, 1890–1925* (New Haven: Yale University Press, 1980); Martin Klein, ed., *Breaking the Chains: Slavery, Bondage, and Emancipation in Modern Africa and Asia* (Madison: University of Wisconsin Press, 1993); Suzanne Miers and Richard Roberts, eds., *The Ending of Slavery in Africa* (Madison: University of Wisconsin Press, 1988). For an exception which looks at women and the ending of slavery see Marcia Wright, *Strategies of Slaves and Women: Life Stories from East/Central Africa* (New York: Lilian Barber Press, 1993).

36   Other studies of women and colonialism have charted the ways in which colonialism involved the lowering of women's status within indigenous societies in Africa. The literature is vast. The pioneering work is Ester Boserup, *Women in Economic Development* (London: Allen and Unwin, 1970). For a recent examination of this theme see Elizabeth Schmidt, *Peasants, Traders, and Wives: Shona Women in the History of Zimbabwe 1870– 1939* (Portsmouth, NH: Heinemann, 1992).

37   Claire Robertson and Iris Berger, "Introduction," in Claire Robertson and Iris Berger, eds., *Women and Class in Africa* (New York: Africana Publishing Company, 1986), 3–26, 9. On the issue of production and reproduction see Elizabeth A. Eldredge, "Women in Production: The Economic Role of Women in Nineteenth-Century Lesotho," *Signs* 16, 4 (1991): 707–731; Margaret Strobel, *Muslim Women in Mombasa, 1890–1975* (New Haven: Yale University Press, 1979), and also Margaret Strobel, "Slavery and Reproductive Labor in Mombasa," in Robertson and Klein, eds., *Women and Slavery in Africa*.

38   See also Elias Mandala, *Work and Control in a Peasant Economy: A History of the Lower Tchiri Valley in Malawi, 1859–1960* (Madison: University of Wisconsin Press, 1990).

conceptualize ex-slaves and different family formations were not debates about abstract labor power but about labor power as it appeared on the market in the form of women, men, boys, and girls.[39] Ex-slaves too did not contest abstract labor power, but labor power in its gendered and racialized nineteenth-century materiality. Ideologies of family were an important image through which different people envisioned their ideas about freedom and labor. Freed people especially saw in liberty an opportunity to consolidate emotional ties which had been officially denied them under Cape slavery. These struggles around the meanings of family in the era of freedom in turn invoked and helped transform other beliefs about the relationship of men and women to one another and to work, and about the categories of and relationships between sexuality, race, and class.

While the study of kinship has been one of the staples of African history and anthropology, a history of emotions, of the interior struggles and lives within kinship or family structures, has been largely ignored. This book tries to unite a concern with ideological contests over family formation with attention to the emotional lives of people freed from slavery. In this respect, the book is much influenced by studies of family and gender relations in the slave family in the antebellum United States as well as the history of the British West Indies.[40]

The ways in which slaves at the Cape were freed in terms of legislation primarily crafted for the British West Indies necessarily draws one into a discussion with the current rejuvenation of British imperial history, and particularly with the ongoing work on gender, empire, and British antislavery.[41] Historians have tended to look to India and the West Indies as sites for a reinterpretation of British history.[42] This book advances studies of gender, race, and emancipation in the British Empire by elucidating how ideas about gender and labor relations shaped emancipation in an African colony tied to the West Indies through their similar experience of slave abolition.[43]

---

39   Fred Cooper, personal communication with the author, November 1996.

40   See particularly Herbert G. Gutman, *The Black Family in Slavery and Freedom 1750–1925* (New York: Vintage Books, 1977); and Jacqueline Jones, *Labor of Love, Labor of Sorrow: Black Women, Work, and the Family from Slavery to the Present* (New York: Basic Books, 1985).

41   For a reconceptualization of empire and colony see Ann Stoler and Frederick Cooper, "Tensions of Empire: Colonial Control and Visions of Rule," *American Ethnologist* 16, 4 (November 1989): 609–621. On gender, empire, and Britain see Hall, *White*; Hall, "White Visions"; and Susan Thorne, "Protestant Ethics and the Spirit of Imperialism: British Congregationalists and the London Missionary Society, 1795–1925" (Ph.D. diss., University of Michigan, 1990).

42   See the special edition of the *Women's History Review* 3, 4 (1994) on feminism and empire. For a sensitive interpretation of how the new British history might be written see Antoinette Burton, "Rules of Thumb: British History and 'Imperial Culture' in Nineteenth- and Twentieth-Century Britain" in the same volume.

43   The silence on the Cape has been echoed in much of the literature on comparative studies of slavery which rarely give more than a cursory mention of the Cape; the pioneering work of Isobel Edwards has had no recent heir. Isobel Edwards, *Towards Emancipation: A Study in South African Slavery* (Cardiff: Gomerian Press, 1942)); Suzanne Miers and Igor Kopytoff, "Introduction," in Suzanne Miers and Igor Kopytoff, eds., *Slavery in Africa: Historiographical and Anthropological Perspectives* (Madison: University of Wisconsin Press, 1977), 14–18. Robin Blackburn does not mention the Cape in his examination of British slave emancipation, *The Overthrow of Colonial Slavery* (London: Verso, 1988). Paul Lovejoy does include the Cape in his discussion of slavery in Africa, *Transformations in Slavery: A History of Slavery in Africa* (Cambridge: Cambridge University Press, 1983), esp. 130–32, 232–34.

Methodology

Histories emphasizing and validating the experiences of colonized people, women, and the working class who lived lives shaped by keenly experienced sociopolitical and economic realities have been central to a new interpretation of the South African past.[44] Yet the emphasis on experience creates its own methodological hurdles. Even as one charts the lives of ex-slaves, for example, one is in danger of reproducing a colonialist argument about the relationship between race and intellect. The archives present a portrait of freed people contributing only "endurance" to the postemancipation colonial order, whereas colonists and colonial authorities contribute ideas: how to encourage ex-slaves to work; how to counter missionary control over the freed people; and how to promote certain cultural habits of industry, morality, and labor.

Recent scholarship has suggested ways of confronting the challenges involved in using experience as evidence. Scott has argued, for example, that experience is discursively constructed, that it is created through language and the assumptions contained in language; experience therefore does not exist outside of historical production.[45] This argument suggests that we attend to the ways in which archival texts, and discourse more broadly, are structured, and it potentially moves us beyond the dichotomy between experience and text. Attention to the production of archival knowledge allows us also to heed the silence in the archival record about the ways in which the documented past was produced and about how it came to be organized and shaped.[46] Silences can be treated as yet another artifact available to the historian. Yet the historical sensitivity to text and the belief in the impossibility of accessing the "real" often seem to create a new silence on political economy and an exclusive embrace of the text.[47]

This book tries to negotiate the tensions between experience and text by attending to both political economy and representation. A methodology merging sensitivity to issues of political economy with attention to cultural practice helps to illuminate the connections between important battles over meanings and material resources in the rural postemancipation Cape. If actions help fashion social structures and cultural identification then historians productively expand their methodological concerns by paying attention to daily social practice.[48] Study of habit, of the social architecture of daily life—the ordering of space in the home, the seating of people at

---

44   For a representative sample of this revisionist writing see the important volumes co-edited by Shula Marks: Shula Marks and Anthony Atmore, *Economy and Society in Pre-Industrial South Africa* (London: Longman, 1980); Shula Marks and Richard Rathbone, eds., *Industrialisation and Social Change in South Africa* (London: Longman, 1982); and Shula Marks and Stanley Trapido, eds., *The Politics of Race, Class, and Nationalism in Twentieth-Century South Africa* (London: Longman, 1986). See also Iris Berger, *Threads of Solidarity: Women in South African Industry 1900–1980* (Bloomington, Indiana University Press, 1992), and Colin Bundy and William Beinart, *Hidden Struggles in Rural South Africa* (Berkeley: University of California Press, 1987).

45   Joan W. Scott, "The Evidence of Experience," *Critical Inquiry* 17 (Summer 1991): 773–97.

46   Ann Laura Stoler, *Race and the Education of Desire: Foucault's History of Sexuality and the Colonial Order of Things* (Durham: Duke University Press, 1995).

47   See for example Comaroff and Comaroff, *Revelation*.

48   Pierre Bourdieu, *Outline of a Theory of Practice* (New York: Cambridge University Press, 1977); Anthony Giddens, *Central Problems in Social Theory* (Berkeley: University of California Press, 1979).

meal times—enables us to "hear" people, particularly women, who have not traditionally "spoken" in the historical archive.[49] A cultural analysis of the daily lives of freed women and men provides insights into the ideas which informed their lives and which they contributed to the postemancipation Cape.

Such an analysis demands that we historicize the archives themselves. The Cape archives have a distinct bias: the voices of farmers, civil servants, and missionaries predominate over those of the freed people, and the voices of men predominate over women. We learn mainly about freed people only once they have become a problem for settlers or bureaucrats (thus all the cases about desertion and drunkenness which turn up under the Masters and Servants Ordinance). The archives structure a view of freed people as living lives of crisis and violence. Freed men do appear as responsible agents in memorials written to the government about land reform and protection of mission stations. But freed women rarely appear since they were not seen by colonial authorities as being capable of representing either their communities or their families.

In order to write a history of freed people we therefore generally have to read against the grain, combing cases about theft, assault, and drunkenness for what they might reveal about people's lives. Women appear mostly in criminal cases both as witnesses and defendants. Their testimonies help give us glimpses into what they thought of emancipation and their lives as workers, lovers, parents, and children. It is nevertheless hard to adequately privilege women's voices without overreaching one's sources. This book tries to balance a concern to write about the experiences of ex-slaves, and particularly women, with respect for the limitations of the material.

Rendering the South African past is made particularly difficult by myriad and shifting forms of identification and racial ascriptions over the course of South Africa's colonial history. Emancipation at the Cape freed slaves into the category "Free Black" which encompassed all people of color native to the Western Cape: "Hottentots" (the colonial term for the Khoi) and "Bushmen" (the colonial term for the San), "Bastards" (white father, Khoi mother), and "Bastard Hottentots" (slave father, Khoi mother), as well as Africans taken from slave ships by the British.

The close cultural and social relations between Khoisan and slaves, which had been fostered in part by the decimation through colonial violence and disease of much of the Khoi population in the early eighteenth century, and the incorporation of the Khoisan into the Cape colonial economy, also contributed to the very heterogeneous culture of the rural poor in the mid-nineteenth century. This very diversity of geographical and cultural origins in part informed the emergence of an official racial terminology which would cover all of these groups. Thus while the category of "Free Black" continued to be used into the 1840s in government correspondence regarding labor legislation, from 1837 the statistical *Blue Books* began listing people of Khoi and San descent, Free Blacks, "Prize Negroes," and freed people under the category "coloured."[50] I use the term "slaves" to refer to those people who were formally enslaved, and the term "dependent laborers" in reference to indigenous people (such as the Khoi and the San) who were kept in a state akin to slavery. Khoi refers to people who would have been considered as belonging to the indigenous pastoralist

---

49   Hans Medick and David Warren Sabean, eds., *Interest and Emotion: Essays on the Study of Family and Kinship* (Cambridge: Cambridge University Press, 1977).

50   Mason, "Fit for Freedom," 589. See Chapter 8 following for a discussion of the rise of this identity.

groups of the Cape. In colonial lexicon they were known as "Hottentots." San refers to people known by the colonists as "Bushmen," hunter-gatherers who lived mainly to the north of the area covered by this book, but who were increasingly exploited for labor in areas such as Worcester through the 1840s and 1850s. The designation of Free Black changed in the course of the nineteenth century. Up to 1834 a person who had been manumitted from slavery was referred to in legal documents as Free Black. And in 1829 the passing of Ordinance No. 50, which gave the Khoi protection under the law from enforced labor and other restrictions on their freedom, liberated the Khoi into the category of Free Black. Emancipation also freed slaves into this category and the freed class was considered as Free Black for legal purposes. However this usage declined very shortly after 1838.

I have used the term Free Black after 1838 only to refer to people with identifiable roots in the Free Black population under slavery, in order to distinguish between people freed by the Abolition Act and those with a longer history of freedom. After 1838 I use the term "freed people" to refer not only to ex-slaves, but also to Khoi and other dependent laborers with whom slaves shared a common culture by the time of emancipation. I have also chosen to employ this term broadly because so many of the records after 1838 rarely tell one if an individual was a recently freed slave. I also use the term "freed people" to refer to white immigrant children who were brought to the Cape in the 1830s, many of whom subsequently married into the freed population. Particularly from the 1850s the term "coloured" became used by colonial officials as a racial ascription describing all people perceived as having a slave past or having roots in the indigenous societies of the Western Cape. Former slaveholders also appear to have used the term "Kleurling" or "coloured" to refer to their ex-slaves. It is unclear, however, to what extent freed people accepted this designation themselves in the period covered by this book so I have tended to avoid the term. I have used it in certain cases with quotation marks to show the tenuousness of the term in the mid nineteenth century. For purposes of clarity, I have used the term "African" only with reference to members of indigenous polities in the interior who came to work in the Western Cape through various labor schemes during the 1850s.

Liberating the Family

This book is divided into three parts which can be read not only chronologically as a conventional narrative, but also as different expositions of the recurrent themes of how people identified themselves through prisms of race, gender, and class in the process of slave emancipation. By the 1830s, Cape urban slavery was already withering away.[51] The slaves who thus experienced emancipation most powerfully as a break between past and future were the slaves who lived on the farms and villages of the Western Cape. For this reason, a history of slaves' emancipation in the rural districts of Stellenbosch, Caledon, Swellendam, and Worcester is the central focus of this book. Chronologically, I concentrate on the period from 1823 when the British intro-

---

51   Andrew Bank, *The Decline of Urban Slavery at the Cape, 1806–1843*, Communications No. 22 (University of Cape Town, Center for African Studies, 1991).

duced legislation to ameliorate Cape slavery, to 1853 when the Cape Colony received a modicum of self-rule through the granting of representative government.

Part I provides a contextual background for the body of the book which focuses on the postemancipation period. It examines the period from the start of amelioration in 1823 to the end of apprenticeship in 1838. In chapters on slavery, amelioration, and apprenticeship I argue that slaves and slaveowners at the Cape, as well as abolitionists in England, conceptualized the meanings of both slavery and freedom in part through the language of family and gender relations.

Part II examines the postemancipation political economy up to 1848 through the lens of gender. It argues that slaves' personal experience of emancipation was partly determined by their access to resources under slavery. I show that gender and the nature of family connections shaped a slave's access to the world of freedom during slavery and emancipation. I also examine the ways in which ideas about masculinity, femininity, and family shaped labor legislation and the cultural worlds of the laboring poor.

The final part of the book analyzes in chronological sequence the tensions which collected around family, race, and sexuality in the postemancipation Cape in the period from 1839 to 1853. In chapters on marriage, infanticide, and rape I argue that ideologies of gender, race, and sexuality themselves helped shape and produce particular colonial narratives and experiences. I show that both settler and ex-slave ideas about the meanings of femininity qualified the freedom of freed women. And I argue that in their struggles to define the meanings of freedom, different groups invoked connections between gender, class, and racial categories which helped define the postemancipation era at the Cape in part as a struggle over the meanings of masculinity and femininity.

PART I

GENDER, FAMILY, AND THE ENDING OF CAPE SLAVERY, 1823–1838

1

Familial Boundaries and Cape Slavery

The premise in Cape Roman Dutch law that "a mother begets no bastard" placed slave women's childbearing capacities at the center of the reproduction of Cape slavery.[1] All children of slave women inherited slave status on the understanding that maternity is evident, while paternity has to be proved or accepted. The ending of the British transatlantic slave trade in 1807 forced slaveholders to attempt to make the slave population self-reproducing. In the last twenty or so years of Cape slavery, maternity thus became even more ideologically central to the perpetuation of slavery in the colony.

The importance of maternity to Cape slavery coexisted with, and to some extent depended upon, a muted recognition of paternity. In particular, male slaveholders stifled recognition of their children born to slave women and did not incorporate these children into the slaveholding family. The child of a slave mother and slaveholder father tended to be placed within the social perimeter of the slave/Khoi family even while being half-sibling with the master's acknowledged children. Children of slave women and masters, however, remained slaves, and came to make up part of the "coloured" population, as many people of slave descent were designated by the end of the nineteenth century. If one's mother was free, then a whole new series of definitions came to bear on determining one's status. In colonial lexicon, the child of a slave man and a Khoi woman became a "Bastard Hottentot"; the child of a Khoi woman and a man recognized as white was labeled simply a "Bastard" which signified explicitly that the child was not accepted as part of settler society.

Recognition of particular ties of family or kin and the denial of others formed one of the key pillars upon which Cape slavery rested. This chapter analyzes the ways in which ideas about family helped shape Cape slavery. And it examines the extent to which slavery depended upon the maintenance of certain fictions as to who constituted family and who did not. It also suggests that one of the ways in which slaves fought against slavery was to have slaveholders recognize precisely those relationships between slaves and other dependent laborers and between slave parents and children which slaveholders perceived as threatening the stability of slavery as a social and economic system.

---

1 Johannes van der Linden, *Institutes of Holland, or Manual of Law, Practice, and Mercantile Law, for the Use of Judges, Lawyers, Merchants, and All Who Wish to Have a General View of the Law,* 5th ed. (Cape Town, 1806; Cape Town: J. C. Juta and Co, 1906), 31

Cape Slavery in the Rural Western Districts

In 1806 the British entered a society which was "no place for a Manichean."[2] They confronted a complex colonial society comprised of indigenous groups such as the Khoisan, settlers with origins in the Netherlands, Germany, and France, and slaves of diverse backgrounds ranging from the Dutch East Indies, to Madagascar, and the east and west coasts of the African continent. In the course of a hundred and fifty years of colonialism, Dutch colonial society had elaborated an intricate social hierarchy determined partly by free or slave status, economic status, cultural origin, and lineage, and "the hierarchies produced by these taxonomies were by no means coincident."[3]

The British took control of a society in which slavery was deeply entrenched. The Dutch East India Company (VOC) which ruled the Cape Colony from 1652 to 1795, introduced slavery very shortly after their arrival. By the end of the seventeenth century, the Cape economy rested fundamentally on slavery. Slaves had been introduced to the Cape because of the reluctance of the indigenous people of the Western Cape, the Khoisan pastoralists and hunter-gatherers, to work for colonists, but by the mid-eighteenth century the Khoisan had been reduced to dependent status. By the time the British arrived permanently in 1806, the Khoisan lived side by side with slaves in a state of de facto slavery.[4]

In the eighteenth century the slave population increased dramatically because of the "expansion of arable agriculture."[5] While in the first half of the eighteenth century farmers tended to mix viticulture and grain farming, the second half of the century witnessed increasing specialization.[6] From the 1830s wool production increased dramatically, but few wine farmers in Stellenbosch district, for example, had sufficient capital to invest in districts such as Swellendam where sheep farming generated a veritable boom in the 1840s.

---

2   Robert Ross, "Structure and Culture in Pre-Industrial Cape Town: A Survey of Knowledge and Ignorance," in Wilmot G. James and Mary Simons, eds., *The Angry Divide: Social and Economic History of the Western Cape* (Cape Town: David Philip, 1989), 46. For an elegant discussion of the fluidity of colonial categories up to 1795 see Richard Elphick and Robert Shell, "Intergroup Relations: Khoikhoi, Settlers, Slaves, and free blacks, 1652–1795," in Elphick and Giliomee, eds., *Shaping*, 184–242. Also see Jean Taylor, *The Social World of Batavia* (Madison: University of Wisconsin Press, 1983).

3   Ross, "Structure and Culture," 46. See also Wayne Dooling, *Law and Community in a Slave Society, Stellenbosch District, South Africa, c. 1760–1820* (Cape Town: University of Cape Town, Center for African Studies, 1992) which shows the important roles that notions of hierarchy and reciprocity played within the Stellenbosch slaveholding community.

4   There is ongoing debate as to whether the Khoi and the San were distinct ethnic and social groups or whether the San hunter-gatherers were poor Khoi who could no longer engage in pastoralism. For an evocative narrative of the Khoisan demise see Richard Elphick, *Khoikhoi and the Founding of White South Africa* (Johannesburg: Ravan Press, 1985).

5   Worden, *Slavery,* 9.

6   In the nineteenth century the opening of the British markets to Cape wines led to increasing production, but the ending of preferential tariffs resulted in a collapse of the Cape wine market in the late 1820s and the wine industry struggled to find its feet through the rest of the century. For a succinct discussion of the Cape economy see Robert Ross, "The Cape and the World Eeconomy, 1652–1835," in Elphick and Giliomee, eds., *Shaping*, 243–80. On the Cape wine industry in the early nineteenth century see Rayner, "Wine and Slaves." For the late nineteenth century see Pamela Scully, *The Bouquet of Freedom: Social and Economic Relations in the Stellenbosch District, 1870–1900* Communications No. 17 (Cape Town: Center for African Studies, University of Cape Town, 1990).

For much of the history of slavery the slave population was overwhelmingly male and the slave population only became self-reproducing in the early nineteenth century. By 1834 there were 36,169 slaves in the Cape with some 50 percent having been born in the Cape since the ending of the British transatlantic slave trade in 1807.[7] Pastoral farmers in the interior regions always depended most heavily on Khoi labor, but, just prior to the ending of the British transatlantic slave trade, even in arable districts such as Stellenbosch, Khoi laborers formed 30 percent of the labor force.[8]

Location within a particular set of sexual and kin relations as well as their gender shaped slave men and women's experience of slavery in the early-nineteenth-century Cape.[9] Both slave men and women experienced slavery as domination. But colonial notions about men and women's capabilities helped shape discrete gendered experiences of slavery. As in many other African slave societies, slave labor confirmed the dominant patterns of the sexual division of labor which operated within slaveholding society.[10] At the Cape men generally worked outside the house while women mostly did domestic labor (although of course slavery enabled both slaveholding men and women to avoid much labor altogether). Slave labor also operated within this framework. Slave men did agricultural work and slave women did domestic work. They only worked alongside men in agricultural work in peak seasons, although this began to change in the 1820s. Women slaves thus avoided the extremes of field labor, but they also became much more subject to the abuses of power precisely because of the intimate living conditions with their owners.[11]

Long inhabited by Khoisan who fought valiant but doomed struggles against the Dutch through the end of the seventeenth century, Stellenbosch, Worcester, and Swellendam districts constituted part of the region known as the Western Cape. This region had had the longest history of colonial conquest and settlement in the Cape Colony.[12] Already by the "1720s there were very few Khoisan to be found within a

---

7   Armstrong and Worden, "The Slaves," 109.

8   Worden, *Slavery*, 35.

9   Van der Spuy asserts that Cape slavery was a patriarchal system, in that authority was invested in the senior male. For an examination of the gendered underpinnings of Cape slavery in the early nineteenth century see Van der Spuy, "Collection," esp. pages 23–27.

10   Claire C. Robertson and Martin A. Klein, "Women's Importance in African Slave Systems," in Robertson and Klein, eds., *Women and Slavery*, 3–25, 11.

11   Slave women were also given less to eat than their male peers, despite the fact that by the 1820s many women were also working in the fields, hitherto a job labeled as masculine. On the smaller rations of slave women in comparison to men, see CA, 1/STB 22/158, Letters Received by APS, "Statement of the amount of labor usually performed by slaves employed in agriculture in the District of Stellenbosch . . . ," 23 July 1830; CA, 1/WOC 19/24, Daybook of APS, Worcester, 8 October 1827.

12   While historians have different conceptions as to what constitutes the region, they generally agree that it comprises those districts which were most rooted in slavery: the Cape, Stellenbosch, Paarl, Malmesbury, Worcester, Caledon, and Swellendam districts. Cape districts were constantly reorganized as the colony grew. By about 1800 the main divisions in the Western Cape had been demarcated: the Cape, Stellenbosch, Worcester, and Swellendam. In 1839 a number of new districts were created to further state control in the postemancipation period: Caledon separating from Swellendam, Malmesbury taking sections from both Stellenbosch and the Cape, and Clan William forming what had been the northwesterly segment of Worcester. In 1848 Tulbagh, which had had an earlier birth and demise, was reconstituted from the western section of Worcester. District boundaries changed considerably even in the eighteenth century, so to speak of Worcester, for example, in 1830 is not to talk of the same geographical expanse as would have applied in 1750. See the contributions to James and Simons, *Angry Divide*, for an indication of the slight differences of opinion as to what constitutes the Western Cape.

distance of fifty to sixty (Dutch) miles of Cape Town."[13] The Cape and Stellenbosch districts, where viticulture and grain production dominated the economy, had significantly higher slave populations than districts such as Worcester, where farmers depended largely on Khoi and other debt peons to continue pastoral farming.[14] Through intermarriage, common financial operations, and posts in the colonial bureaucracy, the slaveholding elites of Stellenbosch, the Cape (where Cape Town was located), and Swellendam districts were always more attuned to political and ideological developments than their poorer peers in the farthest reaches of the Worcester and Swellendam regions.[15]

Huge mountain ranges and wide desolate valleys dominate the region. Throughout the history of Cape slavery runaway slaves and Khoisan sought refuge in the Hantamberge and Cedarberg ranges in the north and west as well as in the Nuweveld, Roggeveld, and Swartberge to the north and east. Mountain ranges also commanded the landscape of Stellenbosch and Swellendam districts. The famous Hangklip, site of one of the few documented Maroon communities in the Cape, was situated at the southern tip of the Hottentots Holland range which ran between Swellendam and Stellenbosch.[16]

Climate varied throughout the Western Cape. Worcester was sufficiently large to have areas in the east which shared the Mediterranean climate of the coastal districts and larger stretches to the west which moved into the semi-desert conditions of the Karoo. Rivers such as the Breede and Doorn created stark contrasts of green among the dry soil of much of Worcester district. Stellenbosch and Swellendam enjoyed winter rainfall which supported such a diverse variety of shrubs and small plants as to make the Cape internationally famous among botanists in the eighteenth and nineteenth centuries. Within a few years of European settlement much of the indigenous bush had been cleared. In the 1820s a visitor's first view of the valleys of Stellenbosch and Swellendam was of vast plains of cultivated land framed by dramatic mountain peaks which were largely left uncultivated owing to their inadequate soil.[17]

Governor Simon van der Stel settled Stellenbosch village in 1679. By 1834, along with neighboring Paarl, Stellenbosch was the center of the Cape wine industry.[18] Slaves, who numbered 8,333 in 1832, did most of the labor there, in comparison to districts further east which depended more heavily on the labor of the

---

13 Nigel Penn, "Land, Labour, and Livestock in the Western Cape During the Eighteenth Century," in James and Simons, *Angry Divide* 2–19, 4.

14 14,365 slaves (39.7 percent of the slave population of the Cape Colony) were found in Worcester and Stellenbosch districts. Swellendam and George districts had only 5,661 slaves (15.7 percent of the total). Armstrong and Worden, "The Slaves," 135.

15 Rayner, "Wine and Slaves," Ch. 2. In 1782, 74.5 percent of farmers in Stellenbosch owned more than one slave. Worden, *Slavery*, 13. On distribution of slaves see also Leonard Guelke and Robert Shell, "An Early Colonial Landed Gentry: Land and Wealth in the Cape Colony, 1682–1731," *Journal of Historical Geography* 9 (1983): 265–86.

16 On Hangklip see Ross, *Cape of Torments*.

17 For descriptions of the Cape see those of the collector Henry Lichtenstein, *Travels in Southern Africa, in the Years 1803, 1804, 1805, and 1806*, 2 vols., translated by Anne Plumptre (1812; reprint, Cape Town: Van Riebeeck Society, 1928).

18 See Rayner, "Wine and Slaves," for a discussion of the boom and bust cycles of this faltering industry.

Khoisan.[19] As in other rural districts, both landholding and population densities were concentrated near the village. Within twenty miles of Stellenbosch lived 273 slaveholders, who owned 2,973 slaves.[20]

Worcester and Swellendam both bordered on Stellenbosch and lay within two days' horseback ride east from Cape Town. At the start of the apprenticeship period in 1834, Worcester still exhibited some of the features of a colonial frontier zone. As in the neighboring districts on the eastern frontier, a small and sparse white population involved predominantly in pastoral production ruled over slaves and dependent laborers with relatively little intervention from the state. Indigenous Khoi and other dependent laborers comprised the majority of the labor force which contributed to the rise of a culture of the unfree which united de jure and de facto slaves.

Swellendam, which bordered Stellenbosch in the west, Worcester in the north, George to the east, and had a southern coastal boundary on the Atlantic Ocean, embodied both the characteristics of the frontier and the more settled areas of the Western Cape. Swellendam farmers used a combination of slave and dependent labor and the population ratios between slave and free were much more akin to the Worcester than the Stellenbosch profile.[21] White wheat farmers near Caledon village in the west owned the majority of slaves. In 1831 there were 624 slaveholders in the district and only twenty-nine owned more than eight slaves.[22]

The district was distinctive in being home to a number of mission stations which predated the emancipation of slaves at the Cape; after emancipation, missionaries also established small stations in both Worcester and Stellenbosch. Missionaries belonging to the Moravian Church, or United Brethren, a Lutheran Pietist church of German origins, had been active in the Cape since the eighteenth century. The Moravians started the first mission station in the Colony in Swellendam district in 1738, which lasted for a short period, and reestablished it again in 1792.[23] By 1834 the Moravians had six stations, mostly among the Khoi in the Western Cape, but also one in Tembuland. They had "thirty-eight missionaries, and claimed 3,099 native converts, all except eight of whom were" Khoi.[24] These missionaries originally intended to minister to the Khoisan population, but the stations of Genadendal and Elim came

---

19   CA, 1/STB 22/159, 29 August 1832, "Statement Shewing [sic] the Number of Slaveowners (or Managers) Belonging to the District of Stellenbosch." In 1832 Stellenbosch village had 1,050 people listed as "black" and 650 as "white." *South African Almanac and Directory for 1832* (Cape Town: George Greig, 1832). For distinctions in labor relations in the Western Cape in the eighteenth century see Worden, *Slavery*, Ch. 1.

20   CA, 1/STB 22/159, 29 August 1832, "Statement Shewing [sic] the Number of Slaveowners (or Managers) Belonging to the District of Stellenbosch." The village of the Paarl to the northwest had a larger population with 426 people owning 4,073 slaves. The most sparsely populated section of the district was the field cornetcy of River Zonder End and Palmiet River where 40 owners lived with 209 slaves.

21   In 1833, 11,822 free people resided in the district as compared to 3,024 slaves. *South African Almanack for 1834*, 136.

22   CA, ZP 1/1/75, PRO, CO 48/142, Despatch Cape of Good Hope, "Slavery No. 30." From Cape Governor, 21 April 1831.

23   Bernhard Kruger, *The Pear Tree Blossoms: A History of the Moravian Mission Stations in South Africa, 1837-1869* (Genadendal: Genadendal Press, 1966), 19.

24   John Galbraith, *Reluctant Empire: British Policy on the South African Frontier, 1834–1854* (Berkeley and Los Angeles: University of California Press, 1963), 79.

to play a crucial role in Caledon's postemancipation world as many apprentices and freed people moved to the missions looking for land.[25]

Travelers to the Cape frequently noted the differences between the settled arable region closest to Cape Town and the sparsely populated pastoral-based societies of the interior. In Stellenbosch and the Cape districts wine and wheat farmers lived "in a decent manner"; of the Dutch settlers living in other areas, John Barrow reported in the late eighteenth century that "few of them, behind the first range of mountains have any sort of convenience, comfort, or even cleanliness."[26] In 1803 Lichtenstein, a traveler to the Cape, wrote of Swellendam district that

> there is a much greater difference between the higher and lower class of the inhabitants, between the masters and the servants, both in their dress and in their habits, than in many other parts, particularly in the Roggeveld [Worcester]. The great trade in cattle, which places the farmers in affluence, and the much more frequent intercourse with the Cape Town, which gives them more idea of polished life, has introduced a sort of luxury and refinement among the higher classes, to which the lower classes, who gain their livelihood chiefly by cutting wood, cannot aspire.[27]

These regional differences in the tenor of slaveholding culture had important implications both for the place of gender and family in slavery and in slaves' experiences of freedom after 1838. There never was one Cape slavery. In Cape Town, social relations and identities were much more fluid than in the rural areas where more than a century of slaveholding, the use of dependent Khoi labor, and the absence of significant free black communities contributed to a greater correlation of racial identities and class status.[28] A slave living in Cape Town with the opportunity to earn wages (indeed, to work under explicit contractual terms), to belong to an Islamic religious community, and to enjoy significant freedoms, would have had a vastly different experience of the peculiar institution than a slave living in Worcester district.[29] There, desolation, violence, the denial to slaves of any formal religious life, and living conditions which might include sharing one room with other slaves and dependent laborers, as well as the slaveholding family, rendered slavery in harsher hues.[30] Conditions also varied in the rural areas. On the wealthier farms of Stellenbosch district, for example, slaves and their owners lived in separate quarters, although individual domestic slaves might well be required to sleep in the main house.

Rural slavery in the Western Cape did have some commonalities. The relative impenetrability of boundaries between slaves and dependent laborers on the one hand, and slaveholders on the other, renders this region somewhat distinctive both in comparison to the relative fluidity of relations between people in urban areas, and

---

25 See Chapters 4 and 7 following.

26 Sir John Barrow, *Travels into the Interior of Southern Africa in the Years 1797 and 1798*, 2 vols. (London: T. Cadell Jr. and W. Davies, 1801, 1804), Vol. 1, 76.

27 Lichtenstein, *Travels in Southern Africa*, Vol. 1, 204.

28 Worden, *Slavery*, Ch. 10, esp. 144–45.

29 See Andrew Bank, "The Disintegration of Urban Slavery at the Cape, 1806–1834" (paper presented to Africa Seminar, Center for African Studies, University of Cape Town, May 1991), 3, 6, 7.

30 Mason, "Fit for Freedom," Ch. 5, provides a helpful discussion on regional variations in Cape slavery in the nineteenth century.

in comparison to slaveholding societies elsewhere in Southern Africa.[31] The small numbers of free blacks in the rural districts by the early nineteenth century facilitated the elaboration of dichotomies which paired "whiteness" and free status as opposed to "blackness" and enslavement. This rigid "polarization" of society was particularly notable in districts such as Stellenbosch where slavery formed the basis of the economy.[32]

Boundaries in Cape Slavery

Slaveholders maintained the division between free and slave partly through violence, in part through an understanding as to the different rights of slaves and free, and partly through an ideology of the slaveholding family which excluded children born of slave mothers and slaveholder men.[33] As Ann Stoler has shown, in colonial societies the pattern of sexual relations through which a child had been produced, through marriage, concubinage, or rape, and the familial structure to which a child was seen to belong, helped situate an individual within the boundaries of the colonized, the colonizer, or in an interstitial position on the margins. In slaveholding colonies, domination became even more intricately woven with issues of family, sexuality, and cultural reproduction.[34]

From the seventeenth century social boundaries in the rural Western Cape were produced and reproduced in part through a discourse on the family, but these boundaries were inherently ambiguous and frequently contradictory.[35] Rural Cape

---

31 Worden has argued that the social structure of the eighteenth-century rural Western Cape was crucially "conditioned by slavery." The "development of social stratification between slaveowners and their labourers provided a basic class division which coincided with racial differences to an extent unknown in other parts of the settlement." Worden, *Slavery*, 138. Historians have generally argued either for the importance of race relations formed under slavery for later racism in South Africa, or for the distinctiveness of the frontier experience in creating racial distinctions. For an astute examination of the issues see William Freund, "Race in the Social Structure of South Africa, 1652–1836," *Race and Class* 18 (1976): 53–67; also Martin Legassick, "The Frontier Tradition in South African Historiography," in Marks and Atmore, eds., *Economy and Society*, 44–79. For the argument advancing the importance of Cape slavery in the formation of race relations see Worden, *Slavery*, Ch. 10; see also Elphick ad Giliomee, eds., *The Shaping of South African Society*.

32 Worden, *Slavery*, 151.

33 On violence see Ross, *Cape of Torments*, and Worden, *Slavery*. For analysis of how notions of community and honor informed slaveholder behavior see Dooling, *Law and Community*.

34 Ann Stoler, "Carnal Knowledge and Imperial Power: Gender, Race, and Morality in Colonial Asia," in Micaela di Leonardo, ed., *Gender at the Crossroads of Knowledge: Feminist Anthropology in the Postmodern Era* (Berkeley: University of California Press, 1991), 51–101, esp. 53. On colonial boundaries and sexuality see Ann Stoler, "Rethinking Colonial Categories: European Communities and the Boundaries of Rule," *Comparative Studies in Society and History* 13 1 (1989): 134–61. For a discussion of the importance of family in colonial cultures see Verena Martinez-Alier, *Marriage, Class, and Colour in Nineteenth-Century Cuba* (Cambridge: Cambridge University Press, 1974; Ann Arbor: University of Michigan Press, 1989).

35 P. J. van der Merwe, *The Migrant Farmer in the History of the Cape Colony, 1657–1842*, translated by Roger B. Beck (Athens, OH: Ohio University Press, 1995), Ch. 2. On the family as a means of maintaining racial and class endogamy see Guelke and Shell, "Early Colonial." Various recent studies have argued that Cape slavery was imbued with a familial ideology. See especially Shell, *Children of Bondage*. For an examination and critique of the notion of paternalism or patriarchy and Cape slavery, see Robert Ross, "Paternalism, Patriarchy, and Afrikaans," *South African Historical Journal* 32 (May 1995): 34–47. Many thanks to Dr. Ross for sending me a copy of his article.

slavery was both intimate and violent.[36] The household formed the fulcrum of most slaves' experience of rural slavery since slaveholding was widely distributed among the settler population with most settlers owning less than eight slaves. Foreign observers of Cape slavery, perhaps more familiar with the plantation slave economies of the West Indies, felt that the proximity of Cape slavery obfuscated the boundary which should exist between slave and slaveholder. John Barrow, for example, felt an improper degree of familiarity existed between white women and their slaves in the interior districts, such as Worcester, which led to the decline of white feminine standards.[37]

The intimacy of Cape slavery, however, did not generate an explicit ideology of paternalism or indeed patriarchy among Cape slaveholders. Cape slaveholders did not elaborate a philosophical argument either for or against slavery. "The stands taken by the colonists were almost always *in reaction* to external initiatives."[38] At least up to the 1820s, when amelioration measures set them on the defensive, Cape slaveholders ruled without an elaborate set of justifications: slaveholding was perceived as necessary, hierarchies as natural. Cape slaveholders in this respect had more in common with many of their African counterparts than with the white slaveholding societies of the Atlantic world. But in comparison to many other Southern African slave societies Cape slavery was strikingly unabsorptive, certainly by the nineteenth century.[39]

Under slavery, an individual's alienation from natal ties constituted the very foundation of his or her enslavement. As Patterson has stated, "slavery is the permanent, violent domination of natally alienated and generally dishonored persons."[40] The natal alienation of the slave resonated particularly in this pre-industrial society where both slaves and slaveholders appear to have conceptualized identity through membership in a community constituted by corporate kin and household relationships. To be free was to be imbricated in dependencies and obligations to a variety of people, and especially to one's family and fictive kin.[41] In self-reproducing slave soci-

---

36   See Worden, *Slavery*, and Ross, *Cape of Torments*, for discussion of the widespread use of violence in Cape slaveholding.

37   "This good lady, born in the wilds of Africa, & educated among slaves & Hottentots, has little idea of what, in a state of society, constitutes female delicacy. She makes no scruple of having her legs & feet washed in warm water by a slave before strangers. . . ." Barrow, *Travels*, 80. See also CA, A602, Diaries of Samuel E. Hudson, Book 11, "Marriages," 1796. For a discussion of Hudson's analysis of Cape slavery as resting upon a collapse of public and private boundaries see Kirsten McKenzie, "Samuel Eusebius Hudson at the Cape of Good Hope, 1797–1807" (B.A. Hons. diss., Department of History, University of Cape Town, 1991), esp. Ch. 4.

38   Andre Du Toit and Hermann Giliomee, eds., *Afrikaner Political Thought: Analysis and Documents*, Vol. 1, 1780–1850 (Cape Town: David Philip, 1983), 34. Italics in original.

39   Miers and Kopytoff have argued that unlike slavery in the West which was founded on the concept of the slave as property, many African societies practiced an absorptive slavery which saw in the slave a "bundle of rights" which could be alienated in a variety of combinations. Miers and Kopytoff, "Introduction," 61. "Absorption" is best seen as one slaveholding strategy among many which invokes the power of a familial ideology to rule over the unfree. See Frederick Cooper, "The Problem of Slavery in African Studies," *Journal of African History* 20 (1979): 103–125. Also Jonathon Glassman, "The Bondsman's New Clothes: The Contradictory Consciousness of Slave Resistance on the Swahili Coast," *Journal of African History* 32, 2 (1991): 277–312.

40   Orlando Patterson, *Slavery and Social Death: A Comparative Study* (Cambridge: Harvard University Press, 1982), 13. See also Chapter 2 following for a discussion of the concept of natal alienation.

41   Miers and Kopytoff, "Introduction." The African literature on family and kinship is vast. For a critical introduction see Jane Guyer, "Household and Community in African Studies," *African Studies Review* 24, 2/3 (June–September 1981): 87–137.

eties such as the early-nineteenth-century Cape, slaveholder power rested upon the power to alienate slaves from their natal ties, to sell them away from their kith and kin. Slaves were the visible outsiders within the slaveholding household: masters denied them permission to marry and or to protect their children or themselves from physical abuse and murder.[42]

In the Western Cape region the ideology of family seldom functioned as a means of reproducing slaveholding society. Slaveholders rarely tried to control slaves by holding out the possibility that they might be absorbed into slaveholding society through marriage, for example.[43] In the rare cases when slave women married into slaveholding families, such marriages generally do not seem to have arisen from any absorptive quality of Cape slavery, but rather from the particular demographics of individual regions at different periods.[44]

In the interior, for a time, slavery assumed a more absorptive cast. In the North Western Cape permanent relationships between slaveholders and Khoi were more common than between slaves and settlers, in part because of the demographic preponderance of Khoi over slaves. These relationships, which were most prevalent in the eighteenth century, produced children called Bastards in settler lexicon.[45] The Bastards occupied an interstitial place between settlers and slaves throughout the eighteenth century, often becoming the clients of settlers. The increasing pressure on land, the insecurity of the frontier, and the settlers' desire to intensify exploitation of slave and dependent labor led to the decrease in status of Khoi, Bastards, and Bastard Hottentots (children of Khoi women and slaves). From the late eighteenth century up to Ordinance No. 50 of 1828, government legislation tied children labeled as Bastard Hottentots through indentures to the farms where their parents worked; in many respects such families suffered the experience of slavery. Many moved in the early nineteenth century across the northern borders of the colony, founding the Griqua state under the leadership of Adam Kok.[46]

Ideologies of family resonated in Cape slavery, but in complex and often inconsistent ways. No one definition of family applies to all participants in Cape slavery. The language of family was prevalent mostly at the level of legal discourse which owed much to the history of Roman Dutch law, rooted as it was in the notion of the paterfamilias.[47] Definition of family and recognition of family ties formed one of the

---

42 This analysis is in contrast to Shell, *Children of Bondage*.

43 On incorporation see Barbara Isaacman and Allen Isaacman, "Slavery and Social Stratification in Mozambique: A Study of the Kaporo System," in Meirs and Kopytoff, eds., *Slavery in Africa*, 105–120.

44 Many of the marriages which did take place involving a slave woman and a white man occurred in Cape Town and involved urban employees of the VOC rather than slaveholders. The incorporation of female slaves into the slaveholding family occurred primarily in the early years of Dutch rule when very few white women settled at the Cape, although a few such marriages did occur in rural areas into the nineteenth century. The marriage usually took place after the woman had been baptized and manumitted. See Shell, *Children of Bondage*, 315–24. For a discussion of marriages and miscegenation see Elphick and Shell, "Intergroup Relations."

45 Elphick and Shell, "Intergroup Relations," 202.

46 Robert Ross, *Adam Kok's Griquas: A Study in the Development of Stratification in South Africa* (Cambridge: Cambridge University Press, 1976). It is almost impossible to discover how many people from these groups moved into the category White. Elphick and Shell, "Intergroup Relations," 202.

47 In some respects Roman Dutch law mediated the "excessive paternal power under the Romans." Van der Linden states that unlike Roman law, Roman Dutch law gave mothers "paternal power" also. Van der Linden, *Institutes*, 30.

consistent sites of struggle between slaveholders and slaves. Slaves used family as a strategy to challenge the atomization of Cape slavery. They saw family as a wide and incorporative ideal of social relationships which helped them forge friendships and ties with people living across the region. Slaveholders, on the other hand, set limits on who counted as family in order to maintain boundaries between themselves and their slaves.

Families defined by biological ties frequently straddled the perimeters of a number of more clearly socially-constituted families. Settler identity activated the social frontiers of family when ties of blood would have meant including slaves as kin. Nonetheless, in practice various nuclear and extended families coexisted enjoying different degrees of slaveholder recognition.

Slaveholders perceived family as a domestic or household group ruled by a patriarch, and as a bloodline.[48] The denial of paternity to slave men constituted one of the hallmarks of slavery. In a culture in which masculinity was formed in part through having authority over one's kin, a slave man experienced a multiple negation of his identity.[49] He was denied participation in the world of men by being robbed of authority. He experienced the threat of or actual natal alienation from his own parents as well as the alienation of his children, particularly if they were the children of a slave woman.

Slave women's relationships with the slaveholding family were differently configured. Slave women suffered sexual abuse at the hands of their owners who in addition to raping slave women as part of their rights as masters also had an incentive to sire children who would add to their slave labor force with the closing of the British transatlantic slave trade.[50] Evidence suggests that slaveholding society condoned but did not encourage sexual relations between masters and their slaves. And where such relations were discussed, they were seen as being the result of the promiscuity of slave women, not as the result of domination by slaveholders.[51] These depictions of slave women as wanton prefaced the discourse about the immorality of slave women which dominated abolitionist campaigns in the 1820s and 1830s. As we shall see in the following chapter, this vision also helped validate the argument by the Cape protector of slaves that Cape slave women did not deserve the same kind of protection as did their slave peers in the West Indies.

Sexual relations between slaveholders and slaves complicates a discussion of "family." The boundaries between the slaveholding household and kinship were constantly transgressed throughout the history of Cape slavery. In general most sexual relations between settlers and colonized under slavery tended to be "extramari-

---

48   For a discussion of the different views of family see Patricia Van der Spuy, "Slave Women and the Family in Nineteenth-Century Cape Town," *South African Historical Journal* 27 (1992): 50–74. Also Jean-Louis Flandrin, *Families in Former Times: Kinship, Household, and Sexuality in Early Modern France*, translated by Richard Southern (Cambridge: Cambridge University Press, 1979), who argues against seeing family as merely a "domestic cell" (p. 4).

49   On masculinity in the 1820s see Van der Spuy, "Collection."

50   See Mason, "Fit for Freedom," 205.

51   De Kock talks of the "loose . . . morals of many of the slave women" being the reason for so much sexual contact between white men and slave women. Victor De Kock, *Those in Bondage: An Account of the Life of a Slave at the Cape in the Days of the Dutch East India Company* (London: George Allen and Unwin, 1950): 118–19. See also Hudson, "Marriages."

tal" and did not confer on the children of slave women any right to claim relations to the slaveholding family.[52] In 1772 "it was stipulated that the mother, as well as the offspring begotten by a master with her, should never be sold, whether the estate were solvent or insolvent, but should be emancipated after the death of the master."[53] But owners rarely manumitted their children or their lovers. In 1832, for example, a slave woman named Philida from Stellenbosch came to the protector of slaves (the official charged under amelioration legislation to look after the interests of slaves) with a classic example of the marriage of violence, sexuality, and intimacy which marked Cape slavery. Philida stated that her owner's son had had a sexual relationship with her for some eight years. That "connexion" had produced four children who theoretically could have been either acknowledged by the father as his own, or at the very least have been freed. Certainly her lover had promised that he would buy Philida's freedom.[54]

However, Philida's owner, who was also her children's grandfather, now banished her from the farm and threatened to sell her far away to someone living in the interior of the colony. Her lover denied that he had ever made promises to buy her freedom and argued that Philida was being sold because she was "impudent" towards his mother. However neither the father of the children, nor his father, Philida's owner, denied that the relationship had taken place. As Philida "had no proof of the promise made by Mr. Brink," the protector recorded that he could not prevent her sale nor enter into any further inquiry of her complaint. However, in acknowledgment, perhaps, of the long-standing nature of the relationship between Philida and Brink, the protector recommended that Mr. Brink have his father "dispose of her in Town which he promised."[55]

A sexual liaison was insufficient to upset the social construction of the slaveholding family. The status of the mother overwhelmingly shaped an individual's experience of colonial life in this slaveholding colony. Three children of one Johan Roode Senior faced completely different fates because of the status of their mothers. Two were destined to be slaves, the other free. Here in one family a sibling became owner of his own brothers through accident of birth. In 1827 Johan Christian Roode Senior admitted to the assistant protector of Worcester that he had had a relationship with his slave woman Clara. They had two children who were now eleven and four years old. The records suggest that this relationship and the children arising from it was the cause of some long-standing tension within the family.[56]

It seems that Clara hoped that an investigation by the assistant protector into the paternity of her children might secure their freedom. While legally children derived their status from their mother, evidence of having a settler father sometimes aided a mother's attempts to have her children manumitted.[57] This step was necessary as

52   Elphick and Shell, "Intergroup Relations," 196, 202.

53   De Kock, *Those in Bondage*, 122.

54   CA, ZP 1/6/6, PRO, CO 53/55; Part 1, Book 1; No. 405, 1832, Report of PS for July–December 1832, Table B: Cases of Injuries.

55   Ibid.

56   CA, 1/WOC 19/24, Daybook of APS, 29 November 1827.

57   Mason, "Fit for Freedom," 210–26. For discussion of the ways in which women's "reproductive labor" within slaveholding households could make them more likely to be manumitted, see Margaret Strobel, "Slavery and Reproductive Labor in Mombasa," in Robertson and Klein, eds., *Women and Slavery*, 111–129, 127.

Mrs. Roode had lied about the children's paternity when she sent in notice of their births to the slave office in Cape Town. One does not know if she did so with the agreement of her husband or whether this arose out of conflict between the couple because of the relationship between Clara and Roode. Roode told the protector that he wished that Clara and her two children could "be made happy, as she has always been a faithful Servant." However, he said that his mother-in-law's will prevented him from doing this. The children, Adriaan and Hendrik, registered as slaves, became, through this will of his wife's mother, the property of their half-sibling, Johan Christiaan Roode.[58] For most slaves biological connection to slaveholding families did not mean social incorporation into settler society. Slaveholders constructed the border between the families of slaveholders and slaves so as to be impervious to challenge based on biology.[59]

Slaves and Family

Up to the 1820s Cape law and slaveholder society did not recognize slave marriages, a common feature of many African slave societies.[60] Cape slaveholders frequently sold slaves away from kin. In 1830 for example, a slave woman called Sarah went to the protector in order to try and gain recognition of her relationship with a fellow slave who now lived six hours away from her. Sarah's owner had made her part from her husband as the owner wanted exclusive sexual access to her. Sarah testified that she had gone to her mistress to try and gain redress but that her master had then tied her and her sister to a "wagon, made them take off their upper garments, and flogged them."[61]

Despite slaveholder opposition, slaves and bonded laborers forged emotional bonds which crisscrossed the farmlands of the Western Cape recognizing few barriers of distance, confinement, or law. Evidence suggests that while relationships were not recognized by law, slaves did accord them respect and counted on spouses for emotional and physical support. Fortuin, an old man and a slave of Isaac van der Merwe of Cold Bokkeveld, depended upon his wife to share her food with him when he was sick, as he got no food if he did not work. Another slave on the same farm said that her husband had given her most of her clothes.[62]

The inheritance of slave status via the maternal line influenced the patterning of slave relationships. The protector of slaves reported in 1831 that "the whole class of Male Slaves seldom intermarry with Slaves."[63] In the rural districts it appears that

---

58   CA, 1/WOC 19/24, Daybook of APS, 29 November 1827.

59   I am grateful to Elizabeth Eldredge for pointing this out.

60   Robertson and Klein, "Women's Importance in African Slave Systems," 7.

61   The reason her master gave for flogging her sister was that, as he said, "her sister and mother had put her up to telling her mistress." CA, 1/WOC 19/24, Daybook of APS, 17 November 1830. See also 1/WOC, 19/24, 15 June 1829, case of Susanna Sophia van der Merwe, and 8 November 1830, statement by Isaac, slave of Widow Ernst Marais.

62   CA, 1/WOC 19/24, Daybook of APS, 2 September 1830.

63   CA, ZP 1/6/5, PRO, CO 53/52, Report of PS for the First Half 1831, 22 November 1831.

slave men more often formed relationships with Khoi women.[64] The demographic imbalance in the century prior to 1820 no doubt contributed to this pattern of relationships, but does not explain its continuation into the 1820s and 1830s when the sexual ratios of slave men to slave women were more equal. Perhaps the most important reason for this pattern was that any children born of the union would be free. This did not necessarily secure for the child a better life in practice, since farmers successfully managed to indenture the children of their dependent laborers even after the passing of Ordinance No. 50 in 1828.[65] But people's awareness of the possibilities of freedom for their children clearly was very powerful.

Partly because of the lack of state concern with slaves' emotional ties, the records on slaves' intimate lives are scarce prior to the 1820s. This is as true for relationships between husbands and wives as it is for parent/child relationships. Earlier scholarship suggested that even where two-parent slave households did exist the role of the father was very weak.[66] Now, however, research suggests the pervasiveness of the various forms of slave families, including two-parent households, although matrifocal families were most prevalent.[67] As we shall see in Chapter 6, at the ending of slavery stable relationships between slaves, and between slaves and nominally free laborers, were evident and in the early 1840s many freed people went to the churches to get legally married.

When talking of the slave family—in terms of its consisting only of slaves—families headed by women were the norm for the Cape. Blood ties to children and to mothers appear to have been a central part of slave women's consciousness of family, but these ties were also imbedded in a wider community of the unfree.[68] Children most often resided on the farm where their mother lived. Young men, unless artisans, were much more likely to be sold to new owners than women and their young children.[69] "[W]hen sale destroyed a family, wives lost husbands, but husbands very

---

64   This is based on analysis of the records of cases brought before the assistant protectors of slaves. For example, Absolom, a slave of Abraham Visser in Worcester district, had been married to a Khoi woman for two years in 1829 when he brought a charge against his owner for denying him food. CA, 1/WOC 19/24, Daybook of APS, 1 September 1829. See also the case of Louis, a slave who had been born in Mozambique, who married a Khoi woman and had children with her. In 1830 he laid charges against his owner for preventing him from seeing his wife. The owner agreed, after the assistant protector of Swellendam ordered him to court, to allow Louis's wife to come and live with him; a rare happy conclusion in the annals of the assistant protector. CA, 1/SWM 16/22, Diary of AP, 9 March 1830.

65   See Chapter 2 for a discussion of the struggle over child labor. This system of indenture had its origins in 1721 when farmers objecting "to feeding the children born from unions between Khoisan women and slave men" petitioned the Council of Policy to permit the indenturing of these children. The petition was refused, but from 1775 a regulation was passed permitting the indentureship of these children up until the age of twenty-five in the district of Stellenbosch. Richard Elphick and V. C. Malherbe, "The Khoisan to 1828," in Elphick and Giliomee, eds., *Shaping*, 1–50, 32.

66   Worden, *Slavery*, 96.

67   See Mason, "Fit for Freedom," for the period from 1806. For an earlier article on family and sexual relations see Robert Ross, "Oppression, Sexuality, and Slavery at the Cape of Good Hope," *Historical Reflections* 6, 2 (1979): 421–433, 426.

68   On slave families in Cape Town see Van der Spuy, "Slave Women." Crais, *White Supremacy and Black Resistance*, Ch. 4, discusses the blurred boundaries between slaves and dependent laborers.

69   Shell, *Children of Bondage*, 132–34.

often lost wives and children."[70] Mothers also lived to see their sons, at the very least, sold into slavery elsewhere.

We should be wary of oversimplifying the matriarchal dynamics in the personal lives of the unfree, however, if only because in those cases where both parents were present it is difficult to talk with any certainty as to the roles played by either parent—the records do not easily reveal the dynamics within the family when the parents were together. The terms of amelioration legislation which allowed slaves to bring cases to the protector and assistant protectors of slaves privilege our knowledge of those slave families which were separated rather than those which remained together or those whose members were were able to see one another.

The paternal absence of slave and dependent laborers created by the circumstances of Cape slavery does not equate necessarily with a feeble paternal presence. The records for the last ten years of slavery at the Cape do suggest that slave men attempted to play an important role in their children's lives. Where mothers and fathers were forced to live separately fathers aspired to visit their families as often as possible. They tried in various ways to maintain contact with their children, often undergoing punishment as a result.[71] Relationships between slaves and between slaves and Khoi across farm and ownership lines, and their own claims to authority over decisions within their families, defied slaveholders' syncretic representations of family, place, and power.

In 1831, the slave Goliah complained that "his . . . Master has named his infant child Aaron contrary to the wishes of himself and his mother who desired that he might be named Goliah. . . ."[72] At issue was the right to name, which signified who had control over the child. By asserting his right to name his child, Goliah challenged the slaveholder's proclamation of exclusive authority over the infant. Goliah's desire to name his child after himself suggests too that he wished to affirm his status as a father. This paternal right and status was denied him through the maternal inheritance of slavery; slavery also denied him paternal status because he was a man who lacked autonomy, a hallmark of masculinity in the nineteenth-century Cape. That Goliah and his wife thought the matter important enough to take to the protector also suggests the importance of personal relationships to slaves' experience of slavery and their struggle against its strictures. Goliah thus elaborated, through his complaint, a critique of slavery and sought to limit the personal power of his owner by claiming his authority in a private sphere of the slave family.[73]

---

70   Deborah Gray White, *Ar'n't I a Woman? Female Slaves in the Plantation South* (New York: W. W. Norton and Co., 1985), 145.

71   For example, Aroulus, a slave from the Worcester district, managed to give his two rations of biscuits to a Khoi man, Klaas, who would be passing his daughter's home. As a result of giving away his rations Aroulus was beaten. CA, 1/WOC 19/24, Daybook of APS, 20 May 1831.

72   The assistant protector wrote to Van Zyl suggesting that he negotiate with Goliah. CA, 1/SWM 16/22, Diary of APS, 24 February 1831.

73   See also CA, 1/STB 2/35, Documents in the Trial of Rex vs. David Johannes Malan for assault, 5 July 1836.

Conclusion

In the 1820s, a discourse about family emerged in the era of amelioration in part because of slaves' history of protest against the separate sales of parents and children and of other loved ones. The personal lives of slaves and the unfree in the rural areas most explicitly challenged slaveholders' attempts to rule through denial of family to slaves and dependent laborers. Extended kin networks crossed farm boundaries, generations, and included both "real" and "fictive" kindred. Family relationships bound slaves and unfree laborers in the communal production of social knowledge about right and wrong, justice and injustice, through mutual obligations between slaves and the unfree.[74] The families forged by slaves also confounded the discourses of abolition which represented slaves as living outside of any family life. While, as in other societies, families were as often sites of struggle and violence as they were oases of calm and support, slaves successfully built a culture of the unfree which rested on intimate relationships denied them by slaveholders and obscured by anti-slavery discourse.

Slavery was premised upon the notion that claims over a person could not be compartmentalized into legitimate and illegitimate areas of interest. Slaveholders expected to have authority over the bodies, labor, and habits of their slaves. Slaves repudiated such total authority. The conflicts over amelioration of Cape slavery in the 1820s and early 1830s, which will be examined in the following chapter, involved precisely slaves' rejection of their owners' attempts to conflate the boundaries of private and public and to interfere in the affective life of their slaves.

---

74 This section owes much to Herbert Gutman, "Afro-American Kinship Before and After Emancipation in North America," in Medick and Sabean, eds., *Interest and Emotion*, 241–65, 246.

2

Gender, Sexuality, and Amelioration

The year 1823 witnessed the resurgence of the British antislavery movement which had first emerged in the late eighteenth century with the campaigns to end the British slave trade. Now, with the formation of the Society for Mitigating and Gradually Improving the State of Slavery throughout the British Dominions (better known as the Anti-Slavery Society), antislavery activists directed their attention to the amelioration of slavery in the British Empire. The efforts of the Society were remarkably successful: In the course of the next eight years Parliament passed a host of legislation aimed at ameliorating slavery. In these laws of the 1820s and early 1830s we see evidence of a widespread faith among British abolitionists and British government officials alike in the moral power of motherhood, the civilizing power of (monogamous) marriage, the hierarchy of men over women within the family, and the spiritual power of religion, to effect a transformation in slavery and to prepare slaves for liberation into an economy based on wage labor. In 1833 slavery was formally abolished. It was followed by what became a four-year apprenticeship in which former slaves and masters were supposed to be prepared for the new world of free wage labor.

Amelioration was a "watershed in the history of Cape slavery" and an era which left an ambiguous legacy to the postemancipation social order.[1] On the one hand, this period from 1823 through to 1834 gave slaves and dependent laborers a tentative stake in the rule of law by allowing them to prosecute their owners. Also, for the first time, slaveholders had to recognize slaves' emotional, physical, and economic rights—as long as these rights did not overly interfere with the prerogative of slaveholders. On the other hand, amelioration also initiated the interventionist legal

---

1 As Davis has stated, with the abolitionist legislation of the 1820s and 1830 the British government "essentially disarmed its opponents by endorsing and absorbing two ideologies—the abolitionist ideology, which called for a wholly new dispensation attuned to moral principles revealed by the collective voice of the Christian public, and the proprietor ideology, which insisted on gradual change, minimal interference with local self-government, and compensation for pecuniary losses." Davis, *Slavery and Human Progress*, 207.

system which was to be a feature of subsequent Cape rural history.[2] This period of the 1820s and 1830s also witnessed the rise of a new "antiliberalism" rooted in an affiliation between slaveholders and an ascendant Dutch-speaking intelligentsia which mounted virulent attacks on amelioration in the 1820s up through 1832.[3] The hostility of officers at the Cape to many of the provisions of metropolitan ameliorating legislation signaled to slaves that liberty when and if it came would be shaped by a colonial order quite hostile to the rights and interests of ex-slaves and colonized people.[4]

This chapter charts the history of amelioration at the Cape by analyzing the ways in which gender ideologies shaped amelioration legislation and by focusing on the slaves' experience of the process. Cape officials limited the scope of amelioration by claiming a sophisticated local knowledge about slaveholding, the behavior of slaves, and especially about the supposed limitations of slave women at the Cape. I argue that colonial officials' notions of gender which were formed in part through contemporary conceptions of race helped to produce, in the process of amelioration, a portrait of slaves as immoral, delinquent and in need of strict supervision. In Part III, we shall see how these images influenced the process of emancipation after 1838 and how freed people constructed their own notions of gender relations.

Gender and Amelioration

Particular associations between gender identity, family, and society pervaded antislavery debates in Britain and similarly affected the framing of the various Orders in Council ameliorating slavery in the 1820s and early 1830s. Amelioration legislation emerged from a belief by government reformers and both male and female antislavery activists that secure family ties, a strong relationship between husband and wife, and the morality of slave women were necessary in order for the slave population to become sufficiently disciplined to be able to handle the responsibilities of freedom.[5]

Abolitionists characterized slavery as having caused moral degeneration of slave society. Fowell Buxton, for example, stated in 1828 that he did not favor immediate emancipation as he believed that "slavery has infused such a moral poison into the negro—has so ground and sunk him to the earth—has so turned him out of the

---

2   See Dooling, "Slaves, Slaveholders, and Amelioration," 63. For an excellent history of amelioration at the Cape see Edwards, *Towards Emancipation*. See also Pamela Scully, "Criminality and Conflict in Rural Stellenbosch, South Africa, 1870-1900," *Journal of African History* 30 (1989): 289-300, for an examination of the hegemonic function of the law in the late nineteenth-century.

3   Bank, "Liberals," Ch. 3.

4   Up to 1853 the Cape government consisted of two tiers. The inner circle consisted of the governor, appointed by the Crown, the lieutenant-governor of the Eastern Cape, the attorney general who had crucial responsibility in framing the laws, and a variety of individuals within the local Colonial Office. Settler interests were most clearly represented by members of the Legislative Council and the Advisory Council, many of whom were settlers themselves.

5   See William A. Green, *British Slave Emancipation: The Sugar Colonies and the Great Experiment, 1830–1865* (1976; reprint, Oxford: Clarendon Press, 1987), 102–103. Also Midgley, *Women Against Slavery.*

race of men, that he is not fit for the exercise of every civil right."[6] The portrayal of slavery as immoral rested partly on an understanding that slavery overturned naturally ordained gender roles. On the one hand, abolitionist tracts described slave men as feminine and childlike precisely because they were deprived of their male rights to be head of a family and prevented from exercising the power that derived from such a position.[7] Indeed, in 1826 the *Anti-Slavery Monthly Reporter* described the horrors of slavery by comparing how an English "peasant" would feel if he looked "at his wife . . . on her shoulder the burning brand which marks her as a *chattel of another* [my emphasis]. . . ."[8] Emancipation would liberate a slave man into masculinity by giving him the right to protect, and indeed to own, his wife. On the other hand, this notion of the slave man as being a man-in-waiting coexisted with, as Clare Midgley suggests, an image of slave men as violently aggressive, sexually licentious, and powerful. This view surfaced particularly around periods of slave rebellions. Freedom, antislavery activists argued, would both tame slave men's unruly masculinity and introduce them to adulthood by conferring on them the right to be head of a family and thus providing them roots in a stable domestic life.[9]

This construction of masculinity depended to some extent on the notion that femininity entailed the willing embrace of a husband, of motherhood, and entrance into the domestic privacy of the nuclear family. This belief arose in England in the late eighteenth century and was fairly widespread in upper- and middle-class circles, from which many abolitionists came, by the 1820s. Women were held to be especially virtuous. It was believed that in bringing up their children and serving as a beacon of morality to their husbands women would influence society from their place in the home.[10] This perspective informed one of the earliest parliamentary debates of the 1820s on West Indian slavery. Supporters of the proposed Trinidad Order assumed that women were the moral pillars of society. Therefore, if one could make women moral, then the rest of slave society would follow. In arguing for the abolition of flogging of women slaves Prime Minister George Canning argued that "to raise the weaker sex in self-respect . . . is the first step from barbarism to civilization." In his

---

6   JL, John Henry Barrow, Esq., ed., *The Mirror of Parliament for the Second Session of the Eighth Parliament of Great Britain and Ireland, Commencing 29 January 1828*, Vol. 1 (London: Winchester and Varnham, 1828), Buxton talking in debate in House of Commons on Manumission of Slaves, 6 March 1828, 550.

7   Hall, *White*, Ch. 1, 27.

8   GL, *ASMR* 1, 9 (28 February 1826): 88. See also Benjamin Godwin, *The Substance of a Course of Lecture on British Colonial Slavery . . .* (London: J. Hatchford and Son, 1830), 52.

9   Hall, *White*, Ch. 1, 32.; Ferguson, *Subject to Others*, 4; Clare Midgley, personal communication, 19 May 1995; Hall, "Free Villages," 110. On the tensions around slaves' definitions and experience of masculinity at the Cape see Van der Spuy, "Collection," Paper 5.

10   This idea found expression in the influential female antislavery campaigns from 1826 in which British women argued that they were especially sensitive to moral outrages. For an extensive study of female antislavery activism see Midgley, *Women Against Slavery*; on women's claims to a unique position of moral critique, see p. 111. Also Karen Halbersleben, *Women's Participation in the British Antislavery Movement 1824–1865* (Lewiston: Edwin Mellen Press, 1993). In 1833 a petition from the "Ladies of Exeter" said that they could "not but feel additionally on account of the deep and foul degradation of their own sex. . . ." JL, 15th Report on Petitions, 30 April 1833, in GB, House of Commons, *Appendices to the Votes and Proceedings 1817–1890*, Reports of the Select Committee on Public Petitions 1833-1900 (Cambridge: Chadwyck-Healey, 1982), microfiche, pp. 559-60.

reply Buxton supported this view saying that "without female virtue, there is no virtue at all. . . ."[11]

The portraits of the man as helpless to stop his wife from being flogged, and of the woman vulnerable to sexual abuse and physical violence helped embellish a mythology: that black slave men and women were indeed "immoral" and living outside the bounds of stable families, and that they were perhaps incapable of being "civilized."[12] While activists pointedly referred to slavery as the cause of moral degradation, this rhetoric nonetheless contributed to the consolidation of a racist body of thought about people of African descent. The racism of the 1850s which emerged partly in reaction to the ways in which freed peoples' lives challenged the norms of British society was already prefaced in subdued tones in antislavery literature.[13] In 1823 William Wilberforce invoked a belief that Africans "notoriously have warm affections" in order to support his argument that slaves welcomed the opportunity to be part of stable relationships.[14] Three years later another antislavery supporter, Moseley, argued that the "poor Negro . . . is a grovelling brute insensible to the finer feelings of nature. . . ."[15]

In addition, activists' belief in women's moral superiority gave slave women a role in reforming slave society, but also potentially blamed them for the purported lack of morality within slave culture. The concern with moral behavior helped focus amelioration legislation on the abolition of the flogging of women slaves and on the legal recognition and protection of the slave family. Abolitionists saw the flogging of naked or nearly naked women as reducing both slave men and women's threshold of shame thus making them more liable to engage in licentious behavior. Flogging made slave men immoral, some writers argued, because men had to witness their wives and daughters being whipped and, unlike free men, could not protect them.[16] *The Christian Record of Jamaica* asserted that flogging led to a "debasement of character, and an utter annihilation, in male and female, of a sense of shame."[17]

---

11   GB, *Hansard Parliamentary Debates*, New Series, Vol. X, George Canning's statement to the House of Commons on "Amelioration of the Condition of the Slave Population in the West Indies," 1097, and Fowell Buxton's response to George Canning, 1116, 16 March 1824. For a discussion of flogging see Vron Ware, *Beyond the Pale: White Women, Racism, and History* (London: Verso, 1992), 60-61.

12   Barbara Bush has remarked with regard to the West Indies, that contemporary portrayals of slave life suggested that "marriage and morality amongst slaves . . . either did not exist, or existed only in unstable 'uncivilized' forms such as polygamy." Barbara Bush, *Slave Women in Caribbean Society, 1650-1838* (Bloomington: University of Indiana Press, 1990), 84.

13   See Ferguson, *Subject to Others*, Ch. 1, p.6, and Conclusion for similar points.

14   William Wilberforce, *An Appeal to The Religion, Justice, and Humanity of the Inhabitants of the British Empire on Behalf of the Negro Slaves in The West Indies* (London, 1823), cited in Edith F. Hurwitz, *Politics and the Public Conscience* (London: George Allen and Unwin, 1973), Document 1, 105.

15   Sir Oswald Moseley, *Speech of Sir Oswald Moseley in Manchester Gazette, March 25, 1826* . . . (Birmingham: Richard Peart Bull, 1826), 8.

16   See Moseley "Speech," 8; Godwin, *Substance*, 52; "*The Christian Record of Jamaica* on Colonial Slavery," *ASMR*, 76 (February 1831): 132.

17   "*The Christian Record of Jamaica* on Colonial Slavery," 131; Wilberforce, "An Appeal," Nineteenth Report from the Select Committee on Petitions, in GB, House of Commons, *Appendices to the Votes and Proceedings 1817–1890*, Reports of the Select Committee on Public Petitions 1833-1900 (Cambridge: Chadwyck-Healey, 1982), microfiche; "The humble petition of the Females belonging to the Congregation of Protestant Dissenters assembling for Divine Worship in Carr's Lane, Birmingham," 780.

Middle-class assumptions, both in England and the Cape, about the centrality of motherhood and family to women and the belief that women needed protection from physical abuse by men not their husbands shaped amelioration legislation at the Cape. But Cape officers in charge of the program of amelioration also merged their ideas about the proper behavior of women with their prejudices against Cape slave women. This marriage of gendered and racial assumptions also importantly helped shape the ways in which amelioration was both avoided and finally implemented in the Cape Colony.

A Token Reform of Slavery

It is not coincidental that the British government proposed the first legislation aimed at ameliorating slavery in 1824, just a year after the founding of the Anti-Slavery Society. Under pressure from Thomas Fowell Buxton, George Canning introduced legislation easing slavery in Trinidad in order to maintain control over the process.[18] This order introduced the office of the guardian of slaves who was to serve as a third party to adjudicate conflict between slaves and their masters. The order also permitted slave marriages, allowed slaves to give evidence in court, and forbade the separation by sale of mothers and children as well as the flogging of slave women. Local legislatures and legislative councils in the various colonies were expected to pass their own versions of the order.[19]

Ironically, at the Cape, a colony which resisted most of the tenets of amelioration, the first legislation ameliorating slavery in fact prefigured the Trinidad Order. Cape Governor Lord Charles Somerset issued the first proclamation reforming slavery some two months prior to the debate on slavery in the British Parliament, perhaps in order to ward off more stringent measures by the Colonial Office. This proclamation was a dead letter. In comparison to the later Trinidad Order, Somerset's proclamation of 18 March 1823 subverted virtually every reform it purported to introduce.

Somerset made Christianity the hallmark of a slave's eligibility for experiencing amelioration: slaves could only marry if they were Christians and with the agreement of their masters. In addition, only men and women who were lawfully married (that is, married in the Christian church) and children of Christian mothers could not be sold separately.[20] These provisions rang particularly hollow since Cape slaveholders had historically denied slaves access to Christian teachings and baptism. Indeed from 1825 to 1829 only six slave legal marriages occurred at the Cape.[21] The proclamation also heralded a reluctance on the part of Cape officials to stop the flogging of women slaves since no mention was made of such a ban.

In 1826, frustrated at the reluctance of colonial assemblies and legislatures to actively address the reform of slavery, the Colonial Office sent out proposed ameliora-

18 Davis, *Slavery and Human Progress*, Ch. 6, 192–93.

19 See GB, *Hansard Parliamentary Debates*, New Series, Vol. X, "Papers Relating to the Amelioration of the Condition of the Slave Population of the West Indies," 1064–1090. On amelioration see Edwards, *Towards Emancipation*; also Watson, *Slave Question*, Ch. 2.

20 Edwards, *Towards Emancipation*, 91.

21 CA, ZP 1/2/2, PRO, CO 714/40, "Analytical Index to Correspondence Received by Secretary of State for Colonies, 1815-1870."

tion legislation to be considered by the colonial governing bodies. Only two clauses in this first order ameliorating slavery throughout the colonies dealt with monetary matters: the right of slaves to own and transfer property and to buy their freedom. Other clauses followed the earlier Trinidad Order in Council allowing slaves to give evidence in court and to marry, and banning the use of flogging against slave women.

Ordinance No. 19, promulgated at the Cape in June 1826, finally realigned Cape amelioration with the intent of the British framers, although the provisions still did not match those contained in the earlier Trinidad Order. Now "heathen" slaves could benefit as much as their Christian peers: no slave children under the age of ten could be separated from their mothers through sale and all slaves could testify in court.[22] Perhaps most importantly for slaves, Ordinance No. 19 established for the Cape the office of guardian of slaves who was to look after the interests of slaves vis-à-vis their owners and was charged with hearing and adjudicating cases brought by slaves against their owners for contravening the clauses of amelioration legislation. As Mason has shown, Cape slaveholders reacted with great indignation to the introduction of this officer with the power to intervene in disputes with their slaves.[23]

Unlike the Trinidad Order which banned the flogging of slave women the Cape Ordinance of 1826 merely stated that a woman should be flogged no more than would a free child. Now slave women could be flogged only across the shoulders. This clause is particularly significant for women's later incorporation into the world of free wage labor. It introduced into Cape labor legislation an equivalence between women and children in the realm of the workplace. Cape legislation thus prefigured the later English protectionist laws which legally made women's and children's working hours subject to the same conditions.

At the Cape, as in many other colonies, the notion of legal protection of slave women from flogging remained a fiction into the 1830s.[24] In 1829 the *Anti-Slavery Monthly Reporter* noted that women slaves at the Cape were subject to punishments such as flogging and branding, as well as working in irons for up to fifteen years.[25] Records of the assistant protectors resident in the rural districts of the Cape Colony show that slaveholders continued to flog slave women despite the limitations put on this practice by the Orders in Council. In 1830 the district surgeon of Stellenbosch examined a slave woman called Rosina who had been brutally flogged. He found

> livid contusions from stripes, on the following parts of her person, viz. the back, arms, shoulders, left breast, loins, hips, posteriors, thighs, belly, and

---

22 In Trinidad children of sixteen and under were protected from separate sale from their mother.

23 See John Edwin Mason, "The Slaves and Their Protectors: Reforming Resistance in a Slave Society, 1826–1834," Journal of Southern African Studies 17 (March 1991): 104–128, for discussion of the office and slave complaints; see also Mason "Fit for Freedom," 105–106.

24 See Colonial Secretary Edward Stanley's remarks in "The Debate in the House of Commons on Colonial Slavery, May 14, 1833," in *The Mirror of Parliament for the First Session of the 11th Parliament . . .* , 1774. Even through the apprenticeship period some colonial assemblies and governing councils tried to circumvent the ban on female flogging. JL, GB, House of Commons, *Report of the Select Committee on Negro Apprenticeship in the Colonies; Together with the Minutes of Evidence, Appendix and Index*, Ordered by the House of Commons to be Printed, 13 August 1836, "Testimony of Mr. Madden," 29 April 1836 (Cambridge: Chadwyck-Healey, 1980-82), microfiche, p. 90.

25 "Cape of Good Hope," in *ASMR* III, 6 (November 1829), 139, 140; See also *ASMR* (January 1827) for similar remarks. See Barrow, *Travels*, Vol. 1.

right groin and, besides the contusions, the skin broken, also from stripes, on the following parts of her person, viz. the left breast, in one place, the belly in two places, the right groin, and the lower part of the back, and the posteriors.

Despite all this evidence of torture, the doctor concluded that these wounds were "of no consequence to life, or ultimately to health."[26]

In 1830, out of frustration that so many of the colonies seemed determined to sidestep crucial aspects of the amelioration legislation, Parliament passed a new Order in Council. The basic provisions remained the same, but the office of Guardian of Slaves now became the Protector of Slaves. The greatest changes for the Cape were that the flogging of slave women was now forbidden and slaveholders had to keep record books of all punishments inflicted on slaves which had to be sent to the protector for inspection twice a year.[27] This Order in Council became law in the Cape Colony in August 1830, but once again the governor, Sir Lowry Cole, attached regulations which limited the effects of the legislation. The resistance of colonial legislatures resulted in the passage of yet another order in 1831 which again prohibited the flogging of women.[28] This order also recognized common-law marriages for the purposes of preventing the separation of slave families.[29]

The first guardian, later protector, of slaves only entrenched the example set by Somerset to forestall any real change in the social order of slavery at the Cape. Major George Jackman Rogers was himself an owner of slaves and "a half-pay British Army officer who had come to the Cape Colony as Governor . . . Somerset's aide-de-camp."[30] In official documents Rogers certainly painted a bucolic picture of Cape slavery, although the cases with which he came into contact would suggest a rather different interpretation.[31]

The protector often seemed to be more an advocate for slaveholders than for slaves. Rogers supported the governor in arguing against the Order of 1830. Rogers argued that the weakness of the bureaucracy at the Cape, particularly in more remote districts such as Worcester, made various aspects of the metropolitan amelioration legislation impractical, such as those focusing on the registration of slaves and the keeping of punishment record books.[32] In 1832 he railed against the Order in Council of 1831 arguing that it was a waste of time bringing people to court when

---

26   CA, 1/STB 22/158, Letters Received by APS, statement of District Surgeon, 21 March 1830; see also 6 April 1830.

27   Mason, "Fit for Freedom," 107.

28   ASR 92 (January 1832), 9.

29   In July 1835, Special Justice Peake, of Worcester, told Nicholas van Wyk, a farmer in the Middle Roggeveld, that his apprentice Absolom had complained that van Wyk was removing him to Cape Town where he would be separated from his wife. Peake referred the farmer to "66 section of the Order in Council of the end of November 1831 wherein it is distinctly stated that Husbands and Wives and parents and children shall not be separated from each other." CA, 1/WOC, 19/60, SJ to Nicholas van Wyk, 23 July 1835.

30   John Edwin Mason, "Hendrik Albertus and his Ex-Slave Mey: A Drama in Three Acts," *Journal of African History* 31 (1990): 423–45; Mason, "Fit for Freedom," 114.

31   See Mason, "Fit for Freedom," for a discussion of the protector and the cases which slaves brought before him. Rogers provided this sentimental representation of Cape slavery: "In the Towns and Villages and on the Estates adjoining Them, the Slaves are amply supplied with Food and Clothing, and I have known some Instances where these have been issued to an Extent almost exceeding belief. . . ." CA, ZP 1/6/6, PRO, CO 53/55; Part 1, Book 2, Report of PS for June-December 1832, 28 May 1833.

32   CA, ZP 1/6/4, PRO, CO 53/51, Report of PS: General Observations, 23 June 1831.

I have strong reasons for believing that very few convictions will be awarded by Jury. . . . the Peace, Happiness and Welfare . . . of this Colony, must be most seriously disturbed by a strict Enforcement of The Order in Council, as it now stands . . . the Dutch Inhabitants considering themselves more grievously Injured, will withdraw themselves altogether and become, if They are not already in a great measure so, a divided People, and that all stimulus to Industry and agricultural or Mercantile Pursuits will be paralyzed . . . if these Orders in Council are to be enforced they are but too fatally framed to doom to Destruction all reasonable Expectation of advancement or Improvement here . . . I hope it may not be Imagined for one Instant that I am not an Advocate for the positive protection and absolute amelioration of the unfortunate coloured Class for whose well being These Orders in Council are purposely, but mistakenly framed. . . .[33]

Rogers advocated that the British government give to the Cape responsibility for framing the laws regarding slave amelioration since the Cape officials were most attuned to the specificity of the Cape slavery.[34] He argued this despite the fact that numerous other government officials themselves owned slaves and were thus unlikely to bring about an emancipation beneficial to slaves.[35] Even Sir Lowry Cole, the governor of the Cape from 1828 to 1833, owned a slave. In defending himself to Lord Viscount Goderich, Secretary of State for Colonies, Cole revealed that he did not entirely share the moral condemnation of slavery that had become commonplace in England. Having bought a slave in Mauritius, Cole argued that "It has always been my *avowed* intention to give him his liberty also on my return . . . from this colony if he conducted himself well. His behavior, however, has, I regret, been the very reverse of what I had a right to expect for what I had done him."[36] Cole did not conceptualize slavery as a moral or philosophical issue. Rather he framed manumission or freedom as a reward for good behavior.

In response to every order sent from England for consideration by the Cape, as one of the crown colonies, both the protector and the governor argued that the special conditions of the Cape, which only local officials could truly understand, made many features of the amelioration laws inapplicable to the Cape, and they especially attended to the proposed ban on the flogging of slave women. Their discussions of slave women expose the ambivalence of colonial officials and of settler society in general about slave women's right to protection because of their status as women, an ambivalence which surfaced throughout the postemancipation period in legal discussions about black and working-class women's rights to equality before the law. Slave women's relatively recent introduction to regular field work, Cape slaveholders's sexualization and abuse of slave women, and slaveholders' rendering of *slave women* as promiscuous contributed to the sentiments expressed by the protector and the governor about the flogging of female slaves.

---

33 CA, ZP 1/6/6, PRO, CO 53/54, Report of PS for January–June 1832, 15 November 1832. For a critique of the protector's handling of slaves' complaints see *ASR* 86 (August 1831), 377.

34 CA, ZP 1/6/6, PRO, CO 53/54, Report of PS for January–June 1832, 15 November 1832.

35 CA, ZP 1/1/75, PRO, CO 48/143, Despatch, Cape of Good Hope, Slavery No. 52, Governor to SSC, 8 September 1831. Enclosure 1, December 1830.

36 CA, GH, 23/10, No. 29, Governor to SSC, 6 December 1832.

Governor Sir Lowry Cole contended that Cape slave women needed physical discipline. In July 1831 the *Anti-Slavery Reporter* argued that Sir Lowry Cole showed "a singular reluctance to take from the planters the power of corporally punishing females." Cole said that people objected to corporal punishment as "tending to lower and impair the sense of respect" but that flogging was necessary to keep women slaves from "debauchery" and "dissipation."[37] A year later Cole again returned to the theme, observing that "the conduct of females . . . is in many instances, in every respect, fully as bad as that of the worst of the male slaves."[38]

The Cape protector echoed the sentiments of his governor and embellished: he labeled slave women as masculine. In 1831 in response to the final Order in Council ameliorating slavery Rogers said, "It is certainly desirable that the flogging female slaves [*sic*] should be wholly discontinued, but some Punishment should be substituted adequate to the degree of the Offences which many of these stubborn Masculine Women commit."[39] He made a similar remark in his next report when talking of criminal cases. He said there were many cases, but none he perceived as serious: "considering how extremely difficult it is to keep some of the masculine Females in any order since corporal Punishment has been prohibited, it is very satisfactory that so few breaches of the Law are committed by Slave Owners."[40] At the same time that Rogers talked of slave women as being masculine he also elaborated an argument as to their hypersexuality. He opposed the Order of 1831 that now forbade the separation from their mothers of children under sixteen years rather than ten years of age which had been the case at the Cape. He argued that "It will have been unknown when this Article was framed—that a female generally arrives at Womanhood in this Climate at about her 12th year and may have one or more children by the time she is 16. Children may safely and very often most advantageously be separated on attaining their 10th year. Many persons are desirous of purchasing clever, active Children about that Age."[41]

The criticisms of Rogers and Cole implicitly held up a vision of how women were supposed to behave, and one against which they found Cape slave women lacking. The emerging gender ideology in both Britain and in Cape settler society which assigned women to a private sphere, and to modest, retiring roles, helped construct these men's perception of female slaves as being unfeminine, in fact, as maybe not being women at all.[42] Roger's use of the adjective masculine suggests that he found some aspect of slave women's bearing offensive and inappropriate.

The fact that in the 1820s Cape slave women began working in the fields on a more regular basis might have produced a fear on the part of the protector that they were becoming masculine through association with male labor. For most of the history of Cape slavery, unlike that of the West Indian colonies, slave women had been employed predominantly in domestic work in the household of their owners. Only in the 1820s, in fact at the very time that slavery at the Cape came under scrutiny, did

---

37   Cole quoted in *ASR* 83 (12 July 1831): 330, 329.

38   GL, *ASR* 92 (January 1832): 8.

39   CA, ZP 1/6/4, PRO, CO 53/51, Report of PS: General Observations, 23 June 1831.

40   CA, ZP 1/6/5, PRO, CO 53/53, Report of PS for July–December 1831, 14 May 1832.

41   CA, ZP 1/6/4, PRO, CO 53/51, Report of PS: General Observations, 23 June 1831.

42   See Edna Bradlow, "Women at the Cape in the Mid-Nineteenth Century," *South African Historical Journal* 19 (1987): 51-75.

women start working in the vineyards and cornfields alongside men on a regular basis. Even in 1827 the practice was sufficiently new for Saartje, a slave in Worcester district, to complain that her owner had made her work "among his male slaves to spread manure on the land."[43] The boom in wine sales which was stimulated by favorable British tariffs contributed to the wider use of female labor and by the 1830s "the presence of women workers in the vineyards was unremarkable."[44]

In addition, Rogers would have met most of the slaves he came into contact with in his capacity as protector of slaves; that is, as a listener and adjudicator of slave complaints about their masters. Slave women appeared to him as masculine possibly precisely because they were assertive: not being loathe to come and complain against slaveholders. This assertiveness contradicted one of the tenets of Victorian gender ideology: that women not represent themselves in court, that they not participate in the public sphere.

Achieving Amelioration

In the light of various officials' hostility to pursuing the provisions of amelioration, slave women and men rather than the protector and assistant protectors became the officers of amelioration. Slaves fought against both the hostility of their owners and the inertia of the protector and of many of the assistant protectors stationed in the rural districts. The "protectors helped those slaves who helped themselves and only those slaves."[45] Analysis of the literature produced by the various district assistant protectors suggests that they too were ultimately reluctant to follow through cases where adherence to the spirit rather than the letter of the law would have facilitated justice.[46]

Slaveholders do not seem to have been willing to abide by the new regulations unless forced to do so by their slaves or, rarely, by the assistant protectors. In fact some owners appear to have punished slaves for amelioration by deliberately refusing to acknowledge slaves' family ties. Slaveholders continued not to recognize common-law marriages despite the revised provisions of Ordinance No. 19. In 1830, in Swellendam, Maart, a slave aged twenty-three who had had four children with his Khoi wife, Anna, whom he had lived with for four or five years, charged that his owner had sent Anna off the farm for no reason.

The assistant protector of that district invoked what was becoming infamous as a Cape interpretation of the law by implicitly inferring that he could not force a slaveholder to accept a slave man's common-law wife if they were not formally married. He argued that he had "no power to oblige a master to receive females on his place, merely because they are living in connection with his slaves—that a slave must endeavour to procure such indulgences by good conduct and submission. . . ."[47] Likewise a year later Tom, a free black man, also complained about being separated

---

43   CA, 1/WOC 19/24, Note in Daybook of APS, 8 October 1827.

44   Mason, "Fit for Freedom," 308.

45   Ibid., 110.

46   See for example, CA, 1/SWM 16/22, Case of Overwacht, slave of Mr F. J. van Zyl, Diary of AP, 23 February 1830; CA, 1/SWM 16/22, Case of Maart, slave of P. F. G. Crots, 21 December 1830.

47   CA, 1/SWM 16/22, Diary of APS, 21 December 1830.

from his wife, Maria, a slave woman living in the district with whom he had had a relationship for over a year and with whom he had a baby.[48]

Slaves had to travel to the office of the protector or assistant protector to make a case against their master, a journey which could take days. But they continued their assault on the customs of Cape slavery. Slaves were more likely to make the trip in the harvest time, and by the 1830s more and more slaves were making this journey of complaint. Mason estimates that some two thousand slaves out of the some thirty-five thousand slaves at the Cape lodged complaints with the protectors. Of those complaints only about one-half went to trial, with maybe one-sixth of the cases resulting in conviction of the masters.[49]

Slaves persisted. They protested the separation of spouses, children, and the bad conditions of slavery, all issues permitted by the 1824, 1826, 1830, and 1831 Orders. A great many of the cases brought before the assistant protectors of slaves from the 1820s related to slaves being prohibited from seeing lovers or children who lived on other farms, or being prevented from choosing with whom they could have intimate relationships.[50] In 1828, for example, a free woman, Saartje, of Worcester, told the assistant protector that she wanted to buy the freedom of a man whom she loved ("with whom she had a connection" in the words of the official) especially as he was ill. She had no money to secure his manumission, but she looked after a young free child who was in the employ of her beloved's owner. The owner, Smith, owed the child six hundred rix dollars, probably under terms of an indenture, and she hoped to secure her friend's freedom by getting the assistant protector to make Smith pay up. Far from intervening on her behalf, he made Saartje go to Smith and demand the money, and asked to be kept up to date on Smith's answer.[51] Two years later a man named Nowel who lived on a farm in Worcester complained to the assistant protector that his wife, who was a slave of another owner, had been prevented from living with him. The case was dismissed, the reason appearing to be that Nowel and his common-law wife, Sara, were not legally married.[52]

Some slaves sought to get married to give legitimacy to their long unions in the eyes of the protectors. In 1830 Carel, a slave from Worcester village, sought a license to marry Fytje Valentyn, a Khoi woman. The assistant protector told him to get written permission from his owner; no further records were found.[53] In the same year Isaac, a slave from the same district, applied to marry Philida Paulse, a free woman who lived a full two-and-a-half hours away on horseback.[54] Like the other case, it

---

48   Ibid., 16 February 1831. See also case of Geduld, who complained that his owner, J. W. van der Merwe of Worcester district, had sold Geduld's wife to a man in Stellenbosch and thus Geduld had "no chance of meeting her." There is no record of how the case was resolved. CA, 1WOC 1924, Diary of APS, Worcester, 26 January 1831; seealso 16 July 1831 and 24 November 1831.

49   Mason, "Fit for Freedom," 111; E. Hengherr, "Emancipation and After: A Study of Cape Slavery and the Issues Arising from It, 1830–1843" (M.A. diss., University of Cape Town, 1953), 11, quoted in Mason, "Fit for Freedom," 123.

50   CA, 1/SWM 16/22, Diary of APS, 3 September 1830, 21 December 1830, and 16 February 1831; CA, 1/WOC 19/24, Daybook of APS, 11 August 1830.

51   CA, 1/WOC 19/24, Daybook of APS, 5 April 1828.

52   Ibid., 16 August 1831.

53   Ibid., 6 November 1830.

54   Ibid., No. 16, 11 November 1830.

appears that this couple were unable to register their application. Very few slaves appear to have been able to register their applications for marriage. In 1830 the protector of slaves reported that only one marriage application, in the Cape district, was made in terms of the Order in Council and he reported none in 1831.[55] In 1832 there is a record of four applications for marriage in Worcester district, but in 1833 the protector reported no slave marriages, at least in terms recognized as legal, in the Cape, Worcester, Stellenbosch, Swellendam, or in many other parts of the Colony.[56]

The protectors seemed generally unwilling to press for slaveholders' full compliance with the law. In the face of such hostility, slaves bargained for at least some acknowledgment of their relationships. In 1830 Onverwacht, a slave from Swellendam, was brought by his owner to the Resident Magistrate's court on charges of deserting the farm. The assistant protector attended the hearing as Onverwacht complained that he had left the farm to press a charge since his owner would not allow him to see Sylvia, his wife and mother of his children, who had been sold away from him. In answer to the magistrate's question, Onverwacht said that he would be "satisfied with permission" to see his wife one Sunday a month, to which the owner's son concurred.[57] The following year, another man called Onverwacht, a slave living in Stellenbosch, bargained with the assistant protector and his master to secure the right to visit his wife and children one Sunday a month.[58] In both cases none of the officers involved in the cases argued that the sale of the slave's wife was in itself illegal—which it was starting with the Order of 1826. The cases was thus settled to the advantage of the owner, a trend which the *Anti-Slavery Reporter* complained about through the 1830s.

Conclusion

The discussions about slavery in the 1820s and the amelioration legislation which was implemented at the Cape had ambivalent ramifications for slave women's experience of freedom after 1838. Discussions around amelioration and legislation rendered slave women as vulnerable and in need of protection. But while legislation liberated women from physical abuse through the abolition of flogging, it also inscribed their inequality as individuals and as workers into colonial legislation. In addition, examination of antislavery literature suggests that while both antislavery activists and some government officials drew a collective portrait of slave women as being vulnerable to sexual and physical abuse, this very portrait embellished another mythology: that black slave men and women, but particularly women, were indeed "immoral" and living outside the bounds of stable families. Abolitionist discourse drew on long histories of racial sexualized knowledge of black women and thus created a double knowledge of slave women as being, like British middle-class women, at the center of morality for society, but also of being immoral women who needed to

---

55   CA, ZP 1/6/4, PRO, CO 53/52, Report of PS for Half Year, 1830, Report of PS for First Half Year, 1831, and Report of PS for Second Half Year, 1831.

56   CA, ZP 1/6/7, PRO, CO 53/55, Book 2, Part 4, Enclosure No.2 to Lieut Col. Wade's despatch No. 2, dated 14 August 1833. Report of APS for Clan William, 28 August to 31 December 1832, 20 January 1833; CA, ZP 1/6/6, PRO, CO 53/55, Book 2, Part 1, Report of PS for January–June 1833, 28 May 1833.

57   CA, 1/SWM 16/22, Diary of APS, 23 February 1830.

be reformed. Cape officials' arguments that Cape slave women were overly masculine and in need of special discipline and control also added to the many contradictory expectations and beliefs about slave women's capabilities and character which
circulated in the course of emancipation.

Slave and dependent laborers' struggles to make amelioration count for something, particularly with regard to their relationships with husbands, wives, and
children return us to the social history of Cape emancipation. The debates over
amelioration at the Cape, especially with regard to the place of women in slave
society, also return us full circle to the centrality of gender in empire-wide discussions about abolition, progress, and free wage labor.

The period of amelioration at the Cape prefaced and informed the many meanings of free wage labor elaborated by slaves, slaveholders, and colonial officials in the
period of apprenticeship from 1834 to 1838 as the Cape was dragged into free wage
labor by the passing of the Abolition Act in 1833. And it was precisely on the terrain
of family, and the role of slave and Khoi women in their capacity as mothers, that the
struggle to determine the terrain of freedom took place.

3

Apprenticeship and the Battle for the Child

In 1833, after increasing extra-parliamentary pressure to end slavery, and well documented evidence of the failure of colonial assemblies and councils to implement the spirit of the amelioration orders, the British government abolished slavery in the British West Indies and the Cape Colony. At the Cape, slavery was to end in December 1834, to be replaced by a period of apprenticeship. Masters were supposed to learn how to be responsible employers and slaves to learn the habits of industry and responsibility which the government saw as necessary for their integration as workers into the subsequent era of freedom. The government appointed special magistrates to districts throughout the colonies to supervise the period of apprenticeship in which former slaves had to remain in the employ of their former masters. In 1838 apprenticeship ended—in August in the West Indies, on 1 December at the Cape Colony.[1]

The period of apprenticeship in the Cape Colony from 1834 to 1838 formed an interregnum in which slavery had not quite ended and free wage labor had not quite begun. In these years the legal erosion of slavery, and the belief of various actors that these years would be crucial in determining the terrain of postemancipation life, led to struggles around power, organization of labor, and notions of contract.

The British operated with seemingly unambiguous definitions of what it meant to be a slave, free person, or free wage laborer. On the other hand, rural Cape slaveholders, and often the colonial officials who implemented amelioration and apprenticeship, saw various ways (not necessarily only slavery) through which labor contracts could bind the freedom of the individual. For slaveholders an externally generated emancipation did not lead to an internal revolution of attitudes towards

---

1 CA, 1/STB 22/31, Proclamation of 6 January 1834. For discussion of this period see Edwards, *Towards Emancipation*, and Hengherr, "Emancipation and After." Also Nigel Worden, "Cape Slave Emancipation and Rural Labour in a Comparative Context" (paper presented at Africa Seminar, Center for African Studies, University of Cape Town, 1983), and "Adjusting to Emancipation: Freed Slaves and Farmers in the Mid-Nineteenth-Century South-Western Cape," in James and Simons, eds., *Angry Divide*, 31-39; Mason, "Fit for Freedom," Ch. 2; and Nigel Worden and Clifton C. Crais, eds., *Breaking the Chains: Slavery and Its Legacy in the Nineteenth-Century Cape Colony* (Johannesburg: University of Witwatersrand Press, 1994). For empire-wide information see Green, *British Slave Emancipation*; and Holt, *Problem of Freedom*, Ch. 2.

the children of apprentices and dependent laborers. Slaveholders in the rural areas built on notions of tied "free" labor which had existed under slavery to redefine apprenticeship as a system of bondage rather than as a preparation for liberation.[2] They conceptualized labor relations in a frame which perceived various categories of dependency as legitimate modes of securing labor. And they particularly looked to children's labor to ease the transition to a wage labor economy.

The precedents of mobilizing Khoi labor power through indenture provided slaveholders with a model through which they could bind apprentices to them without necessarily moving towards a contractual conception of landlord-worker relations. Indentureship of children had been long used as a means of binding Khoi and other legally free laborers to the farm. Indeed the early Cape government confirmed Dutch precedents of tying Khoi laborers and their children to farm labor with the Caledon Code of 1809. The Code brought Khoi within the legal realm, but instituted a pass system which effectively hampered Khoi freedom of movement.[3] As Rayner has suggested, "through indenture schemes and the oppressive pass laws imposed on the indigenous Khoikhoi, the government provided a legislative model for the resolution of the 'labor question' after slavery" in which the rights of employers were secured against those of servants.[4]

This chapter argues that the prior history of indenture shaped the struggles between apprentices and former slaveholders in the period from 1834 through 1838. I show that the freedom that was bestowed on slave children through the Abolition Act of 1833 carried a potential for bondage which former slaveholders seized upon all too frequently. The chapter analyzes how the centrality of maternity to shape a person's status as free or slave under slavery now gave apprentice mothers a particularly important role in the struggle over child labor.

With apprenticeship, the mother-child dyad was severed at least ideologically from its meanings under slavery, and, temporarily, from the coherent contractual system with which the British sought to replace slavery: as such, the relationship between slave women and their children became a point of ideological struggle. The colonial administration had focused on the issue of slave children and labor as early as Governor Somerset's proclamation of 1823. Partly in response to the shortage of labor Somerset had told the Colonial Office that at the Cape the separation of children from their parents by sale in terms of the 1823 law was "limited to 10 years of age instead of 16 as in Trinidad Order. . . ."[5] By doing so the government did not

---

2 See contributions to Eldredge and Morton, eds., *Slavery in South Africa* which argue for the significance in understanding various forms of bonded "free" labor as a form of enslavement in South Africa in the nineteenth and early twentieth centuries. On bonded labor also see Susan Newton-King, "The Enemy Within," in Worden and Crais, eds., *Breaking the Chains*, 225-270.

3 Richard Elphick and V. C. Malherbe "The Khoisan to 1828," in Elphick and Giliomee, eds., *Shaping*, 3–65, 32, 41. See also Du Toit and Giliomee, *Afrikaner Political Thought*, 12, 32, and V. C. Malherbe, "Indentured and Unfree Labour in South Africa: Towards an Understanding," *South African Historical Journal* 24 (1991): 3–30. For a comparative angle see Rebecca Scott, "The Battle over the Child: Child Apprenticeship and the Freedmen's Bureau in North Carolina," *Prologue* (Summer 1978): 101-113.

4 Rayner, "Wine and Slaves," 4. We will discuss the attempt at resolution of the labor issue in Chapter 5.

5 CA, ZP 1/2/2, PRO, CO 714/40, Note in Index, 24 September 1825. For the argument regarding this ordinance and the labor shortage see Van der Spuy, "Slave Women," 20.

explicitly sanction the use of child labor, but did lower the age at which slave children could be considered sufficiently adult to labor.

Slaveholders focused on the mother–child relationship to try to extract labor. For example, they manipulated the apparent contractual rights to a child's labor—legitimated either through indenture of Khoi or through indenture of apprentices' children under the Abolition Act—in order to get a mother's labor too. Apprentices were unwilling to leave their children and thus the ruse often succeeded in procuring the labor of both children and adults. Apprentices also pulled on the maternal relationship. Mothers made complaints to the Special Justices and affirmed their power vis-à-vis former slaveholders in determining the fate of ex-slave children.

Freedom to Labor

Antislavery advocates conceptualized emancipation in the nineteenth century partly as a process of turning slaves into waged workers, of replacing "the discipline of slavery, with the 'discipline of virtue.'"[6] The ending of slavery involved the transition from a world of the slaveowners' personal rule over the bodies of their slaves to the rule of law. Abolitionists also saw abolition as involving the creation of wage laborers who would be governed as much by moral imperatives and economic necessity as by the discipline of imminent punishment. As the secretary of state asserted in 1833 with regard to the slaves about to be released into apprenticeship

> . . . I trust that their masters and the Magistracy, & more especially the Colonial Clergy and Ministers of every Religious persuasion, will all unite in one common effort to dispel any illusions under which the Slaves may be found to labor, as to the real nature of the projected change in their condition, and to inculcate upon them, by the firm but gentle exercise of all legitimate authority and influence, the great duties of industry and subordination to the Laws.[7]

Abolitionists and metropolitan and colonial officials did not envision freedom from slavery as meaning freedom from work, but rather as independence to choose employers in a context in which work was a moral duty. Like their working-class peers in Britain, freed people were not free to relax, only free to labor.[8]

Up to the early 1830s most antislavery activists had campaigned for amelioration rather than outright abolition of slavery. For many years female activists like Elizabeth Heyrick who championed the cause of immediate abolition were very much outside the mainstream.[9] Pressure from the women's committees of the Anti-Slavery Society and the Jamaican revolt of 1831 ultimately pressured the society as a whole to adopt immediate abolition. But even so, many abolitionists and members of Parliament worried that slaves were not yet ready for emancipation. Slaveholders in both

---

6 Holt, quoting Wordsworth, in *Problem of Freedom*, 35.

7 PRO, CO 49/25, ZP 1/3/9, No. 6, 18 July 1833.

8 Davis, *Problem of Slavery*, 357, makes connections between the passing of the New Poor Law and the forces which fueled the ending of slavery.

9 Elizabeth Heyrick, *Immediate, Not Gradual Abolition* . . . (London: Printed by R. Clay, 1824). See also Midgley, *Women Against Slavery*, Chs. 4 and 5.

the West Indies and the Cape also continued to offer significant opposition to emancipation. The Abolition Act which inaugurated apprenticeship represented an uneasy mediation of both slavery and freedom: it looked back to slavery as much as it looked forward to free wage labor.

Ordinance No. 1 of 1835 which ushered in the terms of apprenticeship at the Cape Colony is a good index of the ambivalence contained in the concept of apprenticeship.[10] On January 7, 1834, the acting lieutenant governor of the Cape Colony sent out a circular in which he outlined the desired responses of masters and slaves to the declaration of apprenticeship: "Proprietors should distinctly understand that a cheerful acquiescence in the Provisions of the Law is not only required of them as a positive act of duty, but that their own individual interests . . . are deeply involved. . . ." From slaves, he, "His Majesty is entitled to expect and demand the most tranquil and orderly submission to such laws as shall be framed for their future government, . . . and they will display their gratitude for the favor they are about to receive by carefully abstaining from any insolence or insubordination towards their Masters."[11]

The ordinance established the jurisdiction of the eight special magistrates appointed to the Cape who would fulfill many of the duties of the previous protectors. By 1835 it was clear that this number could not look after apprentices' needs. The Legislative Council's solution, however, contradicted one of the key principles of apprenticeship: that the special magistrates should come from outside of the country. Edwards states that ultimately almost half of the special magistrates were appointed from settler society: nine resident magistrates and five justices of the peace took on the additional duties of special magistrate.[12]

Ordinance No. 1 gave to special magistrates greater power than their predecessors, the protector and assistant protectors. Special magistrates adjudicated cases on the farms and they had to visit farms with more than twenty apprentices to ensure that apprentices were being treated fairly. The clearest departure from slavery rested in precisely the shift of disciplinary power from slaveholders to the special magistrates. Former slaveholders no longer had the right to punish their apprentices.[13] The ordinance also made labor into a commodity by allowing slaves to buy the remaining portion of their apprenticeships and permitting masters to sell that portion to another party.

But the years 1834 through 1838 did not usher in emancipation. Indeed the legislation governing labor relations in this period owed much to the slave laws which preceded it. For example, Chapter 4 of the ordinance stated that employers had a

---

10   CA, CCP 6/3/1/3, Cape of Good Hope, Governor, "Ordinance No. 1 of 1835. For Giving Due Effect to the Provisions of an Act of Parliament . . . entitled 'An Act for the Abolition of Slavery . . . ,' 1 January 1835." For a detailed discussion of the terms of the ordinance and the workings of apprenticeship at the Cape see Nigel Worden, "Between Slavery and Freedom: The Apprenticeship Period, 1834 to 1838," in Worden and Crais, eds., *Breaking the Chains*, 117-144.

11   CA, 1/WOC, 11/12, Circular from Government House, 7 January 1834.

12   Edwards, *Towards Emancipation*, 181–182. The proliferation of such offices produces some inconsistency in titles. Sometimes a person in charge of judicial duties regarding apprentices is referred to as a special magistrate, and sometimes as a special justice. These terms appear to be identical. To ensure accuracy I have followed the usage of the individual archival source, but in general discussion refer to such officers as special magistrates.

13   Worden, "Between Slavery and Freedom," 125.

duty to give apprentices food and clothing, but gave no specified amounts and referred to the standards set by the protector of slaves. Apprentices had to work every day except Sundays and the usual holidays (such as Christmas). The ordinance also bound apprentices to the geography of the farm: apprentices were not allowed to leave the employer's house at night and if found more than a mile away were considered guilty of desertion. This contradicted the stated objective of the amelioration laws to endorse the unity of slave families since many relationships between slaves crossed farm boundaries. The ordinance in general maintained the gap between theory and practice which was an established feature of Cape slavery. The protector of slaves complained in 1834 that the "owners have retained all their old prejudices as to their absolute right over their slaves." The very measures passed by the British Parliament themselves facilitated an ambiguous interpretation of the transition from slavery to freedom.[14]

Apprenticeship created a contest over interests but also over different techniques of mobilizing labor power. Evidence suggests that many slaves and dependent laborers expected all members of the household to contribute to the upkeep of the family. In this respect there was correspondence with colonial officials and settlers who wanted to mobilize as much labor as possible. Yet apprentices also sought to control the terms of their and their children's employment and challenged former slaveholders' attempts to circumvent their independence. This latter independence was to be a locus of tension between farmers, laborers, and the state in the decade after emancipation.

In the years 1834 to 1838 apprentices used their new position as a class of the "almost-free" to try and limit farmers' claims to their children's labor and they strongly protested farmers' attempts to separate families. Freed people's desire to unite families, or to maintain existing relationships, conflicted with former slaveholders' ambition to retain some authority over their former slaves. One realm in which employers tried to exercise that authority was precisely in the realm of emotional relationships. Slaveholders continued, as they had in the period of amelioration, to separate apprentice families as a means of punishing what they saw as unacceptable behavior or as a threat in order to make apprentices indenture their children. For example, Jacobus Stoffberg, a farmer near Worcester village, attempted to send off his farm a baby still nursing at her mother's breast, while another farmer, Charles de Wet, would not allow his apprentice's husband to come and visit her.[15]

Child Indentureship

The battle over the ending of slavery was both a battle over labor and a fight over redefinition of power relations in the familial and the civil sphere. The two spheres were intrinsically connected. The struggle over the slave family was in part a battle for control of slave children's potential labor power. The principal actors in the contest

---

14   CA, ZP 1/6/7, PRO, CO 53/57, "Report of PS for the Western Division of the Colony of the Cape of Good Hope made to His Excellency Major General Sir Benjamin D'Urban KCB Governor of the said Colony for 25 July to 15 December 1833," 20 January 1834.

15   CA, 1/WOC, 19/60, SM to Stoffberg, 16 February 1836; SM to Charles De Wet, 24 October 1835; and SM to Nicholas van Wyk, 23 July 1835.

over slave children between 1834 and 1838 were apprentices, farmers, and the special magistrates. Apprentice women in particular emerged as spokespeople in the cases involving complaints about the illegal indenture of children. The Abolition Act freed all slaves under the age of six and also freed children "subsequently born to slave mothers."[16] However, the thirteenth section of the Abolition Act also provided for the indenture of children below the age of six with the consent of the mother or without her consent if it appeared to the special magistrate that the children were otherwise likely to be destitute.[17] Apprentices' children born after 1 December 1834 were also subject to indenture.

Ironically the very act which liberated the slaves also provided for the continued enslavement of their children. Owing to a loophole in the original Abolition Act of 1833, farmers were able to indenture children for periods extending considerably beyond 1838.[18] For many children, free status became a condition of extended servitude. In the three-and-a-half-year period ending in April 1838 1,464 apprentice children were indentured in the Western Cape. The final total amounted to 2,364.[19]

Criteria which shaped Cape legislation shaped the dynamics of the battle over the child. Special Magistrate Major Longmore argued in 1836 that the fact that all Cape slaves were listed as "non-praedial," or as domestic and urban slaves, had significant results for the fate of their children. Under the terms of the Abolition Act only praedial or field slaves, such as many slaves in the West Indies were labeled, were entitled to fifteen hours per week in which they could work to support their families. Longmore concluded that apprentices at the Cape thus had little alternative but to indenture their children to their former owners in order to make sure that the children were fed and housed.[20] A year later the special magistrate of Stellenbosch was moved to write a letter to the governor explicitly detailing the ways in which former slaveholders sought to gain access to both adult and child labor. He said he had had

> frequent occasion to remark the injurious tendency of the system . . . of binding indiscriminately the children of recently emancipated Slaves as apprentices without due regard to the Spirit of the Act which applied merely to cases of necessity. . . . It should likewise be observed that as a parent will be naturally inclined to continue to reside with his child during the apprenticeship of the latter (a feeling particularly strong amongst the colored population & duly appreciated by the master) on any terms however unfavorable which the employer may be disposed to offer, the provisions of the local Acts will have the effect of imposing on the parent the painful alternative of either parting with his child or continuing himself in a state of servitude, worse, in some respects than Slavery, during perhaps the term of his natural life.[21]

---

16   Edwards, *Towards Emancipation*, 169.

17   CA, 1/WOC 19/60, SM to Isaac de Vries, Hex River, 11 March 1835.

18   Edwards, *Towards Emancipation*, Ch. 8, discusses child indentureship.

19   CA, GH 23/12, SG to USSC, 18 April 1838, Enclosure No. 1; CA, GH 23/12, No. 52c, Governor to SSC, 1 October 1838. I found no figures for the number of children emancipated by the act.

20   CA, GH 1/110, No. 59, SM Longmore to SSC, 9 April 1836, enclosed in letter from SSC to Governor, 11 July 1836.

21   CA, GH 1/118, No. 14, SM to SSC, 13 November 1837, enclosed in letter from SSC to Governor, 27 November 1837.

Former slaveholders' attempts to bond children to them for twentysome years arose in part from an ongoing crisis in the economy of the Western Cape. From the late 1820s farmers, and particularly wine farmers, witnessed economic stagnation and crisis caused by bankruptcies, falling wine prices, and the problem faced by a slave-based economy with low prices and rising costs.[22] Poorer settlers used their own children in farm labor and the Dutch Reformed Church bemoaned the poor attendance of settler children at school, saying that it "may be chiefly attributed to the real distance at which many of the inhabitants reside from the schools & also to the parents which obliges them to use their children in their farming occupations."[23] In 1834, therefore, slaveholders were keen to indenture apprentice children as a means of retaining cheap labor and as a way of securing a future free of manual labor for their own children.

Some former owners' attempts to control children's labor had virtually no limits: in 1835 a farmer in Swellendam asked James Barnes, the special magistrate, if he could not indenture the *unborn* child of his apprentice, who was in a "far advanced state of pregnancy," until the child was twenty-one.[24] The following year, a Mosterd of Paarl threatened to throw off his farm the children of two of his women apprentices unless they indentured the children to him.[25] These threats represented practical application of the economic power held by the former master class after emancipation, even in the years before the state came to their aid with the Masters and Servants Ordinance.

During the apprenticeship period apprentices and Khoi parents sought to gain control over their children. Most clearly parents tried to bring together family members who had never been able to live together under slavery, or to reunite families torn apart by the manipulation of the child indentureship clauses of the Abolition Act. Apprentices and Khoi parents also sought to gain access to their children's labor as part of a broader household economy in which all members of the family were expected to contribute to the support of the household. For example, the nine records of free black parents indenturing their children in Stellenbosch suggest an emergent household economy in which the labor of children was seen as contributing to the household; free black parents might have seen indentureship of their children as a legitimate option to bring in income.[26]

Sometimes apprentices' need to be free conflicted with their role as parents: the freedom of one family member sometimes could only be gained at the expense of another's. For example, despite the urging of the official present, Caroline, an apprentice in Tygerberg, made a verbal agreement with her master to buy her own freedom. The terms of her buying her freedom and that of her youngest child was that she leave her two other young children on the farm of her former owner.[27] This

---

22   Rayner, "Wine and Slaves," Ch. 4.

23   CA, DRC, G2 2/6, Return of the Number of Schools, 1826, District of Swellendam.

24   CA, CO 441, No. 69, SM to CO, 6 July 1835.

25   CA, CO 2799, No. 65, Acting Special Justice, Paarl, to SG, 21 July 1836. See also the case of Sarah below.

26   This observation is tentative, since the patterns of indentureships after emancipation do not correlate with this observation: in the period from 1838 to 1853 Stellenbosch parents were less likely to apprentice their children than their peers in Swellendam and Worcester. See Chapter 5 for a discussion of the household economy.

27   CA, CO 465, No. 69, Office of SJ, Tygerberg, to SG, 10 July 1837.

pattern occurred throughout the Western Cape. In May 1836, an apprentice named Lea, mother of three children, came to an agreement with her master, Daniel Rouseau, of Paarl, to buy her freedom as well as that of her children. However the children's freedom was compromised at the very moment it was bought. Lea agreed that upon attaining her family's liberty she would then indenture her two boys for five years each to Rouseau under terms of Ordinance No. 50 which had regularized labor contracts pertaining to people defined as Khoi. What considerations led Lea to indenture her sons as the price of her and her daughter's freedom? Was this a comment by Lea on the possible sexual violence inherent in situations of tied labor? Did she perceive the boys as laborers rather than her daughter? The prospects of employment for herself might also have shaped her choice. The official in the special justice's office in Paarl worried about legalizing the discharge, as it placed "the minor children of the discharged apprentice in such situation as will protract the term of their service much beyond that fixed by the Abolition of Slavery." The attorney general, however, said that the discharge could go ahead.[28]

Often, apprentices had little choice but to indenture their children. Sarah, an apprentice of W. C. Rossouw, also of Paarl, stated in a memorial in 1836 that as a result of her refusal to bind her children to him until they were twenty-one, he sold her. Her new owner refused to allow her to bring her children with her. Rossouw now argued that since the children were not indentured to him he would, according to Sarah, "put them in the bushes, and if she does not like that, she may make application where she pleases."[29] Sarah put her children in the care of "some people of color," and while there, one of the children, an infant of some nine months, who was not yet weaned, became very ill. Sarah then brought the baby back to Rossouw and agreed to have it indentured. However, now that the baby was ill, Rossouw declined the indenture and sent the child off the farm. Sarah left too and soon had to bury the child she had tried so valiantly to save.[30]

The workings of the law which made no provision for the protection of family exacerbated such conflicts and colonial officials tended to side with the letter rather than the spirit of the Abolition Act. For example, in 1837 a Worcester apprentice bought the remainder of her and two of her children's apprenticeship. She asked the special justice "to direct that one other of her Children that has been Indentured shall be given up to her." Responding to the special justice's enquiry, the attorney general replied on 9 October, 1837, that "the 10th section of the Abolition Act does not apply to this case. The indentures of a child are not to be broken because a change takes place in the status of the mother."[31]

Indenturing of children did not occur uniformly throughout the colony nor remain consistent through the period of apprenticeship. Only one apprentice child was indentured in Swellendam district in the entire period while the majority of apprentice children in the Cape Colony were indentured in the special districts of Tygerberg, Stellenbosch, Paarl, and Worcester. And, at least in Cape Town, Stellenbosch, and Paarl,

---

28   CA, CO 452, No. 51, Office of SJ, Paarl, to SG, 28 May 1836, and Opinion of AG, 7 June 1836.

29   CO, 3990, No. 31, Memorial of Sarah, 28 July 1836.

30   CO 3990, No 31. Letter from Acting SJ to SG, 4 July 1836. See also CA, CO 5177, from SG to Acting SJ at Paarl, 18 August 1836.

31   CA, CO 465, No. 116, SJ Worcester to CO, 1 December 1837; AG to SJ, 9 October 1837.

the majority of indentureships in this period occurred in 1835 with numbers falling thereafter.[32] In contrast, in Worcester, the number of children indentured under the Abolition Act increased each year of apprenticeship: 41 in 1835, 81 in 1836, and 144 in 1837.[33] It is unclear what led to this difference. Cape Town certainly offered an alternative to farm employment and one might have expected farmers to be even more anxious to secure labor. On the other hand, the Cape and Stellenbosch districts were the most densely settled in the colony and slaveholders perhaps felt less anxious than their Worcester peers that former slaves and their families would be able to farm independently after emancipation.

Former slaveholders did not only target the children of apprentices for extended indenture. Many Khoi and free black children were also indentured.[34] Khoi children tended to be older than six when apprenticed. In contrast the majority of apprentices' children were much younger: the terms of the Abolition Act forced farmers to indenture these children at a very young age in order to secure their labor as adults.

Comparison of these indentures of Khoi and free black children shows some distinctions in the districts with regard to the status of the children. In Stellenbosch parents witnessed nine out of the twenty-one indentures. In Worcester, on the other hand, the seven Khoi children indentured that year were all recorded as being orphans. And of the total number of forty-nine indentured in Worcester, thirty-eight were recorded as orphans.[35] Employers in Worcester more easily asserted children's orphan status because of the size of the district and the difficulties faced by parents in coming to court to contest indenture. It is difficult to discuss these indentures with any degree of certainty, however, since some of the records are incomplete and the information far from specific.

Settlers indentured children without the consent of the parents precisely on the grounds that they needed the children's labor to offset the costs of feeding them. Of the

---

32 Only 158 apprentice children were indentured in Cape Town, but there were 265 in Tygerberg, 220 in Stellenbosch, 318 in Paarl, and 269 in Worcester, while none were indentured in the special districts of Simon's Town, Beaufort, Albany, Somerset, Fort Beaufort, and Colesberg. In Stellenbosch, 68 boys and 86 girls were indentured in 1835, 15 and 7 in 1836, and 7 boys and 7 girls in 1837. For Paarl similar proportions pertain: 85 and 75 in 1835; 9 and 13 in 1836; and 30 boys and 23 girls in 1837. CA, GH 23/12, SG to USSC, Enclosure No. 1, "Return of Apprenticed Children . . . who have been indentured by the Special Justices under the Slavery Abolition Act," 18 April 1838.

33 CA, 1/WOC 19/60, List of indentures between 1834–1836, 11 October 1836. GH 23/12, SG to Under Secretary of State, Colonial Department, 18 April 1838, Enclosure No. 1.

34 The children of slave men and Khoi mothers as well as those of free parents did not turn up in the lists focusing on children indentured under the Abolition Act, but appear in a different set of indenture books. In Swellendam district, 1 Khoi or free black child was apprenticed in 1834, 2 in 1835, 3 in 1836, 3 in 1837, and 9 in 1838. In Worcester a total of 49 Khoi children were indentured between 1834 and 1838 which, including apprentice, Khoi, and free black children, brought the total of all Worcester children indentured to 315. The indentures of free children followed a similar pattern as those of apprentices's children. Sixteen children were apprenticed in 1834, 6 in 1835, 7 in 1836, 4 in 1837, and 16 in 1838. CA, GH 23/12 SG to Under Secretary, Colonial Department, 18 April 1838, Enclosure No. 1; 1/SWM 13/7, Register of Apprenticeship Contracts 1829-1853; 1/WOC 16/42, Register of Apprenticeships 1828-1845.

35 In Stellenbosch in 1836 one boy under six was indentured, five girls and fifteen boys over six. Nine of these children were orphans, and three were regarded as destitute. The following year the numbers of children indentured in this way fell to nine. One indenture by an apprentice parent was registered in the Stellenbosch Indentureship book. CA, 1/STB 18/188, Indentureship Contracts 1836–1839, Pursuant to Ordinance No. 50. All were performed by Frederick Dickinson, CP; 1/WOC 16/42, Register of Apprenticeships 1828-1845.

159 apprentice children indentured in Worcester alone from 1835 through January 1838, 40 of their mothers were listed as objecting.[36] In 1838 Special Magistrate Mackay stated that "it appears from the records of this office that very many children . . . have been indentured against the wishes of the mothers."[37]

Maternity and Morality

For many apprentice women, attempts to prevent the illegal indenture of their children involved convincing special magistrates that they were fit mothers and better able to take care of their children than their former masters. These cases expose the ideals about family, gender relations, and motherhood which special magistrates brought to their evaluations of the cases. The legal determination of children's status according to that of the mother under slavery had bolstered the maternal relationship and weakened the legal rights of fathers. In addition, the Abolition Act of 1833 gave mothers the power to indenture their children under the age of six. This perhaps explains why most of the appeals against child indentureship were made by mothers rather than both parents together, or fathers alone, even when the child involved was older than six. The legal affirmation of mothers' rights over young children provided apprentice women with a powerful ideological weapon against the claims by farmers, and other freed people, to control of children's labor.

This claim was echoed by the antislavery *South African Commercial Advertiser*. In an article on the child indentures the newspaper stated that "The feelings of nature, have . . . in several instances, been outraged, and the helpless mother has been compelled, by harsh and cruel means, to surrender her infant to a prolonged period of servitude."[38] The endorsement of motherhood was a double-edged sword: the responsibility placed on mothers to organize or protest the indenture of their children also meant that women had to confront some of the most painful decisions cast by the ending of slavery.

The terms of indenture under the Abolition Act of 1833 made examination of women's morality central to the special magistrates' evaluations of how to proceed in cases of illegal indenture. In such cases the power to decide between the claim of the employer or the mother lay with the special magistrate. The Abolition Act charged special magistrates with determining whether children were indeed destitute; that is, whether the mother was able to take care of her child. Their determinations inevitably involved both explicit and implicit judgments regarding the lifestyle and morality of the mother, and they echoed the sentiments expressed by Governor Cole and Protector Rogers in the early 1830s.[39]

---

36   CA, 1/WOC 16/40, Apprenticebook 1836–January 1838. Neither Stellenbosch nor Swellendam archives contain detailed records on these apprenticeships. Stellenbosch only has a book recording indentures of Khoi and free black children. Lea of Tulbagh in the district of Worcester, for example, protested that her child was illegally detained by her former master, Jacobus Theron. CA, 1/WOC, 19/60, SM Peake to Jacobus Theron, 16 June 1835.

37   CA, 1/WOC, 19/61, Mackay to Wouter de Wet, 30 March 1838.

38   *SACA*, 1 March 1838.

39   See Chapter 2. Cases involving the indenture of Khoi children were ostensibly handled by the clerks of the peace, although in practice the special magistrates often indentured these children also.

In 1837, Edward Molesworth, the special justice of Worcester, indentured one-year-old Diana as a housemaid to a widow despite the objection of the mother. The special justice permitted this indenture because he regarded the mother as irresponsible or unable to care for Diana. He wrote at the bottom of the indenture: "Mother objects, but has nine children."[40] Molesworth perhaps interpreted the size of the woman's family as being too large for her to be able to support another baby, or, perhaps, made a pejorative judgment that she had already had too many children. Other records contain more overt judgments on the character of the mother. For example, Molesworth wrote on the indenture form of Thomas, aged four, that "Mother objected, a bad character," as if this was sufficient to wrest the child away from her and to negate her objection.[41] In neighboring Stellenbosch the clerk of the peace endorsed the indenture of a Khoi child, Griet, aged ten, to the widow W. C. Spykerman in 1836. In so doing he also therefore endorsed the widow's view that Griet's mother, Leentje, lead "a wandering life."[42] In this record we see the trace of an argument about the unfitness of some freed people to enjoy the benefits of freedom since they refused to live their lives according to the dictates of settler society which some settlers made particularly after 1838 in order to secure bonded labor.

These cases also show the pervasiveness in British society and settler society at the Cape of contradictory attitudes towards women. On the one hand women's maternal feelings were believed to be central to female identity as nurturer of society. Yet on the other hand this belief in the purity of motherhood coexisted with an assumption that female sexuality needed to be contained since unleashed it threatened to degrade society and tempt men into immorality. The comments by the colonial officials in these cases also echo the stereotypes of the immoral slave and Khoi woman which were widespread in settler society, and indeed in imperial antislavery discourse. A remark by the attorney general with regard to a case involving the separation of spouses in 1837 illustrates the ways in which these prejudices could shape the lives of freed people. Special Justice James Barnes of Swellendam reported that an apprentice had had a child by one man but had separated from him and formed a relationship with a man living about an hour away. Her employer then sold her to a farmer living ten hours away from her partner. Barnes stated that, "The husband falls sick, she is anxious to visit him, applies to her employers for leave, and is refused. Was the first Employer justified in so selling her services and if so, is the second authorized to refuse her leave to visit her husband?"[43] Despite the explicit statement of the Order-in-Council of 1831 which recognized slave relationships even where they were not legally solemnized, the attorney general tersely responded, "I consider the woman under consideration simply as a whore, and not the wife of any person whatever; therefore that the first employer was justified in selling her services, and the second is authorized to refuse her leave to visit the man with whom she cohabits."[44]

---

40   CA, 1/WOC 16/41, Indentureship Contract, 10 October 1837.

41   Ibid., Indentureship Contract, 23 November 1837. Also 25 November 1837 Molesworth writes, "Mother absent a bad character."

42   CA, 1/STB 18/188, "Indenture of Apprenticeship of a destitute child," 5 August 1836.

43   CA, CO 465, No. 3, SM to CO, 3 January 1837.

44   CA, CO 465, No. 3, AG to SJ, Swellendam, 7 January 1837.

Yet what "woman" meant was always in flux.[45] The same woman might be represented both as overtly sexual, and in need of discipline and control, but also as a helpless victim of powers beyond her control. Colonial officials' conflicted representations of women of the slave and later ex-slave population had significant repercussions in the postemancipation era. As we shall see in Part III, various colonial officials and missionaries saw freed women as potential bearers of both morality and stability to the rural working class, but they also perceived women's sexuality as the very instrument of the perceived degradation of the ex-slave population.

Conclusion

It appears that the Cape was unique in the proliferation of indentures of apprentices' children between 1835 and 1838. Glenelg, the Secretary of State for Colonies, stated that as "far as the returns have been received from other Colonies, it appears that this power has been most sparingly exercised elsewhere and in some Colonies no such indentures have been executed."[46] Cape settlers' long history of using bonded Khoi child labor no doubt facilitated the ease with which farmers turned to indenturing apprentices' children as a means of obtaining labor. Special magistrates also were overworked and spread thin, and perhaps unable to give the cases of indenture the attention they deserved in making sure that parental consent had really been obtained, or that a child's orphan status was correct. The magistrates' terms of evaluation of women as mothers also affected the high rate of indenture.

In 1837 a resolution of the British House of Commons called for "Copies of Returns of all the Children who have been apprenticed in the Colonies under the provision of the Abolition Law."[47] The indentureship of children became a *cause célèbre* and in 1838 Glenelg demanded a special enquiry into child indentureship at the Cape. He told the governor that

> the number of children who have been apprenticed in most of the Districts of the Cape under the 13th Section of the Abolition Act, is far greater than I had any reason to believe, and I much regret that it should have been thought necessary by any of the Special Magistrates to exercise so largely the power vested in them in this respect, and which was intended to be exercised solely for the benefit of the children, in rescuing them from destitution.[48]

The Abolition of Slavery Act of 1838 outlawed the indentures of apprentice children beyond August 1840. In fact, Governor D'Urban abolished child indentureship

---

45 See Denise Riley, *"Am I that Name?" Feminism and the Category of 'Women' in History* (Minneapolis: University of Minnesota Press, 1988).

46 CA, LCA 9 15, SSC, to Govenor, 30 Apr., 1838.

47 CA, GH 1/118, Circular from SSC to Governor, 1 December 1837. The figures called for by the British Colonial Office only reflected children indentured under the age of six; this did not include older apprentice children who were also indentured in terms of the Act. Thus, the apprenticeship book for Worcester reveals that in fact 55 rather than 41 children as listed by the Colonial Office were indentured in 1835 and that 88 rather than 81 were indentured in 1836. The count for 81 includes the 9 children indentured in both 1835 and 1836 who were born after 1 December 1834. CA, 1/WOC 16/40, Apprenticeship Contract Book, 1836.

48 CA, LCA 9, No. 15, SSC to Governor, 30 April 1838.

as a whole on that day. This meant that despite slaveholders' wishes, apprentices' children were also freed on 1 December 1838. The practice of using bonded child labor continued, however, in a different guise under the Masters and Servants Ordinance of 1842 and in the de facto slavery practiced by those farmers who brought African children illegally from the interior into the Cape.[49]

In the end, the period of apprenticeship, that twilight world between slavery and freedom, was a decisive period in defining some of the contours of the freedom which would follow. Ex-slaves demonstrated through their charges at the offices of the special magistrates that they were prepared to fight to limit employers' claims to their children and indeed to their own labor. In the decade after final emancipation, freed people sought to move off the farms and to start a life of independent labor.

Yet between 1834 and 1838 former slaveholders had given notice of their determination to try and limit the significance of the coming freedom. In many ways they succeeded. Of all the colonies in which slavery ended, only the Cape maintained production levels akin to those of slavery. In fact, in the two decades following emancipation in 1838, the Cape actually witnessed a "boom in the agricultural economy." This was owing in part to the leverage that Cape slaveholders were able to exert over the lives and labor of ex-slaves. And, as Ross has shown, this control was so successful because it was "based on the experience, acquired over two or three decades, of holding the officially free Khoisan effectively in bondage."[50]

Women's position as key actors in the struggle over child labor declined in the postemancipation period with the passing of the Cape Masters and Servants Ordinance of 1842 which gave the decisions for child indentureship over to the father. Yet the representations contained in some of the special magistrates' reports about some women being deficient and irresponsible, which again invoked earlier European and settler commentaries on slave women, continued to exert a powerful role in the responses of colonial officials to the family formations and social lives of freed people in the postemancipation period.[51]

This then was the period of apprenticeship, a time in which former masters lied, fraudulently tied apprentices and children to their farms, and sustained the violence of servile relationships. Freed people signaled that independence of farm labor constituted one central meaning of freedom. They also indicated that personal relations would remain a central focus of the redefinitions of society in the postemancipation period.

Part II analyzes the social and geographical landscapes of emancipation. It argues that the relationships slaves had formed under slavery and apprenticeship shaped their experience of emancipation and were crucial to the formation of a working class. I also argue that freed people's conceptions of the household as a complex social and economic unit, and their ideas about women's place in the workforce, critically informed labor relations and colonial discourses on labor in the postemancipation period.

---

49 See Chapter 5.

50 See Robert Ross, "'Rather Mental than Physical': Emancipations and the Cape Colony," in Worden and Crais, eds., *Breaking the Chains*, 153, 161.

51 See Part III.

PART II

LIBERATING THE FAMILY?
1838–1848

4

Landscapes of Emancipation

The relationships which slaves and dependent laborers had established before emancipation importantly fashioned the road which individuals traveled after 1838. For a slave man a relationship with a free woman had meant that their children were free. A slave woman's relationship with a free man involved in skilled work had opened up the possibility that he could save sufficient money to manumit their children or herself. In the Western Cape such relationships facilitated ex-slaves' movement into an economy based on wage labor in the years after 1838.

Slavery in the rural districts had been characterized by a relatively low level of labor specialization as compared to the quite large group of skilled slaves in Cape Town, and men almost invariably filled the few skilled occupations such as carpentry and wagon-making.[1] For female or male slaves who had been involved predominantly in agricultural work, or who were unskilled, the limited employment opportunities of the villages of the Western Cape prohibited easy assimilation into the town unless friends or family could aid in the transition to labor of a different sort or provide them with entry to a mission station.

This chapter shows the measures taken by freed people to find their children and other loved ones in the years after 1838. Freed people made claims to land, moved to new districts, and manipulated the labor market to increase their flexibility and bargaining position in the postemancipation world.[2] After 1834, some ex-slaves took advantage of short-lived government schemes to make land available to freed people; others bought individual plots in villages, and many freed people saw in the mission stations the best way of gaining land. Missions came to play a central role in the postemancipation political economy. The chapter concludes by examining the significance of family ties in securing some ex-slaves entrance to the mission station and by showing how the establishment of new stations catering to ex-slaves only temporarily enabled freed people to avoid farm labor.

---

1 Andrew Banks, "Slavery," Ch. 1, 47. For a discussion of slave labor in the nineteenth century see Mason, "Fit for Freedom," 307.

2 For a discussion of the multiple ways of approaching a study of emancipation see Rebecca Scott, "Exploring the Meaning of Freedom: Postemancipation Societies in Comparative Perspective," *Hispanic American Historical Review* 68, 3 (1988): 407–428.

Family and Freedom

On 1 December 1838, the slaves of South Africa woke up as freed people no longer the possession of others. People celebrated the day either in religious services or in other festivities with relatives and friends. In Stellenbosch, "not withstanding the inclemency of the weather, the missionary chapel . . . was crowded to excess at three different services during that day and many who could not gain admittance, remained outside, near the door, and windows endeavouring to catch some portion of the service."[3] G. A. Zahn of the Rhenish Missionary Society in Tulbagh recorded that "at two o'clock in the afternoon the old and the young, known and unknown, could be seen with joy on their faces. And here and there one could see a tear of thankfulness flowing over black cheeks. . . . Triumph, triumph . . . now they are free, free from slavery."[4] In nearby Worcester, the resident magistrate, P. J. Truter, wrote, "New Epoch in Colony, slavery abolished, all Apprentices this day emancipated. Happy event for the future generation!"[5]

While missionaries reported Emancipation Day as one of complete happiness for slaves, Katie Jacobs, a rural slave remembered the first of December as a day filled with conflicting emotions, dominated by tension rather than overwhelming happiness:

> I know there was rain that day. . . . I recognized my husband in a violent temper. His *baas* was cruel and *sjamboked* his slaves as often as he fed them. He was mad with rage on the day of our emancipation. Early in the morning he armed himself with a gun, mounted his horse, and drove every ex-slave off his farm. At the boundary he warned them that the first one that was found trespassing on his land would be shot down. Soaking rain had fallen since daybreak, so that when Jacob [her husband] reached me he was drenched to the skin. No wonder he spoke to me so harshly on that day of joy, humiliation, and prayer.[6]

On emancipation the some twenty-five thousand slaves emancipated in the Western Cape left clear signposts as to how they saw the ending of slavery.[7] Former slaves imagined freedom through personal relationships—both between members of

---

3   CA, CO 476, No. 123, SJ to SG, 10 December 1838. The *SACA* similarly reported, "On Saturday the places of Public Worship open to them [freed people] in the forenoon and evening, were filled to the doors by most orderly and attentive congregations. . . ." SAL, *SACA*, Bound Volume, 5 December 1838, 197–198.

4   CA, DRC, P42 1/2 Diary of G. A. Zahn, 1 December 1838. The original was in Dutch.

5   CA, A 79, Diary of P. J. Truter, 1 December 1838.

6   CA, Press Cuttings, Volume 14, Interview with Katie Jacobs, *Die Banier*, 2 June 1963. The interview was conducted by an English interviewer who translated Ms. Jacob's Dutch into English (at the time of the interview it appears). The article did not contain information on the interviewer. Other farmers displayed similar punitive behavior on the day of emancipation; for example see CA, CO 476, No. 124, SM, Worcester, to SG, 11 December 1838.

7   Of the approximately 39,000 slaves freed on 1 December 1838, 25,000 came from the Western Cape. John Carel Marincowitz, "Rural Production and Labour in the Western Cape, with Special Reference to the Wheat Growing Districts, 1838–1888" (Ph.D. diss., University of London, 1985), 28. The *SACA* estimated that of those 25,000 a full 20,112 lived in the Cape and Stellenbosch districts alone. SAL, *SACA*, Bound Volume, 28 November 1838, 187.

an extended family and between friends.[8] That grandparents, aunts and uncles, friends, and fellow freed people involved themselves in recovering children after 1838 demonstrates indeed that slave families comprised wide and complex emotional relationships in which community and family were in some senses one and the same.[9] The freed people who appear in the Western Cape records seem to have had a fair idea of where to find their children and other relatives. Possibly the relatively small geographical area of the Western Cape enabled slaves to stay in closer contact with their kin even if this was only through secondhand knowledge of their whereabouts. For example, Katie Jacobs knew that her mother had been sold to an owner in Frenchhoek, but Katie's owner prevented Katie from visiting her mother, and they never saw each other again after her mother's sale.[10] In an age when the only transport available was by foot, horse, or wagon, the struggles of parents and other relatives to find children in different districts meant overcoming not only the objections of employers, but also often the rigors of a long journey.

After 1838, the office of clerk of the peace took over some of the functions of the special magistrates and handled the investigation of illegal indentures.[11] These records provide information on the early years of emancipation and on freed people's efforts to get in touch with family members and to free children from illegal bonded labor to former slaveholders. The attorney general's office in Cape Town does not seem to have gone to any great pains at all to establish the veracity of the claims to familial status made by people appealing to the clerks of the peace. The determinations of parenthood were often very subjective. Fathers in particular had difficulty proving their relationships because the legal status of a child had been determined by that of the mother with the paternity of both slave and Khoi men being unrecorded. It is possible that people who stated that they were uncles and aunts might sometimes have been old friends or fictive kin.[12]

---

8   For similar points in other contexts see Holt, *Problem of Freedom*; Jones, *Labor of Love*; Leon F. Litwack, *Been in the Storm So Long: The Aftermath of Slavery* (New York: Alfred A. Knopf, 1979); and Rebecca Scott, *Slave Emancipation in Cuba: The Transition to Free Labor, 1860–1899* (Princeton, N.J.: Princeton University Press, 1985), especially Ch. 7, 167. The literature on Africa has focused very little on the emotional concerns of slaves and freed people, but for a brief discussion see Wright, *Strategies*.

9   The information presented by the appeals to the clerks of the peace show the dimensions of the search by former slaves to reconstitute their families. CA, 1/STB 22/37, "Memorandum by RM, Paarl, of Statements made by Moos, Manuel and Mina, persons of colour relative to some of their children and relatives who have been indentured to the masters of their deceased mothers without the knowledge and contrary to the wishes of the Deponents," 1839. Also 1/STB 22/45, CP to Mr. L. P. D. van der Poel, Moddergat, 3 December 1838; 1/STB 22/45, No. 242, CP to Mr. C. Lombard, Swartland, 7 December 1838; 1/SWM 16/33, CP to Barend Kogelman and Heyn Mulder, 19 December 1838; CO 4000, No. 172, "The Memorial of Eva late an apprentice of Mr. Ponte Haupt of Vlagenberg in the District of Stellenbosch," 4 December 1838.

10   CA, Press Cuttings, Volume 14, Interview with Katie Jacobs, *Die Banier*, 2 June 1963. In the Cape Colony one does not find the extensive advertisements in newspapers asking for help in finding relatives as one does in the USA: possibly this is also testimony to a less newspaper-oriented culture.

11   For examples of successful cases see CA, 1/STB 22/45, CP to L. P. D. van der Poel, 3 December 1838; CP to Jan J. le Roex, 4 December 1838; and CP to P. A. Cloete, 5 December 1838; also 1/SWM 16/33, CP to D. F. Joubert, 11 December 1838; and 1/SWM 16/28, CP, STB, to CP, SWM, 9 December 1839.

12   For a claim by a grandmother see Clara's memorial in CA, CO 4000, Memorials A–E, Volume 1, 1839, 25 February 1839. CA 1/STB 22/36, Acting AG to RM, 26 June 1839, Report on Memorial of Clara.

The battle over the child before 1838 had mainly involved women in their positions as mothers. After 1838 fathers also instituted proceedings to end illegal indentures: a circular of 14 December 1838 allowed children to be placed in the custody of any relative who would look after them.[13] After emancipation fathers appear more frequently in the records. For example on 18 December 1838, just seventeen days after Emancipation Day, an ex-slave man, Saul, told the clerk of the peace of Worcester that he was the father of a child who had been illegally indentured to Saul's former owner. The former owner had claimed that the child, Theunis, was an orphan. Now that Saul was free, and working on a farm where there was a schoolmaster, he wanted to have his child freed from the indenture so that he could "place him under the Care of the schoolmaster."[14]

In 1839 another father, originally a slave in Stellenbosch district, but who had been sold to the Beaufort district in the interior, returned to Stellenbosch in order to fetch his children. Moos told the clerk of the peace that

> when he became free in December last he returned with as little delay as possible with the intention of taking away his children but the Widow Pepler told him that they had been indentured to her, and that the Girl was then living with her daughter, Mrs. Malherbe of Swellendam, and that she would keep the boy Africa in her own service, whom, he Moos saw at the time almost naked and who complained to him about being extremely ill-treated.[15]

Other relatives also acted to bring children into the fold of the freed family. In 1839, Mina July and her husband, Platjes, from the Hex River field cornetcy in Worcester district secured the freedom of Mina's younger sister, aged twelve, from an indenture to a Hans Brewer of neighboring Swellendam.[16] Mina and Platjes July's journey from Hex River in Worcester to Swellendam would have entailed at least a twelve-mile walk or wagon ride to the village of Worcester and then a long journey up through the Breede River valley to Swellendam: a trek taking many days.

Even people who might not have had formal family ties to children sought to bring them into the fold of the ex-slave community after emancipation. At Groenekloof mission station in Malmesbury, "eight or nine of the sixteen children who entered Groenekloof on their own, entered when the agreement for their fostering by members of the institution, possibly relatives, had been completed." In fact the fostering of children "by established Groenekloof couples" predated emancipation. Residents took in children and adopted them as their own.[17]

Yet kin did not automatically wish to be united. In 1839 the uncle of a five-year-old slave girl, Dina, refused to take her "on the grounds that he had several children

---

13   CA, 1/STB 22/35, Circular from CO, 14 December 1838. The Colonial Office stressed to local magistrates that indenture should be avoided unless absolutely necessary, a caution no doubt arising from the distinctive history of the Cape in having so many children indentured during apprenticeship.

14   CA, CO 2779, No. 161, CP, Worcester, to AG, 18 December 1838.

15   CA, 1/STB 22/37, Memorandum by H. Piers, RM, Paarl, of Statement of Moos, 1839.

16   CA, 1/SWM 16/33, Note in Letter Book of CP, 15 January 1839.

17   Helen Ludlow, "Missions and Emancipation in the South Western Cape: A Case Study of Groenekloof (Mamre), 1838–1852,"(M.A. diss., University of Cape Town, 1992), 62.

of his own."[18] The desires of children raised under slavery also did not always coincide with their parents' and grandparents' wish to reunite family members. In December 1839, a year after emancipation, a freed man, Hans of Stellenbosch district, traced his four sons, Hans, Abraham, Ezau, and Marthinus to different farms in neighboring Swellendam and applied to the clerk of the peace in Stellenbosch to aid him in reuniting his family.[19] By January Hans had arranged to have the children brought to the farm on which he was working, making solicitous and careful arrangements to secure the children's safety by giving the clerk of the peace at Swellendam nine pence to cover their travel expenses on the road to Stellenbosch.[20] But Hans's search for his children ended in disappointment. Three of his children had left Swellendam and only Marthinus, who appears to have been the youngest of the sons, remained in the district waiting to be reunited with his father.[21]

Evidence also suggests that a few ex-slave children remained at the homes of their former owners. It is difficult imagine this occurred free of coercion. In the Western Cape cases of children staying with their owners rather than going to their families are almost solely confined to Swellendam district.[22] This suggests that particular pressures existed in this region which influenced children's "choices." The strong presence of mission stations in Swellendam district, which offered freed people a place of refuge from farm labor after 1838, also might have encouraged farmers there to pay attention during the apprenticeship years to bribing apprentices' children with good food, clothes, and promises of a better life. Walter Harding, the Swellendam clerk of the peace, might also have been more willing than his colleagues to take children's claims of loyalty to former owners at face value.

In deciding on the merits of individual cases Harding invoked many of the assumptions which had governed the assessments of the special magistrates during the period of apprenticeship. On 16 December 1838, barely a fortnight after Emancipation Day, a Christoffel Coetzee brought Mariana, aged ten, to Harding. In his record Harding listed Mariana as an orphan in the records even though she told him that her grandmother lived nearby. Mariana stated that she did not want to leave Mr. Coetzee. Apparently Harding had asked her grandmother to appear before him so that he could better adjudicate the case. We learn only that the "Grandmother (an old woman) appeared & stated that her wages were Rds 3 a month. Mariana to remain with Mr. Coetzee. . . ."[23]

Harding does not seem to have tried to find out the extent to which Mariana might have been coerced to say she wanted to remain with Coetzee. Coetzee was privileged in any competition as to whom could provide better for the child by virtue of his former ownership of slaves. Virtually any former slave would lose in this calculation. Former masters summoned their professed knowledge of their former slaves

---

18 CA, 1/SWM 16/33, Note in Letter Book of CP, 12 January 1839.

19 CA, 1/SWM 16/28, CP, STB, to CP, SWM, 9 January 1839.

20 CA, 1/STB 22/45, CP, STB, to CP, SWM, 21 January 1840.

21 CA, 1/SWM 16/28, CP, SWM, to CP, STB, 30 April 1839.

22 CA, 1/SWM 16/33, CP to Hendrik Swart, 16 December 1838; CP to Christoffel Coetzee, 16 December 1838; and CP to Barend Kogelman and Heyn Mulder, 19 December 1838; 1/SWM 16/33, Note in the Letter Book of CP, 10 January 1839, and 12 January 1839.

23 CA, 1/SWM 16/33, CP to Christoffel Coetzee, 16 December 1838.

in arguing their case against parents and Harding seems to have been very willing to believe former owners' claims. Barend Kogelman, a Khoi laborer from the Karoo, came to Harding on 19 December 1838 asking for his daughter, Apalom (known also as Mietje), to be returned to him. Apalom had been apprenticed to Heyn Mulder, the owner of her late mother. According to Mulder, the mother had left Kogelman because he was an alcoholic and had taken another wife. Mulder claimed that "on her Death bed he was made to promise . . . that Mietje should not be given up to Barend but was remain with Muller [sic] . . . & that he promised to have her taught & christened."[24] Harding recorded that "Mietje alias Apalom stated that she wished to remain with Mr. Muller in preference to Barend Kogelman her reputed father."[25] Harding did not query Muller's account and the child therefore remained.

It is possible that some children genuinely did decide to stay on the farms in which they had lived most of their lives. The children like Apalom who chose not to go to relatives probably knew the other laborers and former apprentices on the farm better than their relations. However, the kinship offered by other laborers rather than any allegiance to a former owner probably prompted children to stay.[26]

Land and Freedom

Clearly emancipation freed slaves into a political economy in which settlers fundamentally controlled the means of production and in which the Cape government supported the interests of settlers over those of ex-slaves and newly colonized peoples. The slave population of the Western Cape could not draw on a significant peasant breech to give economic meaning to freedom.[27] Up to 1834 some slaveholders had allocated small plots to their slaves allowing them to accumulate livestock and farm land on their own accord although the evidence for this practice in the Western Cape is scarce.[28] Further east, in districts such as Worcester and particularly in the Eastern

---

24   CA, 1/SWM 16/33, CP to Barend Kogelman and Heyn Mulder, 19 December 1838.

25   Ibid.

26   Walter Harding's letter book of the cases he covered as clerk of the peace contains many other such ambiguous cases. In January 1839, a young man named Pieter was able to identify where many of his siblings lived, and yet stated, according to Harding, that he preferred to live with his former master. CA, 1/SWM 16/33, Note in Letter Book, 24 January 1839. See also CA, 1/SWM 16/33, Note regarding letter from CP to Hendrik Swart, 16 December 1838. See also case of Caatje, in CA, CO 2801, CP, SWM, to SG, 9 March 1841.

27   See Johannes Stephanus Marais, *The Cape Coloured People, 1652–1937* (New York: AMS Press; Longmans, Green and Co., 1939), 167.

28   The evidence of such garden plots in the Western Cape comes from a couple of reports by the protectors of slaves, and thus must be used with some caution. For example, in 1833 the assistant guardian of slaves in Stellenbosch reported that slaves were able to market the produce from their gardens in both Stellenbosch and Cape Town, and in the same year the protector for the Western Division stated that rural slaves sold the produce of their gardens. CA, 1/STB 22/158, "Statement of the amount of labor usually performed by slaves employed in agriculture in the District of Stellenbosch . . . " by Assistant Guardian of Slaves, 27 July 1833; CA, ZP 1/6/6, PRO CO 53/55, Report of PS, Western Division, 28 May 1833. Mason suggests that a peasant breech was widespread in the Western Cape but relies on the references by the protector and assistant protector which were also the only ones I found. Mason, "Fit for Freedom," 322 passim. The original secondary reference seems to be Marais, *Cape Coloured People*, 167, but he is also citing the protector's report for 1830.

Cape the practice was more common. Slaveholders allowed slaves to farm on their own accord as a means of encouraging them to remain in a situation where the possibilities of escape were much greater than in the more closely settled areas of the Western Cape.[29]

Emancipation freed slaves in the Western Cape into a predominantly agrarian economy where self-employment or urban work was the exception, not the rule, and where most of the best agricultural land was already owned by whites. Of the districts under consideration, only Worcester had large tracts of unused land. In Stellenbosch settlers had long ago seized most of the land.[30] Settlers' control of land, and particularly their increasing ability to shape government policy, meant that freed people were ultimately unable to establish a peasantry on the same scale as their peers in Jamaica, for example.[31] If such a peasantry arose it did so on the mission stations, and even there by the late 1840s people increasingly had to work on the farms throughout the year in order to support themselves.

Prior to the 1820s three forms of land tenure had existed at the Cape: freehold tenure, loan farms or *leeningsplase*, and quitrent. Up to 1813, when Governor Cradock introduced the system of quitrent, farms had been granted to individuals as loan places which could be converted into freehold tenure.[32] While rents were supposed to be charged, the general inefficiency of administration under VOC rule allowed farmers to run up enormous debts. Cradock's reforms failed to raise revenue in large measure because of the weakness of the colonial state. After the commission of enquiry into the state of the Cape in 1828, land tenure, like the judicial system and labor relations, underwent a reform and quitrent became the predominant form of land tenure throughout the Cape.[33] Quitrent involved the payment of annual minimal fees to the government and facilitated the registering of land. Quitrent registers recorded all transactions regarding a parcel of land including the subdivision and transfer of land and the payment of quitrent.

Very few people outside of the settler group had formal titles to land prior to emancipation. In the rural areas the free blacks had always formed a tiny minority,

---

29 For a discussion of the peasant breech at the Cape see Clifton C. Crais, "Slavery and Freedom Along a Frontier: The Eastern Cape, South Africa, 1770–1838," *Slavery and Abolition* 11 (September 1990): 201–203; and *White Supremacy and Black Resistance*, Ch. 4, esp. 70–73. Also see John Edwin Mason, "Fortunate Slaves and Artful Masters: Labor Relations in the Rural Cape Colony during the Era of Emancipation, ca. 1825 to 1838," in Eldredge and Morton, eds., *Slavery in South Africa*, 67–91.

30 For example in 1844, while sixteen farms totaling nearly seventy-eight thousand acres were awarded in Worcester district, in Stellenbosch only two farms were so granted totaling just over one thousand acres. Subsequent years showed similar trends. CGH, "Return of Lands Granted and Sold During the Year 1844," *Blue Book 1844*, 354–356; *Blue Book 1845*, 360–363; *Blue Book 1846*, 410–413.

31 For the Caribbean see Sidney Mintz, "A Note on the Definition of Peasantries," *Journal of Peasant Studies* 1 (October 1973): 91–106. For a general overview of the Cape economy see Robert Ross, "The Origins of Capitalist Agriculture in the Cape Colony: A Survey," in William Beinart, Peter Delius, and Stanley Trapido, eds., *Putting a Plough to the Ground: Accumulation and Dispossession in Rural South Africa 1850–1930*, (Johannesburg: Ravan Press, 1986), 56–100.

32 In 1717 the VOC board had stopped the practice of converting loan places into freehold in order to discourage European immigration, but renewed the practice in 1743. Leonard Guelke, "Freehold Farmers and Frontier Settlers," in Elphick and Giliomee, eds., *Shaping*, 66–108, 78.

33 This information is taken from Peires, "British and the Cape," 502–503.

and only a small minority of them owned land before 1838.[34] In the northwestern Cape some people of Khoi and white descent, the "Bastards," had "held on to land, whether registered or unregistered, in isolated areas in . . . the Cedarberg. . . ."[35] Manumitted slaves and free blacks also bought land in other districts before 1834. For example, Leander, a slave who had bought his freedom "after many years and exertion," became "proprietor of the Loan place Olynebosch situated in the Onder Roggeveld" of Worcester District.[36] The quitrent register for Paarl village shows grants to people of Khoi/slave descent dating back to 1817.[37] In 1834 a David Jephta bought one morgen, and S. J. Willemse six, of the twenty-six morgen farm of the "Bastard Hottentot" Carel Fortuin who had received the land in 1817.[38]

But in 1838 freed people had few opportunities to farm independently. On emancipation only some one thousand people, roughly 4 percent of the ex-slave population of the Western Cape, settled independently on public land.[39] In 1841 Governor Napier wrote that in the whole Colony only five million acres were

> considered in any degree fit for occupation. The whole Colony contains about eighty seven millions, so that considerably more than a half consists of mountain or wilderness. Now as it happens . . . the remaining available portions of land are to be found either intervening between the portions already occupied, in patches generally unsuitable for the formation of new farms or interspersed amongst the 64,000 square miles of utterly useless country.[40]

A year later a missionary at Elim Moravian station in Caledon concurred: "We can hardly expect, that the Hottentots will ever attain to affluence: the finest and most fruitful portions of the land of their fathers, have been for more than a century in possession of European settlers."[41] In 1851, a good decade after emancipation, the governor remarked that "Except at the missionary institutions, very few of the coloured people own or occupy any property, but are principally labourers living on the farms of their employers."[42]

---

34 Worden, *Slavery*, Ch. 10, 144–147. In 1838 Stellenbosch had a free black population of 358. *Cape Almanack of 1838*, 96. For information on free black communities in the seventeenth and eighteenth centuries see Guelke and Shell, "Intergroup Relations," 220–224.

35 Martin Legassick, "The Northern Frontier to 1840," in Elphick and Giliomee, eds., *Shaping*, 358–420, 373; Marais, *Cape Coloured People*, 12.

36 CA, CO 3980, Memorial of Leander, 12 May 1835.

37 CA, 1/STB 11/1, Folio 27, Quitrent Register, Grant of 2 morgen to Saartje, "Bastard Hottentot," 1 July 1817; Folio 148, Grant of 26 morgen 208 square roods to "Bastd. Hott." Carel Fortuin, 27 October 1817.

38 CA, 1/STB 11/1, Quitrent Register, No. 148, 10 June 1834.

39 Marincowitz, "Rural Production," 33. Thus, 4 percent of slaves in the Western Cape settled as free holders compared to the 60 percent in Jamaica where there were 20,000 "new freeholders" after emancipation. Green, *British Slave Emancipation*, 171.

40 CA, GH 23/13, No. 19, Governor to SSC, 15 March 1841.

41 HA, "Letter from Brother Genth, Elim Station, 9 July 1842," *PA*, XVI, CLXXVII (December 1842).

42 GB, Parliament, House, "Further Papers Relative to the Establishment of a Representative Assembly," Parliamentary Papers 1851 (1362) Despatch from Governor Sir H. E. Smith to Earl Grey, 21 January 1851. At the time of the 1865 census only 10 percent of all farmers in the Western Cape were considered coloured, with most of these probably being accounted for by the populations of the mission stations. Marincowitz, "Rural Production," 116.

As elsewhere after the ending of slavery many former slaves wanted to achieve actual as well as legal freedom.[43] Freed people sought economic freedom in part because it helped them achieve autonomy and self-determination in every aspect of their lives. They wanted to give economic meaning to freedom and this ideally entailed independent access to, or ownership of, land, and manipulation of the labor market to ensure giving credence to the notion of free labor. Of the some twenty-five thousand slaves freed in 1838 in the Western Cape some seven thousand ex-slaves left the farms in the decade thereafter. Three thousand settled in villages such as Stellenbosch and Worcester, while three thousand went to live on the old mission stations such as Genadendal and Mamre, as well as on the new ones which were created for freed people.[44]

In 1838 the government did offer a few fortunate families land free of ties to former slaveholders. Up until the late 1840s the Colonial Office and "friends of the natives" such as William Porter, the attorney general, favored a form of peasant ownership by ex-slaves as one way of producing a stable rural society in the aftermath of emancipation. Worcester witnessed the most concerted effort, which predated emancipation in 1838, by both government and local officials to settle Khoi and other freed people.[45] A few months prior to the initial abolition of slavery one Ernestus J. Visser of Worcester complained that "Bastard" families had occupied the farms Brakfontein and Rietfontein in Worcester which actually belonged to him. The governor and the local civil commissioner supported the families' claims, the governor writing that "the Bastard families . . . are entitled to the places in question. . . ."[46] Similarly, in 1836, the government authorized the settlement of some five hundred to six hundred families in a location in Du Toit's Kloof in Worcester even though it meant the dispossession of two loan farms belonging to the farmers Daniel and Charles Theron.[47]

But officials did not perceive freedom from slavery as automatically conferring the right to land ownership. The colonial office made applications for land by Khoi and other free blacks conditional on behavior and expected that the land grants would help create good work habits. When, in 1836, the civil commissioner of Worcester authorized ten Khoi families to buy land near the village the governor approved of their being so settled as long as "due regard" was paid "to character, and to the probability of their turning the advantage thus conceded to them to good

---

43 See Cooper, *From Slaves to Squatters*, Ch. 2. "Slaves in general also seem to have preferred working their own land or self-employment, which allowed them to control their own work rhythms, to wage labor or tenancy arrangements." Richard Roberts and Suzanne Miers, "End of Slavery in Africa," in Miers and Roberts, eds., *End of Slavery in Africa*, 3–68, 57.

44 See Marincowitz, "Rural Production," 33; Ludlow, "Missions and Emancipation"; Tessa van Ryneveld, "Merchants and Missions: Developments in the Caledon District, 1838–1850" (B.A. hons. diss., History Department, University of Cape Town, 1985); Marais, *Cape Coloured People*, 191; and Ross, "Origins," 82.

45 CA, 1/WOC 11/13, SG to CC, 18 March 1836; CA, CO 2779, No. 11, CC to SG, 15 January 1838; CA, 1/WOC 19/61, SJ of the Peace to CC, 25 June 1838.

46 CA, 1/WOC 11/12, Acting SG to RM and CC, 24 June 1834. "Bastard" families living on the northwestern border of Worcester, in the Clan William area, also received favorable consideration by the Assistant CC in 1836 for their application for titles to pieces of government waste land on the grounds that they had already occupied the land for some years and also deserved recompense for their military service on behalf of the colony. CA, CO 2765, No. 91, Assistant CC for Sub District Clan William, to SG, 8 December 1836.

47 CA, 1/WOC 11/13, SG to CC, 18 March 1836; also SG to CC, 27 May 1836.

account." The commissioner subsequently granted the land next to the village on the stipulation that no canteen be allowed "to be erected therein or that any Canteen keeper shall be permitted to become the proprietor of any of these allotments to prevent their coming in immediate Contact with the Venom of immorality and Vice."[48] Special Justice Mackay of the district also sponsored the application for a plot of land by ex-apprentices in the Klein Roggeveld because they "appear to be respectable persons" and he continued, that it was "obviously of great importance at this moment that respectable persons of this class should meet every encouragement that may be calculated to incite them to industry."[49] In 1839 when freed men made their application for allotments near to the village of Worcester, they were careful to emphasize their respectability. They apparently said that they wanted "an opportunity of sending their children to the Missionary Chapel."[50]

Freed people also purchased land after 1834 without government aid.[51] "coloured" people who were reputed to be "the illegitimate children" of a white farmer owned Kopjeskasteel, a large farm of between eight to ten thousand acres in size, about thirty miles from Genadendal mission station.[52] Kopjeskasteel had been owned originally by a *landdrost* of Swellendam who used it as a grazing ground.[53] According to the superintendent of Genadendal, this *landdrost* had given the farm to a "Hessian" who had been

> a faithful servant to him. . . . After the death of the latter, seven or eight years ago, his eldest son, and two Hottentot sons-in-law, took the farm, which they have managed in a very creditable and successful manner. They employ four Hottentot families besides, all of whom are in connection with us. . . .[54]

In neighboring Caledon district, which was separated from Swellendam in 1839, only one farm was owned by so-called "coloureds": Houtkloof. In 1841 the farm was granted to ten Khoi and/or ex-slaves by the name of Van der Heyde.[55] The chronology and details of the grant to the slave/Khoi branch of the Van der Heyde family are very unclear. The quitrent register shows only the names of the grantees, not the grantors, and the register provides no reason for the transfer. Local folklore seems to

48 CA, 1/WOC 11/13, SG to CC, 18 March 1836; CA, CO 2779, No. 11, CC to SG, 15 January 1838.

49 CA, 1/WOC 19/61, SJ to CC, WOC, 25 June 1838.

50 CA, CO 2788, No. 31, CC, WOC, to SG, 12 February 1839. The document is marked confidential and private. See also CA, 1/WOC 19/61, 25 June 1838, for evidence of apprentices wanting land.

51 Examination of the Caledon and Stellenbosch quitrent records and letters from resident magistrates to the Colonial Office archives regarding landholding after emancipation formed the basis of my study.

52 Evidence of JP, CAL, Mr. T. B. Bayley, in CGH, Select Committee of the House of Assembly on Granting Lands in Freehold to Hottentots. *Minutes of Evidence taken before the Select Committee of the House of Assembly on Granting Lands in Freehold to Hottentots*, S.C. 13. (Cape Town: Saul Solomon and Co., 1856), 7–8.

53 Until 1828, when they were replaced by magistrates, the *landdrosts* were the chief administrative officers in the rural districts serving as head of the police and the local militia.

54 HA, "Journal of a Visit by Hallbeck to Clarkson in September and October 1839," *PA*, XV, CLXVIII (September 1840), 256.

55 Van Ryneveld cites eleven owners, but I count ten. Van Ryneveld, "Merchants and Missions," 37; CA, 1/CAL 7/1/1, Folio 762, Return of Farms in Caledon Division, 15 March 1841.

suggest, however, that the families of Houtkloof were descended from a white Dutch-speaking farmer who had had a "coloured" wife.[56]

Kruger states that when the former owner and his wife died the Moravian brethren "assisted the children in the payment of the estate duties, in order to preserve their property rights."[57] It is uncertain if the transfer Kruger mentions is that of 1841. The deed of 1841 shows that people of the name Van der Heyde lived as a community sharing the name, the resources, and the ownership of Houtkloof.[58] Like Kopjeskasteel the farm had no water during much of the dry summer season and the community of up to a hundred people supported itself through agricultural production and pastoralism.[59] In 1841 a hundred people lived on the station. A Moravian missionary stated that they "live, for the most part, on their own little properties, and some have dwellings here also."[60]

After 1834 people probably of ex-slave or free black status also bought land in Paarl and Stellenbosch villages.[61] The case of a David Alexander suggests that previous relationships with the free black communities of the villages, and also perhaps the white community, helped ex-slaves to buy land. In 1824 David, "a slave of Antoon Fick," was baptized "David Frederics" in the predominantly white Dutch Reformed Church. By being baptized, and presumably also manumitted since the two acts often followed one another, David Frederics became a member of a small group within the free black community which worshipped at the white church rather than the Rhenish and Wesleyan mission chapels. An 1829 report on religion in Stellenbosch stated that the regular attendance at the predominantly white Dutch Reformed Church was three hundred whites, sixty "free blacks or coloured," and forty slaves. It is difficult to say with any precision how many of the people mentioned in the earlier DRC lists were slaves themselves as this is not always clearly stated.[62]

---

56 Mr. Vigne's remarks in the Minutes of Evidence, 9 December 1854 in ASL, CGH, *Report of the Select Committee on Granting Lands in Freehold to Hottentots*, S.C. 11 (Cape Town: Saul Solomon and Co., 1854), 22. He does not mention Houtkloof by name, but refers to a farm with forty people living on it.

57 Kruger, *Pear Tree*, 188–89.

58 The farm was 1,994 morgen 300 roods. The Caledon register records the grant as dated 15 March 1841; this might have been a formal registration of de facto ownership. The owners are listed as Adolph van der Heyde, Eva van der Heyde, Domingo van der Heyde, Rosalyn van der Heyde, Christiaan van der Heyde, Sartje van der Heyde [Jantje?], Cobus van der Heyde, Steintje van der Hyde, Greetje van der Heyde, and Klaas, minor child of Klaas van der Heyde. CA, CAL 7/1/1, Folio 762, 15 March 1841.

59 Van Ryneveld, "Merchants and Missions," 37.

60 HA, "Letter from Brother Genth, Elim, October 1841," *PA*, XVI, CLXXV (June 1842), 135.

61 It is difficult to chart exactly the manner in which people moved off the farms into the villages. The land records rarely indicate whether a person was a former slave or had always been free black. Also the indenture and other wage contract records do not give one any indication of a person's previous history (slave or free) so one cannot determine if a person entering employment in 1839 in a village was formerly a slave. Yet we know from demographic statistics of the rural villages that many freed people did move to the villages after 1838. See Marincowitz, "Rural Production," Ch. 1.

62 The number of communicants (people accepted into full membership in the church) was smaller: 100 whites, 10 free blacks or coloured, and no slaves. CA, DRC G2 1/7, "Return showing the places of worship at Stellenbosch, in connection with the established church . . . on 31 December 1829," 12 July 1830. Also DRC G2 11/2, List of Sitting Places in the Church, 12 March 1856. The free black community was relegated to the twelfth row. The last name "Van de Kaap" indicated that the person was of slave ancestry. CA, DRC G2 6/2, Membership List Book, DRChurch, Stellenbosch. CA, DRC G2 6/1, Membership List of the DRC, Stellenbosch, 24 December 1828.

David Frederics' membership in the community appears to have secured him access to status, and later to land in Stellenbosch village. In 1833 he married in the church under the name of David Fredericus Alexander. He wed Magdalena Geertruida Fortuinse, a woman listed as free black.[63] It is possible that the Alexanders' "respectable" status as married individuals and as members of the white Dutch Reformed Church strengthened their bid to buy land. In 1842 David Alexander bought six morgen from white farmers Philip Wouter de Vos and Christoffel Ludolph Neethling. However, the following year Alexander transferred 287 roods to a Carel Jacobus Fortuin and a year later another 546 roods to Adam Jacob Mozes, both of whose names suggests that they were ex-slaves.[64]

The transfer of land from white owners to those of free black of ex-slave status appears in other records, although not with great frequency. In Moddergat, near Stellenbosch, a Gerhardus Ignatius Delport, whose name suggests he belonged to the white community, transferred the piece of quitrent land of 227 morgen, which was considered "waste land," to one Ronet on 19 November 1839. In the 1840s further subdivisions of land from settlers to "coloured" owners occurred.[65]

Men overwhelmingly dominate the quitrent records of the districts with which this study is concerned. Settler women very rarely appear in the quitrent registers and when they do it is as widows.[66] Black women rarely owned land in their own right.[67] However it is striking that when a woman's name does appear in the quitrent register it was far more likely to be the name of a free black woman than her settler counterpart. The register for Houtkloof shows that women and their male partners owned plots together. For example, Adolph and Eva van der Heyde are listed as owners, as are Domingo and Rosalyn van der Heyde.

Freed people possibly registered women as co-owners of land because they recognized the importance of landownership to securing independence and having both parties register their names might make it more difficult for the land to be taken away. Possibly this spoke also to a more egalitarian conception of gender relations within the freed family than existed either in mission teaching or in British colonial discourse. In general after 1838 both freed women and men contributed to the household by working for money—women were not confined to the private sphere in the

---

63   CA, DRC G2 8/1, Marriage Register, 20 January 1833. For a lengthy discussion of marriage and family see Chapter 6.

64   CA 1/STB 11/1, Folio 35, Quitrent Register, 13 September 1842. CA, 1/STB 11/1, Folio 45, Quitrent Register, 8 December 1843; 20 August 1844. These men's last names suggest that they were either former slaves or free blacks. I have been unable to trace them in the records.

65   CA, 1/STB 11/2, Quitrent Register, No. 235, 19 November 1839. CA, 1/STB 11/1, Quitrent Register, Folio 148. For similar trends see Folio 93, 2 January 1816, six subsequent transfers of one particular parcel of land, and on 26 August 1841, Cornelis Laurens Goosen transferred the land to Abraham February and Abraham Johan George. See also Folio 125, 1 July 1817. There were three subsequent transfers, and on 16 November 1847 the land was transferred to Slammat Arendse. Also Folio 253.

66   One instance I found of a settler woman owning land appeared in CO 4000, No. 77, Memorial of Aletta Margaretha Burger, 11 April 1839, who inherited the quitrent place Steenbergs Hoek from her uncle Jacobus Abraham Burger.

67   Some rare examples are CA, 1/STB 11/1, Folio 127, Quitrent Register, Grant of 2 morgen to Saartje, Bastard Hottentot, Paarl area, 1 July 1817; Folio 148, Grant of 6 morgen 61 roods to Mariana and her four children, 3 December 1847.

same way as their settler counterparts.[68] Another case also suggests the importance that freed people placed on legal title. In 1840, the clerk of the peace in Swellendam found a group of people living on government ground with one hut already built and another being erected. A Khoi man, Fielander, his wife, Roslyn, and their two children lived in the hut as did the wife of a Khoi man who was in prison and another girl. Upon the clerk of the peace "enquiring by what authority they built, and resided upon this spot, Pamella produced the letter and certificate which I now enclose."[69]

Where people could not get legal tenure they squatted on government land or on the farms, or moved constantly between the districts avoiding permanent farm labor, always under the threat of being penalized for vagrancy and squatting by virtue of the coercive legislation enacted in the 1850s. The most extensive squatter settlements of the three districts occurred in Worcester, but people also squatted "between Somerset West beach and the Government grounds near Elim, particularly in the Zondereinde Mountains, Hottentots Holland Mountains and the mouth of the Bot River. These settlements constituted a semi-circle on the peripheries of the commercial wheat-farming area in the vicinity of Caledon. . . ."[70] In 1843, for example, the field cornet of the Klein Roggeveld region of Worcester complained of his "fruitless attempts to dispossess certain wandering Hottentots & others from the Government Land occupied by them. . . ."[71]

Moving to Missions

The symbolic and practical significance of familial connections in shaping the trajectories of emancipation is clearest with regard to freed people's movement off the farms and on to the mission stations.[72] The importance of missions at the time of emancipation testifies both to the weakness of Islam in the rural Western Cape and to

---

68 See Chapter 5 for analysis of gender and labor after 1838.

69 CA, 1/SWM 16/33, CP to SG, 31 August 1840.

70 Marincowitz, "Rural Production," 44. Squatting was rare in Stellenbosch but there is anecdotal evidence that some people continued to squat there in the 1830s. For an example of squatting see CA 1/STB 2/35, Documents in the trial of Kiewiet Windvogel, Hans David, Paul Kuipers, and Annaatje Windvogel, 5 September 1835.

71 CA, 1/WOC 14/78, No. 681, CC, WOC, Report on Memorial of Andries Esterhuijze, 16 December 1843. It is difficult to chart accurately the economic life of those freed people residing neither on the mission stations, nor permanently on the farms, nor engaged in regular work in the villages, and one relies on evidence gleaned from memorials to the Colonial Office, quitrent registers, and letters between colonial officials. As Marincowitz has suggested, official statistics of the postemancipation period record only those people of "fixed abode" and did not count people on the move, or those involved in fishing, "subsistence cultivation" or casual labor. Marincowitz, "Rural Production," 42.

72 This is owing mainly to the excellent record keeping of the missionary societies: the Moravian Missions are particularly good. See *PA*. For studies of specific mission stations see Kruger, *Pear Tree*; Johannes W. Raum, "The Development of the coloured Community at Genadendal" (M.A. diss., University of Cape Town, 1952); Van Ryneveld, "Merchants and Missions"; and Ludlow, "Missions and Emancipation." For a general study of missions and ex-slave communities see Jane Sayles, *Mission Stations and the Coloured Communities of the Eastern Cape, 1800–1852* (Cape Town: A. A. Balkema, 1975). Also Marais, *Cape Coloured People*. For discussion of the Missions see also John Carel Marincowitz, "Proletarians, Privatisers and Public Property Rights: Mission Land Regulations in the Western Cape" (paper presented to the African History Seminar of the Institute for Commonwealth Studies, SOAS, University of London, 23 January 1985).

the success of missionaries (both Moravian, Wesleyan, and Rhenish) in having established themselves particularly from the 1830s as champions of the rights of slaves to religious observance and education.

In the six weeks following emancipation on 1 December 1838, 456 people moved to the Moravian mission station of Genadendal in Caledon district.[73] In February 1839 Genadendal and Elim missions were "full, almost to an overflow."[74] The superintendent of the Moravian Missions in South Africa indicated that at all the missions, but particularly Genadendal, Groenekloof (in Malmesbury District near Cape Town), and Elim, "the augmentation [of population] appears to have been considerable."[75] The numbers of people at the Moravian stations increased from 3,772 to 4,389 in the year following emancipation.[76] The mission population of six thousand in 1838 grew to twelve thousand in 1850. "By 1860 . . . about eleven thousand, of a total mission population of about 14000, resided in the commercial wheat-growing regions" of the Cape, Stellenbosch, and Swellendam.[77]

The decision to move to a mission was generally a family one. The mission was "used, in the post-emancipation era, as a place where families could be reconstituted and/or secured." At Groenekloof mission in Malmesbury district, north west of Stellenbosch, freed people reassembled the very relationships and friendships which had been forged in defiance of various farm and district boundaries. As Helen Ludlow has shown, the movement to the mission involved not only an attempt to assemble or reassemble "family units" but also to reconstitute "a wider community of fellow workers."[78]

Twenty-five percent of the newcomers to the station after 1838 had prior connections to the station. Some had been born there, others had lived there earlier and were returning with spouses and children, and others were joining relatives already living at Groenekloof. That relationships could be reestablished on the missions depended in part on whether people had a family member who was already an inhabitant of a station. In January 1840, Vytje and Lakey Janeiro moved to Groenekloof mission bringing with them their baby boy and three of Vytje's children from a former relationship. In the next year another of Vytje's children and his common-law wife and two other sons received permission to settle at Groenekloof.[79]

Freed people's movement to other stations in the Western Cape followed a similar pattern. At the Moravian mission of Genadendal, for example, ex-slaves with wives or husbands and children already at the station were accepted before others.[80] Likewise at the London Missionary Society station of Pacaltsdorp, people with friends or relatives at the station were more likely to be approved. In Decem-

73   Van Ryneveld, "Merchants and Missions," 46.

74   The baptism class grew from fifty-two candidates in 1835 to "three times that number" in 1839. CA, CO 2784, No. 33, Acting RM, CAL, to SG, 19 February 1839.

75   See Van Ryneveld, "Merchants and Missions," 45.

76   It is not totally clear to which year Hallbeck is referring, but I gather it is 1839. HA, "General Remarks on South Africa," PA, XV, CLXVII (June 1840), 238. The Genadendal population grew from 1,446 in 1837 to 2,846 twelve years later. Van Ryneveld, "Merchants and Missions," 45.

77   Marincowitz, "Rural Production," 49, 122.

78   Ludlow, "Missions and Emancipations," Ch. 2, 59, 73.

79   The information in this paragraph comes from Ludlow, "Missions and Emancipation," 60–65.

80   Kruger, Pear Tree, 196.

ber 1838 Booy Floris, a man living on the station whom the missionary described as a "Hottentot of good character, owner of 8 oxen and 16 Breeding Cattle," left the mission station to fetch his wife, two daughters, and their eight grandchildren who had been slaves of a Mr. Vivier, and brought them home.[81] Floris's wife's prior relationship with her Khoi husband who lived on a mission station played a crucial role in her experience of freedom as well as that of her children and grandchildren. Rather than stay on the farm, or move to a village, these ex-slaves became part of the burgeoning population of the mission stations of the Western Cape. By 1846 the ratio of Khoi to freed people at Genadendal mission was estimated to be two to one, whereas prior to emancipation people defined as Khoi had been in the overwhelming majority.[82]

Slaves with no former ties to missions were able to move there too. Shortly after the ending of slavery, Charlotte Toa, a slave from the East Coast of Africa who had been "carried off when young," moved to Genadendal with her husband, Timothy. He had been born in Mozambique and, like her, had grown "old in a state of slavery." Although Charlotte Toa had children, we do not know their paternity nor their fate: "her master sold her children away from her" and she never saw them again. Mr. Toa died in November 1842, just four months after his baptism, a free man. Two years later Charlotte also died, a full communicant in the church.[83] Nearly a decade after the ending of slavery, missions of various denominations still drew members of the rural poor into their fold. In 1847 Katharina Bryan and her common-law husband Saul Patience, probably of Khoi descent, and a former laborer on the farm Leeuwenklip, were married at Saron mission station in the Worcester district.[84] Katharina, Saul, and their child, Patiens, were among the first families to rent land along with their neighbors (and probable relatives), Adonis Patience, Sina Faroe, and their four children who lived on plot thirty. Saul rented *erf* (lot) number twenty nine, leasing land at Saron from 1847 through to 1884. The two families together established a sizable lineage. Saul and Katharina alone had nine children.[85]

So many ex-slaves wanted to go to the missions that from 1841 missionaries established a host of new mission stations to accommodate freed people. As in the West Indies, one of the catalysts behind the establishment of new stations was an attempt to halt the scattering of congregations caused by the movement of former slaves off the farms. Missionaries' concern that freed people would be attracted to Islam, which was particularly strong in Cape Town, also influenced the establishment

---

81 CA, CO 485, No. 29, Reverend W. Anderson, Pacaltsdorp, to Reverend John Philip, Cape Town, 21 March 1839.

82 Raum, "Development," 51.

83 Information on the Toa family was pieced together from "Diary of Genadendal, 1846," *PA*, XVIII, CXCVII (March 1848), 239; "Diary of Genadendal, 1842," HA, *PA*, XVI, CLXXXII (March 1844), 515.

84 Helen Ludlow has noted that with "rare exception, the mission records do not distinguish slave from non-slave." Ludlow, "Missions and Emancipation," 57. I have also found this to be the case in my research. Earlier in that year the Rhenish Missionary Society bought Leeuwenklip in Worcester district, turning it into the Saron mission station as a haven for freed people and Khoi.

85 All the information on the Patience family was supplied by M. D. Nash. I am very grateful to Ms. Nash for sharing her research on this family and the Solomon family. M. D. Nash has counted approximately one hundred baptisms of children with the last name Patience in the Saron register between 1847 and 1890. Personal communication.

of Christian religious communities after 1838.[86] In 1846 G. A. Zahn, the Rhenish missionary in Tulbagh, reported with satisfaction that he had "much reason to believe" that at the mission station (Steinthal) "the Labours of the Missionaries have been an effectual Check on the spread of Mahemotism [sic] among the emancipated class."[87]

In 1838 Groenekloof was the only mission in the Cape and Stellenbosch districts, but between 1841 and 1846 four new stations were established "intermittently and strategically along the perimeter of the western-cape's commercial farming heartlands."[88] Where no established mission existed on which to welcome freed people, missionaries at the Cape, like their peers in the West Indies, endeavored to buy up farms and subdivided them into lots so as to form the nucleus of a religious community.[89] In Worcester, where formal missions to the slave and Khoi population previously had been lacking, the Rhenish Missionary Society founded at least two missions in the decade after emancipation.[90] In 1846 Reverend Zahn bought two pieces of land near the village of Tulbagh at the foot of the Witzenberg Mountains for five hundred pounds and thereby started Steinthal mission station. It was to be divided "into small allotments and to form a settlement for the Colored class of people residing in and near Tulbagh who belong & and are attached to the Rhenish Missionary Society and thereby to enable them to have a fixed residence, a home to return to and to become good and peaceable members of society."[91]

In the course of the 1840s the Moravians also started founding missionary outposts on farms to preach to members of the freed population. Freed people who already owned land seem to have been keen to establish links with the missions both through formal transfer of land and through allowing their farms to serve as outposts. In Stellenbosch district, a woman called Ronet, who might have been a former slave, transferred just over two hundred morgen of land she had recently acquired near Stellenbosch village to Edward Edwards, a Wesleyan missionary in November

---

86   See CA, DRC R1/1, Report on Religion, Paarl, 1828, 293–294; DRC R1/2, Report on Religion, Tygerberg, 1831, 178; Report on Religion, Tygerberg, 1834, 360. Also SOAS, *Report of the Wesleyan-Methodist Missionary Society for the Year Ending April, 1837* (London: P. P. Thoms, 1837), 27. CA, GH 1/117, Enclosure No. 2, Governor to SSC, 7 November 1837.

87   CA, 1/WOC 14/28, No. 689, Memorial Book of Resident Magistrate, Report on memorial of G. A. Zahn, Missionary in Tulbagh, 10 May 1846.

88   Marincowitz, "Rural Production," 38. The new stations were Pniel in Groot Drakenstein, Saron in Worcester, Steinthal in Tulbagh, and Goedverwacht near Piquetberg. The Rhenish missionary society established Pniel near Groot Drakenstein in Paarl district in 1843. For Pniel see CA, 1/STB 11/2, No. 346, Quitrent Register, Grant of 22 morgen 76 sq. roods, worth 12s. per year, transferred from Adrian Hermanus Louw to the directors of the Pniel Institution on 4 December 1843.

89   Green, *British Slave Emancipation*, 171.

90   For Saron, see CA, CO 550, Memorial of Johann Heinrich Kulpmann, Rhenish Missionary residing at 24 Rivers in the district of Worcester, 8 December 1846. The farm Leeuwenklip out of which Saron mission station was created was divided into 102 plots on which Khoi and ex-slave families settled. The families rented the land from the Rhenish Missionary Society, living off wages from farm labor and from the produce of their plots. By 1860 there were one thousand inhabitants at Saron. This information on Saron was kindly provided by M. D. Nash in a communication she has written on the Solomon and Patience families of Saron. Also see Elfriede Strassberger, *The Rhenish Missionary Society in South Africa 1830–1950* (Cape Town: Struik, 1969).

91   CA, 1/WOC 14/28, No. 689, Report on Memorial of G. A. Zahn, Memorial enclosed, 10 May 1846.

1840.[92] In 1845 Barnabus Shaw, also a Wesleyan missionery, bought additional land in order to minister to farm laborers in Moddergat cornetcy, but the Weslayan Missionary Society decided not to formally maintain Raithby as a mission station. The land was divided into individal lots, but people appear to have seen themselves as constituting a religious community.[93]

The farms Houtkloof and Kopjeskasteel, which, as we have seen, were both legally owned by people of settler, Khoi and possibly slave descent, also became outposts for the Moravians. Since 1830 church meetings had been held at Kopjeskasteel in Swellendam "which were attended by many Hottentots and slaves from the neighbourhood."[94] Reverend Hallbeck remarked in 1839, "That place now exhibits one of the most striking triumphs of the Gospel. It was in past years, a scene of sin and debauchery; it is now quite the reverse, and several of the neighbours have expressed their astonishment at the change that has been effected."[95] The people at Houtkloof had become members of Elim mission station—on the southern tip of Caledon district—as early as 1833 in accordance with "the diaspora plan," and the ties between the community and Elim became stronger in the decades after emancipation.[96] In 1841 Houtkloof was described as a "flourishing outpost."[97]

The owners of Kopjeskasteel and Houtkloof prudently perceived that their future was best protected by becoming part of a mission station community. In the 1840s the colonial office still tended to protect free blacks' rights to land, but in that decade, and particularly in the 1850s, white farmers launched a significant attack on the independence of the stations. Most white farmers had never supported government plans to give land to freed people. For example, J. J. du Plessis of Worcester— where the government plan to make land available to freed people was most extensively implemented—specifically blamed grants of land to freed people as "causing scarcity, idleness, and poverty."[98] Farmers from Stellenbosch, Paarl, Worcester, and elsewhere rejected the sanguine views that freed people would learn the proper habits of wage labor and instead called for stringent measures to enact anti-vagrancy and squatting legislation which would force freed people into poorly paid wage labor.[99]

---

92 As we have seen, Gerhardus Igantius Delport transferred the piece of quitrent land of 227 morgen, which was considered "waste land," to Ronet on 19 November 1839. CA, 1/STB 11/2, Quitrent Register, No. 235, Ronet transferred the land to Edwards, 6 November 1840. In Worcester, Saron mission station had similar origins, being established on farms purchased by the Rhenish mission society in 1846. CA, CO 550, Memorial of Johann Heinrich Kulpmann, Rhenish missionary residing at 24 Rivers in the district of Worcester, 8 December 1846.

93 CA, 1/STB 11/2, Quitrent Register, Folio 35, 6 February 1845 . See 1/STB 20/95, RM to SG, 9 March 1849 for discussion of the station.

94 Kruger, *Pear Tree*, 188–189.

95 HA, "Letter from Reverend Hallbeck, 12 November 1839," *PA*, XV, CLXVI (March 1840), 171.

96 Kruger, *Pear Tree*, 188–189.

97 HA, "Letter from Brother Genth, Elim, October 1841," *PA*, XVI, CLXXV (June 1842), 135.

98 CA, LCA 33, Reply by J. J. du Toit, to Masters and Servants Ordinance questionnaire, 1848; also Reply by JP, WOC, H. A. du Toit.

99 CA, LCA 6, No. 35, Memorial of Inhabitants of Paarl, Drakenstein, Franschehoek, Wagenmakers Vallei, Stellenbosch District, 29 July 1834; No. 30, Memorial of Inhabitants of Hottentots Holland and Somerset, Stellenbosch District, 1834; LCA 10, No. 17, Memorial from the inhabitants of Wagenmakers Valley, 7 September 1839.

In 1844 the secretary to government acknowledged a memorial of a settler from Worcester which asked that steps be taken, in the words of the secretary, to "dispossess certain wandering Hottentots & others from the Government Land occupied by them." The secretary replied that "if any specific charge of sheep or cattle stealing is brought against these people they can be punished, but beyond that, no interference can be exercised by the government."[100] But in the same year the secretary hinted at future policy—the dividing of rural people into "farmer-landholders or illegal squatters."[101] In referring to applications by farmers for legal rental of various "Leg Plekke," or loan farms, the secretary stated that the governor was

> desirous of securing legal occupancy to the parties interested, until the land be required for government purposes or sale, and to prevent as far as practicable, through their medium, the practice which appears to exist, of persons without the least claim to such an indulgence, settling thereon or moving from one part to another to the annoyance and injury of the farmers who have been hitherto allowed to make use of them.[102]

Conclusion

Personal connections forged under slavery and reaffirmed after 1838 were so decisive because the options available to freed people were so narrow. Freed men and women looked to ownership of land as a means of securing economic independence for themselves and their children. Freed women, like men, had some success in securing titles to land and in this regard emancipation promised a measure of real independence for freed women and suggested an area of equality between men and women.

But, as we have seen, by the 1830s the possibility of independent ownership of land was limited , and from the 1840s white farmers successfully lobbied the government to tighten access to land. Thus, very soon after emancipation, freed women and men again found themselves working for white settlers in the villages and on the farms. Freed women, in particular, found that their entry into regular waged work was limited by the constraints set on women's work by postemancipation labor legislation. Yet, as the following chapter also shows, ex-slaves and dependent laborers forged their own routes back to employment with the former slaveholding class. Freed people in the rural areas of the Western Cape used various strategies to widen their options in a political economy in which former slaveholders held so much power. Freed women and men juggled different types of work to generate income for their families, apprenticed their children to learn skills and earn money, and avoided as much as possible permanent labor on white-owned farms. The following chapter examines debates about labor between officials in the metropole and in the colony, and the ways in which freed people created their own worlds of labor.

---

100   CA, 1/WOC 11/15, SG to CC, 5 January 1844.

101   Marincowitz, "Rural Production," 145.

102   CA, 1/WOC 11/15, SG to CC, 15 March 1844.

5

Laboring Families

No single ideology about gender and labor completely dominated the Cape poste-mancipation economy. In the nineteenth century assumptions that women were minors in the workplace gained ascendancy in the legal sphere. In practice, however, groups with different notions about how to reconcile women's potential capacities as both productive laborers and mothers constantly struggled to define how women would participate in the postemancipation economy.[1]

Evidence suggests that freed people's ideologies of gender and labor saw moth-erhood and certain forms of waged work as complementary rather than antagonistic. I show that freed women and men themselves made a break between slavery and emancipation by trying to end women's waged work on the farms. But this apparent confining of women's work opportunities by freed people themselves is deceptive. The abandonment by women of domestic work on the settler-owned farms seems to have emerged out of a history of struggle against former slaveholders' sexual abuse of slave women, and not out of a patriarchal dynamic within the freed family. Women continued to engage in waged labor in order to help support their families, but in conditions of their own choosing, where possible.

Various colonial officials' notions of work and labor cut a different swath between the lines of reproductive and productive labor. Legislators tended to reify the purported natural roles of women as mothers and wives. They also assumed that childrearing could not easily coexist with waged work. Masters and Servants legisla-tion thus consolidated the attention to "woman" as a special category of worker which had already been evident in the laws ameliorating slavery.[2]

If postemancipation labor law was framed with reference to an idealized order in which men engaged in waged work and women stayed at home, this just did not conform to the pattern of social relations among the freed population. Freed women headed families, and even if in a long-term relationship or marriage, often were in charge of the family during the week while the husband worked elsewhere. For

---

1 For the debates on production and reproduction see particularly Zillah Eisenstein, *Capitalist Patriarchy and the Case for Socialist Feminism* (New York: Monthly Review Press, 1979), and Michele Barrett, *Women's Oppres-sion Today: Problems in Marxist Feminist Analysis* (London: New Left Books, 1980). For a view on the impor-tance of this debate for South African history see Elaine Unterhalter, ed., *Women in South African History* 1, (January 1981): 1–24.

2 See Chapter 2.

many, and maybe most, freed women and men, the notion of an independent house-hold or home and family remained a myth under the working conditions of the postemancipation economy. The tension between ideology and practice is further complicated by the desires of former slaveholders to employ freed women. They wanted freed women to engage in permanent domestic labor and did not necessarily support the idea of a sexual division of labor premised upon women's primary responsibility to their own children and household.

This chapter examines the ways in which different freed communities, the colonial state, settlers, and missionaries tried to organize freed men and women's participation in the wage labor market after 1838. Beginning with a discussion of postemancipation labor law, I argue that Cape labor legislation in the period 1838 to 1842 validated the assumptions current in both settler society and in British abolitionist and government circles that the worker who had been freed by emancipation was a man. If men were workers, then what roles were women to play in the free wage labor economy? The chapter concludes with a discussion of the ways in which freed people organized work and suggests that all members of the family, women, children, and men were expected to contribute in some way to the well-being of extended or nuclear families.

Legislating Labor, Race, and Gender

Farmers, missionaries, and secular advocates of free wage labor advocated the benefits of patriarchal power relations within the freed family.[3] Missionaries championed a gendered division of labor and authority. Women would ideally stay at home and look after children and the house while men worked for wages outside of the home. For former slaveholders, emancipation threatened some of the foundations upon which labor relations had previously operated. Yet, drawing on their experience of indenturing Khoisan children and adults under slavery, and on their success in apprenticing the children of their slaves and Khoisan laborers during apprenticeship, white farmers entered the era of free wage labor with some skills at circumventing the spirit of emancipation.

In general, former slaveholders continued to see access to the labor power of a male worker's wife and children as a crucial means of surviving in a wage labor economy. This therefore meant supporting the notion of patriarchal power within freed families. However, farmers in the rural Western Cape did not necessarily support the propagation of nuclear family arrangements precisely because this limited the number of dependents of an individual laborer. Many former slaveholders appear to have viewed freed men not only as workers, but also as recruiters and suppliers of cheap labor when necessary. When farmers hired a male worker they expected to be able to have access to the labor of his wife and family when needed.

For example, Governor George Napier said in a letter to the Colonial Office in 1841: "I verily believe . . . the great body of the South African farmers would rather

---

3 See Chapters 6 and 7 for analysis of missionaries' and colonial officials' views on women's appropriate roles in society. Edna Bradlow provides an early examination of the place of women in Cape society and attitudes towards work in "Women at the Cape," esp. 74.

maintain a native servant with his wife and children paying him from 10 to 20 shillings a month, than pay to an English labourer a crate of wages a little higher in appearance, but less in reality. . . ."[4] The Reverend W. A. van der Lingen, a Dutch Reformed Minister at the Paarl, saw labor as being part of a social contract between a male laborer and an employer which was based on an understanding that the worker could mobilize the labor power of his entire family. He argued that by refusing to work, freed women upset the whole premise of wage labor. Assuming that family labor could be mobilized through the formal employment of only the man, Van der Lingen outlined the advantages for farmers in employing families which did not conform to the monogamous or nuclear model advocated by missionaries. He recommended forcing women and children to work, since otherwise "[t]he hirer would be obliged to pay for the service of one man alone as much as he would have to pay to one man, with one, two, or three wives, and some children, when working together ought to earn."[5]

Imagining the existence of patriarchy within the freed family enabled settlers to fantasize about how easy it was for the senior male to make his family work for the farmer. This version of a reserve army of labor accorded to freed men the kind of power over the bodies and will of their wives and children which they, the former slaveholders, had once exercised over both freed women and freed men. In a sense these slaveholders shifted the responsibility for freed women and children onto the shoulders of the men whom they had formally owned. The colonial state helped mediate this transition through its inscription of patriarchal responsibility into the postemancipation labor legislation. The male worker thus became the centerpiece of labor legislation, and the core of settlers' strategies to gain access to cheap seasonal labor.

Postemancipation labor legislation bore many of the hallmarks of the apprenticeship laws, which were themselves rooted in the amelioration laws which had governed the last decade of Cape slavery. Cape labor legislation also reinscribed the suppositions about women as special kinds of workers which had been first raised in amelioration legislation against the flogging of women. Most importantly, gender hierarchies within the family which had been alluded to in the amelioration laws of the 1820s, and first mentioned in Ordinance No. 1 of 1835 which introduced apprenticeship to the Cape, became legally engraved into the very fabric of labor relations in the postemancipation era.

The 1842 Cape Masters and Servants Ordinance was the product of three years of struggle about how to accommodate ex-slaves and the former free black population of the Western Cape in the new era of wage labor.[6] That battle revolved around

4 CA, GH 23/13, No. 143, Governor to SSC, 21 December 1841.

5 ASL, CGH, *Master and Servant. Documents on "The Working of the Order in Council of the 21st July 1846 . . ."* (Cape Town: Saul Solomon and Co., 1849), replies of W. A. van der Lingen, minister at Paarl, question 6.

6 This legislation had a rather tortuous history. It had local roots in the abortive Vagrancy Ordinance of 1834 but was first drawn up as a local Cape ordinance by the attorney-general in 1839. It was rewritten in 1840, and again in 1841, the final version being authorized by the British government in 1842. The new Cape Legislative Assembly passed a revised act in 1856 and a variety of amendments in the latter part of the century. The act was only repealed in South Africa in 1974. Various historians have written on the disciplinary sections of the ordinance and latter acts; I am not going to repeat that discussion here. For an incisive history of this legislation see Colin Bundy, "The Abolition of the Master and Servants Act," *South African Labor Bulletin* 2, 1 (1975): 37–46. Marais, *Cape Coloured People*, Ch. 6, provides detailed discussions of the various provisions.

determining, if every worker was equal before the law, the extent to which race could be the category which marked the workers needing discipline from those who did not, and whether particular familial networks could "rescue" an individual from the racial category to which he or she would otherwise be ascribed.[7] Examination of the debates around the ordinance reveals the extent to which settlers, officials in the Cape, and the Colonial Office in England, accepted the subordination of women to their husbands and fathers. Proposals which suggested making race a criteria for whether a person was to fall under the legislation or not were challenged and abolished by the secretary of state for colonies in London. But the clauses which made women workers subject to the authority of their husbands passed without comment, and were written into law.

The Masters and Servants Ordinance of 1842 occupied an ideological position between the ideas which had grounded slavery and those which generated the idea of wage labor. As Colin Bundy has argued, "many features of the master/slave relationship continued to be reproduced in the system of free labour that succeeded" slavery. In fact the criminalization of several actions on the part of the servant derived from the slave codes. The ordinance laid the foundations for later acts which discriminated against farm workers and further consolidated employers' power over employees.[8]

If the Ordinance of 1842 represents agreement between advocates of slavery and wage labor as to the need to discipline labor, it is also very clearly the product of a new era of labor relations grounded in economic principles of which Adam Smith would have approved.[9] Masters and Servants legislation was disciplinary and class specific: the ordinance was not merely a consolidation of the power of former slaveholders over their former slaves, but also was part of the elaboration of new forms of discipline and punishment aimed at the reformation and regulation of working-class behavior. The conduct of the working class was regulated and prescribed; that of the employer scrutinized only in terms of whether the wage had been paid, or specified clothing given. For example, the ordinance (and subsequent acts) criminalized various behaviors on the part of the servant ranging from "insolence," "scandalous immorality," and drunkenness, to negligence. The servant could be fined one months' wages, or face a prison term of up to fourteen days with or without hard labor.

The preamble of the Cape draft of 10 July 1839, written by the attorney general, explicitly placed Europeans outside of the scope of the law with its coercive features of punishment against servants. It also made a distinction between Africans from the Eastern Cape who could be employed only under the terms of Ordinance No. 49 of 1828, and "people of colour" native to the Western Cape.[10] The ordinance thus explic-

---

7 For a more extended treatment of the cultural and sexual boundaries of race see Chapter 8.

8 Bundy, "Abolition of Master and Servants Act," 38; Erica Boddington, "Domestic Service: Changing Relations of Class Domination, 1841–1948. A Focus on Cape Town" (M.Soc.Sci diss., University of Cape Town, 1983), 139. Act No. 18 of 1873 made a distinction between farm and other servants and the former received higher penalties than their urban counterparts. For a first offense a "generic" worker was fined £1 while a farm worker was fined £2. Scully, *Bouquet of Freedom*, 60.

9 In an editorial welcoming the coming era of wage labor, the *SACA* quoted Adam Smith admiringly. *SACA*, 26 July 1837, 41–43.

10 The preamble stated that the term "person of colour" did not refer to "any Caffre, Gonaqua, Tambookie, [or] Griqua." CA, LCA 10, Appendix, Item No. 16, Draft of Masters and Servants Bill, 10 July 1839.

itly disciplined only those people newly freed from slavery and the Khoi who techni-
cally entered free wage labor with Ordinance No. 50 of 1828. This demarcation
legislated through contract the historic claim of former slaveholders to the ex-slave
and free black population of the Western Cape. By so doing the draft wrote in a new
language of contract an older premise of domination.

Ironically, such a formulation also suggests the beginnings of colonists' ambivalent self-identification with former slaves and free blacks native to the Western Cape,
the oldest part of the colony. In distinguishing between Africans and free blacks (ex-
slaves and Khoi) the ordinance can be read as a cultural overture by Dutch-speaking
white farmers to other people who spoke Dutch, and who had complicated family
connections—however strongly denied by former slaveholders—to many colonists
in the Western Cape. In a new era, former slaveholders invoked older claims to their
former slaves, now written in a language of geography rather than property. But, as
under slavery, the claims made by settlers in the Western Cape to a special relationship to ex-slaves and Khoisan, generated not feelings of empathy, but rather a desire
to discipline and produce distance between freed people and themselves.

The determination as to who was a "person of colour" derived not only from
supposed racial or geographical markers, but could also be gleaned from a particular
configuration of gender and genealogy. The preamble specifically excluded from the
designation "person of colour" a woman who had been or was about to be legally
married to "any European, or person of, or reputed to be of, pure European descent."
It further stated that

> every such woman so married or person so procreated as aforesaid shall
> respectively be deemed and reputed in Law to be of some descent and con-
> dition and shall have and enjoy some rights and privileges in this colony as
> her said husband or his or her said hereinbefore described parents.[11]

The draft serves as an interesting marker of the elaboration of racial thought in
the Cape colony. The histories of race in the nineteenth century British empire always
involved an ambivalence as to whether race was tied to biology alone, or could be
mediated by culture.[12] This particular interpretation elevated culture as securing
racial identity; culture rooted in gendered individuals and specific social practices.
The draft acknowledged the ongoing practice of marriages between white men and
free black women. It also spoke to the sex-specific directions of cultural incorporation: a free black woman could be incorporated into white society through marriage
to a white man, but a white woman married to a black man was to be culturally
absorbed into his racial community. The draft contained a warning to those white
men who were involved in relationships with black women, but who were not formally married. It threatened by implication that white men who continued to cohabit
with "coloured" common-law wives would see their children and their wives subjected to humiliating labor legislation, which would in turn come to define the men
as of lower status in the white community.

While the draft spoke of protecting women married to white men, in fact, the
clause really secured the protection of white men. A white man's status could not be

---

11   CA, LCA 10, Appendix, Item No. 16, Draft of Masters and Servants Bill, 10 July 1839.

12   See Chapter 8, and Pamela Scully, "Rape, Race, and Colonial Culture: The Sexual Politics of Identity in
the Nineteenth-Century Cape Colony, South Africa," *American Historical Review* 100, 2 (April 1995): 335–59.

lessened by marriage to a black woman. A white woman enjoyed no such protection. The latent hostility displayed in this draft to relationships between white women and black men is unsurprising given that most racially stratified postemancipation societies regarded sexual relations between black men and white women as unforgivable.

By identifying those members of the free black community who should be freed from subjection to the discipline of Masters and Servants legislation, the framers of the draft signaled that all members of society were not to be equal before the law in the postemancipation world. Ascription of white racial identity would exempt a person from disciplinary legislation, and family alliances and gender could work to mitigate the significance of race. Crucially, the draft indicated that even through marriage a black woman could only be accorded "some rights" since marriage rendered her only of "some descent." As we shall see in the final part of the book, the undercutting of rights through racial ascriptions had implications for women's status and rights in both economic and social relations.

However, overt racial distinctions undermined the notion of a disinterested civil sphere of contract, unfettered by ties of race, which was one ideological pillar of emancipation: neither the 1839 draft nor its successor found favor in London.[13] The 1841 version which was ratified by London in 1842 made no reference to race although as Governor Sir Harry Smith remarked in 1852, "the population of the Cape Colony essentially consisted of two Classes . . . .the White and Black or in other words the Master and Servant."[14] In the postemancipation period class became a metonym for race. "'Master' and 'Servant' supplied the objective and thus 'neutral' or depoliticized legalistic categories liberal discourse required, and enabled a whole range of historical actors to talk of race without every saying it. . . ."[15] Postemancipation labor legislation thus consolidated "race domination."[16]

If race became a silent discourse in labor legislation, class and gender explicitly framed the contractual sphere of work. Married women produced a real dilemma for framers of labor laws in the nineteenth century both in Britain and the Cape. Married women lost their abilities to be free agents because, through marriage, they became subject to the law of coverture which prevented women from making contracts.[17] The state recognized that in theory married women slaves could not enter into public contracts because of their status as minors—the law thus needed to specify that in terms of *work* contracts, women were to be regarded as competent. Ordinance No. 1, which introduced apprenticeship to the Cape, had remarked explicitly on the subordinate status of women slaves created through marriage. Because women who were married became unable to enter into contracts, Chapter 6 of this ordinance stated that "Every married woman, notwithstanding her covertude . . . shall be competent to enter into [labor] contracts."[18] As we shall see this legal exception provided the basis for a differential construction of gender in the experience of middle-class and working-class rural women.

---

13   Marincowitz, "Rural Production," 58–59.

14   CA, GH 23/20, Governor to SSC, 12 February 1852, cited in Crais, "Race," 16.

15   Crais, "Race," 16.

16   Bundy, "Master and Servants Act," 38.

17   Rose, "Protective Labor Legislation," 5.

18   Ordinance No. 1, 1835.

The Masters and Servants Ordinance of 1842 legislated a particular view of the relationships between women and the workplace by demarcating a distinction between slavery and freedom through protection of the "private sphere." The ordinance protected the privacy of the worker's home, and thus in a sense "invented" a new private space. For example, the wife and children of a male servant could live with him on the premises of his master, but the master could not call the family members to work just because they lived on his property.[19] The ordinance protected and created a private sphere of the family against the labor claims of the employer and exposed exactly that arena in which abolitionists had sought to break slaveholders' power.

That familial sphere was explicitly created as one in which men held power over other family members. The various versions of the Masters and Servants legislation from 1842 engraved into labor legislation married women's status as minors under the authority of their husband. This was a status already inscribed in both Cape Roman Dutch civil law and British common law, alluded to in the amelioration legislation which had raised women's status as mothers into a special category, and now a status which written into the world of "free" labor. Cape labor legislation thus reproduced the notions of waged work as masculine activity which were gaining currency in the metropole. Like their British peers, married women laborers were incorporated into the sphere of wage contract first as wives, then as workers.[20]

Both single and married women could enter into work contracts, but a married woman did so only as the wife of a servant (again this meant that a woman was first a wife, then a worker). In cases where a man and his wife and child were hired into service, if the man died, the contract for the wife and child would become void after one month. Thus married women and children were hired under the contract of the man.[21] Chapter IV of the ordinance explicitly dealt with "the effects of the death of the Master or Servant or Apprentice, of the Insolvency or change of Residence of the Master, and of the marriage and pregnancy of Female Servants and Apprentices." If a single woman was married after the start of a contract of service, her husband could dissolve the contract "if he shall think fit so to do, and shall be entitled to claim the wages and other remuneration which may have become due to her for services previously to such removal."[22] In addition, if a woman became pregnant or got married, her employers could dissolve the contract.[23]

The sections regarding apprenticeship and indenturing also legally confirmed the paternal power implicitly conferred to slave men on emancipation.[24] The ordinance

---

19 Masters and Servants Ordinance of 1842, Chapter 1, Section XV.

20 Pateman, *Sexual Contract*, Ch. 5.

21 Cape Masters and Servants Ordinance, Ch. 1, Sections XIII–CIV.

22 Ch. IV, Section XII.

23 Ch. IV, Section XIII. See Chapter 7 of this book on infanticide for the implications of this clause: women resorted to desperate means to avoid losing their jobs.

24 While the 1842 Ordinance reflected a victory of sorts by former slaves and free blacks over farmers in the battle for the child, subsequent acts reneged on this achievement. It continued to allow the indenturing of children, but strengthened parents' rights. Children could be apprenticed as rural laborers until the age of sixteen, and destitute children between the ages of ten and sixteen could be apprenticed until the age of twenty-one.. The magistrate, as state guardian of children, had to give a child to a parent or guardian if such a person came forward, and parents could prosecute for illegal indentures of their children and would receive the fine. Edwards, *Towards Emancipation*, 207; Marincowitz, "Rural Production," 126.

transferred the responsibility for the apprenticeship of children which women had enjoyed hitherto to the father.[25] Now only in cases where the father was absent or dead could the mother exercise her rights as a parent.

The Ordinance of 1842 also recognized that many freed people lived in familial and marital units which did not conform to the dominant colonial ideals of the nuclear family bound through marriage. In this regard the ordinance is a testimony to freed people's success in redefining the world of freedom. In contrast to the stipulation of "lawful marriage" in the 1839 draft, the preamble of the 1842 Ordinance now stated that "the words 'father, parent, relative, husband, and wife,' shall respectively be construed and understood to comprise reputed fathers, parents, relatives, husbands, or wives, as well as actual parents and relatives, and lawful husbands and wives."[26]

Labor law framed freed people's postemancipation world, but so too did the material conditions of freedom. In Stellenbosch, where settlers had long dominated landholding, freed people either had to move to the villages or to the missions to avoid farm labor. On the outskirts of Stellenbosch, freed people grew gardens and became market gardeners supplying the local and the Cape market. But even some residents of the villages worked on the farms as weekly laborers coming back to their homes on the weekends. In Swellendam the rise of wool farming in the 1840s generated a boom which drove up wages and made farm labor somewhat attractive to the men living on the missions. In Worcester district, as we have seen, freed people had greater success gaining access to land than their peers in Swellendam and Stellenbosch, but markets remained small until the development of the railway at the end of the century. For most freed people, and particularly for freed women, in all these districts, farm labor remained the main source of employment.

The Political Economy of Labor

The thirty years after emancipation witnessed a realignment of economic relations within the rural Western Cape. Poorer white farmers who had been farming on credit found themselves increasingly marginalized. But wealthier farmers were able to take advantage of the opportunities opened up by the development of public works near Cape Town and the diamond mines in the Northern Cape from the 1860s. All sectors of the settler farming class demanded that they would be able to secure laborers to work for them at very low wages. In 1839 settlers from Tulbagh pleaded for strict Masters and Servants legislation which would "enduce [sic] persons bred to agriculture to take service instead of wandering about in idleness" while a petition from settlers in Paarl nine years later blamed the "natural propen-

---

25 Ch. III, Section III.

26 CA, 1/STB 19/9, Preamble to Ordinance, "For Amending and Consolidating the Laws regulating the Relative Rights and Duties of Masters, Servants, and Apprentices," 27 August 1842.

sities of the coloured population" for freed people's unwillingness to engage in regular labor.[27]

In Stellenbosch district, which had both a diversified economy and a strata of very wealthy farmers, wine farmers who had expanded their farming operations through ownership of wheat farms survived the trough in the market through the 1860s, but continued to look to the sphere of labor relations to lower the costs of farming. In the wheat-growing districts of Swellendam and Caledon the postemancipation period witnessed increasing stratification and the emergence of poor white sharecroppers. By the 1840s wool farming predominated in the district and formed the basis for the rise of a new commercial elite.[28]

In general white farmers' cries of labor shortage derived more from a shortage of labor on their terms than from a real absence of labor, although in 1838 and 1839 substantial numbers of former slaves did avoid farm labor. High monthly wages in the two years after emancipation reflected farmers' vulnerability in the wake of emancipation. Male workers received 25s per month up to 1841, with wages falling dramatically the following year to 10s. Commercial areas such as Stellenbosch and Swellendam enjoyed higher wages since farmers there were better able to pay wages in cash: in Worcester much of the wage was actually paid in "a variety of commodities and rights" and so was not reflected in the wage scales.[29]

This period of relatively high wages also witnessed an increase in production of both grain and wine products. Robert Ross has shown that while the harvest of wheat and oats was temporarily negatively affected in 1838, possibly caused by the bad drought, from 1842 yields increased so much so that in the period 1842–1846, production was 35 percent higher than in the period 1829–1834. Similarly, while wine farming had suffered greatly in the 1820s, farmers recovered, pressing more "wine between 1838 and 1841 than in any other four year period, for which there is information between 1806 and 1855."[30]

In general agricultural yields in the colony as a whole increased in the 1840s and 1850s. But freed people did not enjoy the benefits of that boom. Perhaps the high wages they had received in the period 1838 to 1842 had contributed to the particularly good yields of those years, but white farmers certainly did not make the connection. From 1842 a dramatic lowering of monthly wages occurred, in part because so many ex-slaves now returned to farm labor in the face of few alternatives. In 1848 men engaged in monthly contracts in Wellington near Worcester were earning 7s 6d to 18s with board and lodging while women earned 3s to 15s.[31] By the mid-1840s most men on the stations were employed as farm laborers for at least part of the year, and by the next decade missions were clearly serving as labor

---

27   CA, LCA 10, Appendix, Item No. 17, Memorial of Inhabitants of Wagon Makers Valley, 7 September 1839; LCA 21, Appendix 21, Petition from Paarl farmers regarding the Masters and Servants Regulations, 28 March 1848.

28   Van Ryneveld, "Merchants and Missions," Chs. 1 and 2; Scully, *Bouquet*.

29   Marincowitz argues that farmers suffered a shortage of labor for "ploughing, harvesting, threshing, sowing, and transporting wheat." Marincowitz, "Rural Production," 54, 32; Figure 2 (no page number), 50.

30   Ross, "Rather Mental Than Physical," 153.

31   ASL, CGH, *Master and Servant*, JP, Wellington, 65.

reserves, though at least ones in which the inhabitants could shape the pattern of labor relations.[32]

The 1840s witnessed a general move towards day work in the rural Western Cape.[33] The justice of the peace at Swellendam lamented that "Daily labourers are in general to be had, if allowed to take their own way and go and come as they please; but herds, household, and stable servants are with the most difficulty obtainable."[34] Freed people seem to have preferred the flexibility offered by day labor, perhaps because short-term contracts clearly distinguished between slavery and freedom. Governor Napier mused that aversion to long-term employment "probably originated . . . amongst the coloured classes, that by continued services they might thereby fall into a state of bondage. . . ."[35] A farmer in Swellendam said that "few men will engage for more than a day" and that only "English labourers" would "engage for any certain period beyond a month"[36]

Farmers preferred long-term contracts. Such agreements tied laborers more permanently to the farm and made them subject to regulations which placed them more firmly within the farmer's domain. For example, Masters and Servants regulations prevented workers from receiving visitors without the farmer's permission. This assertion of control also facilitated a farmer's access to the labor of the worker's family who were more likely to live with a laborer working permanently on the farm (owing to the provision of a cottage) than day laborers. Marincowitz argues that day wages rose inversely relative to the declining value of monthly wages. By the 1850s the wages of resident farm laborers employed by the month had hardly reached their 1838 level. People who had not been able to gain a foothold on the missions or in the villages and who lived on the farm and engaged in monthly contracts therefore remained among the most vulnerable members of the rural working class.[37]

The seasonal pattern of agriculture in the rural Western Cape had traditionally enabled farmers to draw on the same pool of labor. Wheat farmers in Caledon and Swellendam particularly required laborers in the harvest season from October to December while wine farmers needed laborers from January with the start of the picking season. The pattern of sharing labor had its roots in slavery when farmers loaned out their slaves in the off seasons.[38] The ending of slavery, however, created a new dynamic in the older processes of labor: now laborers themselves could exercise some degree of choice regarding for whom they wished to labor.

---

32   Marincowitz, "Rural Production," 122; and Van Ryneveld, "Merchants and Missions," Conclusion.

33   Marincowitz, "Rural Production," 50. Wage statistics for the postemancipation period are virtually non existent for the period 1838 to 1853 and day wages are only formally recorded after 1853. The only real information I have found is in the replies to the questions sent out by the government to various officials and individuals in order to ascertain the workings of the Masters and Servants Ordinance. ASL, CGH, *Master and Servant*. Therefore any discussion of labor relations in this period is painfully hampered by the paucity of archival sources.

34   ASL, CGH, *Master and Servant*, 82.

35   CA, GH 23/12, No. 40, Governor to SSC, 22 June 1838.

36   ASL, CGH, *Master and Servant*, JP, SWM, 82. See also CO 4024, No. 26, T. B. Bayley, farmer at Swellendam, to SG, 24 February 1845.

37   Marincowitz, "Rural Production," analyzes this transformation, Ch. 1, 52; 138.

38   Mason, "Fit for Freedom," Ch. 5.

This created difficulties for some white farmers since their demand for labor varied throughout the year. Most wheat farmers, for example, employed about six laborers throughout the year and needed double that number in peak periods.[39] In this context, farmers sought new means of attracting laborers especially during the peak seasons. In the aftermath of emancipation farmers used cash advances, the payment of wages partly in wine, and systems of tied rent to try and lure laborers to the farms. Farmers offered workers wages in advance on the understanding that the laborers would then refuse other offers of work in the interim. Wealthier farmers with cash to spare clearly benefited from this system, but poorer farmers could not compete. Workers benefited by playing employers off against one another and by arguing that they could secure a better advance somewhere else. Advocates of white farmers not surprisingly complained that the advance system gave too much power to laborers and upset the balance of the labor market.[40]

In general employers paid lower wages for women, even when women were employed in domestic work—an occupational category which began to suffer great demand and short supply. Marincowitz states that in 1838 a man could earn a monthly wage of £1.6s in farm labor, while his female counterpart in domestic service earned £1.2s.[41] While it is difficult to establish a general pattern of wage rates either across the districts or between men and women in the scarce records existing which detail wages in the period from 1838 to 1853, one can tentatively say that women generally received less than men, although there were exceptions.[42] In Swellendam the "usual rate of wages" in 1849 was between 15s and 20s for farm servants and only 6s to 9s for female servants. In Groot Drakenstein near Stellenbosch women workers received significantly less than men and sometimes less even than adolescents. While men from Pniel mission station earned on average 9d per day working full-time for farmers, women earned 4_d per day. In the pressing season, when wine farmers needed extra labor, men earned also 9d. Women's wages could go as high as 6d per day, reflecting the demand for their labor. The teenage boys who were also employed at pressing time earned up to 9d per day for similar labor.[43]

By the latter half of the nineteenth century the expectation that wine would be given as part of the wage had become a given among laborers on the farms of the Western Cape: wine held a pivotal role in both the economic and the social worlds of

---

39 Marincowitz, "Rural Production," 106–115.

40 ASL, CGH, *Master and Servant*, RM, CAL, 37. Marais, *Cape Coloured People*, 196, also discusses the new methods farmers used to secure labor.

41 Marincowitz, "Rural Production," 49–50.

42 For example in 1849 the justice of the peace in Wellington near Paarl stated that wages for women servants were generally between 3s and 15s and men 7s6d to 18s; he paid an ex-slave woman fifteen shillings, in comparison to her husband who earned only nine shillings. ASL, CGH, *Master and Servant*, JP, Wellington, 65.

43 ASL, CGH, *Master and Servant*, JP, SWM, 113. In Riversdale in Caledon, one employer paid his senior domestic servant 15s per month, and the young cook 4s6d. He also employed a man as a groom and gardener at 20s per month. ASL, CGH, *Master and Servant*, Individual Replies, Riversdale, George Ebeleigh, Surgeon, 152. ASL, CGH, *Master and Servant*. *Addenda to the Documents of the Working of the Order in Council of 21st July 1849* . . . . (Cape Town: Saul Solomon, 1849), Lists of laborers working for farmers and during pressing time, provided in Memorandum by G. W. Stegman and J. W. Stegman, missionaries of Pniel Mission Station, 24 April 1849. I am grateful to Robert Ross for sending me a copy of this document.

rural labor.[44] Slaveholders had long given cheap wine to slaves throughout the day as a form of labor control. The giving of wine as part of the wage became more widespread in the postemancipation period. The amounts given daily also increased as farmers sought both to rid themselves of excess wine in a time of overproduction and to lure laborers to the farms.[45] In the mid-nineteenth century marginalized farmers who struggled to find laborers at cheap wages increasingly looked to the tot system as a bulwark against the capitalization of agriculture.[46] Former slaveholders sought to accelerate a process of proletarianization among freed people partly by producing a class of alcohol-dependent laborers. In 1849 a farmer in Caledon gave laborers two bottles of wine each per day during the harvest time. He maintained that without this wine "they will not work."[47]

Farmers with sufficient land also increasingly offered laborers various sorts of tenancy arrangements. A number of wealthy farmers owning multiple farms and large amounts of acreage offered houses and plots of land in return for a commitment to work on the farm during peak seasons.[48] In Worcester there is evidence that some farmers continued to pay wages as much in kind as in cash into the 1850s.[49] In Swellendam and George sharecropping unconnected to labor tenancy was more common.[50] White farmers in Swellendam and Caledon increasingly complained of freed people's unwillingness to work for them. For example, the justice of the peace in Swellendam complained in 1848 that he was unable to attract laborers to the farm even with offers of "cottages and gardens" and he echoed many farmers in the district in blaming the missions for providing freed people with an alternative to farm work.[51]

---

44   Pamela Scully, "Liquor and Labor in the Western Cape, 1870–1900," in Jonathan Crush and Charles Ambler, eds., *Liquor and Labor in Southern Africa* (Athens, OH: Ohio University Press, 1992), 56–77. For examples of freed people's perceptions of the pervasiveness of liquor in economic and social relations see CA, 1/STB 2/37, Documents in the trial of Josephus and Alie for cellar breaking and theft, 1 July 1840; 1/STB 22/38, Statement of Cornelis, "person of color", before JP, 4 March 1842; 1/STB 22/38, Letter from J. Edgar, Somerset West, 23 February 1843; 1/WOC 2/16, Preliminary examination of Saartje Salomon vs. Augus Salomon for assault, 19 November 1858.

45   Rayner, "Wine and Slaves," Ch. 4, discusses the wine industry; on the increase of the tot system after emancipation see Marais, *Cape Coloured People*, 196.

46   Marincowitz, "Rural Production," 121.

47   ASL, CGH, *Master and Servant*, JP, CAL, 73. His counterpart at Zoetendal's Valley in Swellendam gave his laborers a bottle of wine and a glass of brandy. *Master and Servant*, 79.

48   Marincowitz, "Rural Production," 37.

49   CA, 1/WOC 16/37, Hottentot or Free Person of Color. Contract of Hiring or Service, 8 February 1833; Laborers given mares in lieu of wages, 24 February 1851..

50   In the latter district, east of Swellendam, both free blacks and people defined as white farmed on the share. Marincowitz, "Rural Production," 47. For a discussion of rural stratification and white poverty in the second half of the nineteenth century see Colin Bundy, "Vagabond Hollanders and Runaway Englishmen: White Poverty in the Cape Before Poor Whiteism," in Beinart, Delius and Trapido, eds., *Putting a Plough to the Ground*, 101–128.

51   ASL, CGH, *Master and Servant*, JP, SWM, 82. For a discussion of missions and labor relations see below, and Chapter 7.

"Women's Work"

For ex-slaves freedom was flawed, but welcomed. Freed women and men forged identities in relation to former owners, new authorities, and each other. While labor legislation tended to assume specific patterns of masculine authority within a nuclear family this did not always accord with the distribution of power in the families and communities which freed people reaffirmed and constructed after 1838. Ex-slaves freed themselves in ways which sometimes meshed and some times exposed the tensions implicit in the distinctions between private/public, home/work, and the association of freedom and patriarchy which dominated colonialist discourse after 1838.[52]

Freed people embraced a nuanced interpretation of the relationship between gender, family, and waged work. This overlapped, but did not strictly accord, with the separation that missionaries, and some abolitionists, advocated between the male sphere of waged labor and the feminine domestic sphere of household work. The family economy constructed by freed people, particularly on the missions, for which we have the most information, established discrete spheres of male and female labor, but certainly depended upon the contributions of both men and women. Perhaps this arose because they saw some work as more suited to men, but it also arose from the different histories which men and women had experienced under slavery.

Under slavery women had worked as domestics, wet nurses, and cooks, and from the 1820s increasingly in the fields. After 1838 commentators remarked on the withdrawal of married women, and in some cases, young unmarried women too, from regular farm labor, and particularly from domestic waged work. In 1838 Governor Napier stated that there was a "considerable" demand for female labor.[53] Ex-slaveholders' complaints about freed women's refusal to labor possibly arose because the withdrawal of black women's labor upset a social hierarchy which was signified in part through the labor of women. White farmers and their supporters particularly protested that *their* wives and children were having to work while the families of laborers did not. The justice of the peace at Caledon stated in 1849 that

> The Boers, in order to gain a bare subsistence, are compelled to employ their own children of both sexes, from the most tender age, in field labour, and in the most menial offices. It is miserable to see these unfortunate children worn down with exertions beyond their strength, and growing up in a state of more complete barbarism than the Hottentots about them. All this time, the Missionary institutions are swarming with boys and girls old enough for work, but wanted at *school*; with women who will not take service, and with men who will remain idle, as long as they can subsist without work.[54]

In one sense the labor of black women and children helped to separate white farmers from ex-slaves and other free blacks. The use of family labor also demarcated

---

52 See Poovey, *Uneven Developments*, for an exposition of the multiple ambiguities and tensions within Victorian gender ideology.

53 CA, GH 1/121, Answers by Governor Napier to questions posed by SSC, in SSC to Governor, 20 May 1838.

54 ASL, CGH, *Master and Servant*, JP, Caledon, 74.

boundaries between wealthy white farmers who employed laborers to work for them, and poorer white farmers who used family labor to survive.[55]

But in the decade after emancipation married freed women and children appear to have worked on white-owned farms only at harvest time or where they had no other options.[56] On the missions and on the large farms where farmers offered male laborers houses with plots, married women were more likely to be able to avoid regular farm labor. Freed women did not want to work in conditions akin to slavery. The movement from domestic work for employers into domestic work for one's own household came to signify liberty from slavery, and an entry into womanhood for some freed women.[57] In addition, the fact that women earned lower wages than men probably did not encourage them to enter farm work. A decade after emancipation, however, overcrowding on the mission stations and lack of economic opportunities forced freed people into the farm labor market in greater numbers. More women seem to have started going out to work with their husbands as well as entering domestic service although it appears that they tried to protect their daughters from such work.[58] In 1854 a farmer in Malmesbury district complained that female servants were scarce since "the parents are not anxious to let the girls go from their care."[59]

Mission communities most clearly operated according to a gendered division of labor. In 1841 Brother Genth of Elim in Caledon stated that "Nearly all the male inhabitants of this place are employed as day-labourers on the neighbouring farms; the wives and children remain mostly at home. . . ."[60] A survey of households at Genadendal in 1849 lists only 16 married women working off the station of the 468 households in which the man and woman were either formally married or in relationships of reputed marriage. On the other hand, in this case, daughters were much more likely to work off the station. Of the same households, out of the 110 which had daughters, 72 had daughters working outside the home.[61]

---

55 See the case of a Caledon farmer whose wife worked threshing grain, quoted in Van Ryneveld, "Merchants and Missions," 59. Also CA, 1/STB 2/36, No. 15, Documents in the Case of Regina vs. Adam alias Willem Patience, for rape, 5 January 1838.

56 Boddington, "Domestic Service." See Edwards, *Towards Emancipation*, 206, for an early reference to the reluctance of freed women to work in domestic service. Marincowitz, "Rural Production," 53, and Mason, "Fit for Freedom," Ch. 8, also make reference to this.

57 Pamela Scully, "Gender, Emancipation, and Free Wage Labor Ideology: The Cape Colony, 1830–1860" (paper presented to the Eighth Annual Graduate Women's Studies Conference, University of Michigan, Ann Arbor, March 1991); also Mason, "Fit for Freedom," 568–69.

58 This statement has been drawn from anecdotal evidence: As Erica Boddington has suggested, "domestic service was an important point of incorporation into wage labor" for women but it did not appear in nineteenth-century statistical records. Boddington, "Domestic Service," 135, 71. See CA, CO 503, No. 53, Justice Kekewich to Governor regarding trial of Galant for murder of his wife Delie, 14 June 1841; 1/SWM 2/26, Printed Indictment of case of Queen vs. Lys for murder, 23 March 1842; 1/STB 18/183, Wage Contract, 19 November 1845.

59 ASL, CGH, Select Committee, *Granting Lands in Freehold to Hottentots*, S.C. 11, 1854, 23; Also ASL, CGH, *Master and Servant. Addenda*, Barnabus Shaw to W. Hope, Clerk of Councils, 2 May 1849, 49.

60 Two years later Kolbing of Genadendal mentioned that he had spoken to seventy-seven women whose husbands were absent from the station. HA, *PA*, XVI, CLXXV (June 1842), 134; *PA*, XVI, CLXXXII (March 1844), 518.

61 ASL, CGH, *Master and Servant. Addenda*, numbers compiled from "Information Relative to the Laborers and Their Families, Residing at the Institution, Genadendal." The precise meaning of the term "going out to work," which was used in all the tables in the 1849 survey is unclear. I have taken it to mean women working off the station, as sometimes when a woman was listed as not going out to work, her occupation is stated to be "housemaid" or "teacher."

The wealth of the inhabitants and the labor and market opportunities in any given area were crucial in determining if married women worked for wages outside the home. Economics rather than ideology mainly seems to have determined the nature of married women's work. Even on different mission stations where similar ideas about the necessity of women remaining at home prevailed, one sees very different patterns of employment. At Zuurbraak, for example, a relatively wealthy station where men worked as artisans and could also earn money selling wood and engaging in day labor when necessary, most married women did not work on the surrounding farms. In 1849 the missionary there said that "married women do not go out to work as a general rule. They have all families, and they reside at home to attend to their households, manufacture mats, etc."[62]

In contrast, at poorer Saron station in the Tulbagh district (established in 1847), a different pattern emerges. In 1849, out of 112 households headed by men who were either married or reputed to be married, a full seventy of those women worked outside the home. The figures provided do not give a breakdown of the number of households with daughters, but only four are registered as having daughters going out to work.[63] At Pniel mission station in Groot Drakenstein near Paarl, which had very little land to offer its members, of the forty-three households including both a man and a woman, fifteen women worked regularly off the station while nine did so occasionally.[64]

In part the ability of married women to avoid working for farmers was related to the economy of the mission station on which they lived. By 1849, when the survey of missions was done, Genadendal and Zuurbraak had been established for well over fifty years, and even Elim was a good ten years old. Genandendal and Zuurbraak in particular had flourishing communities on the station which provided internal markets for women to work from the home in washing, and making mats and other products. Saron, on the other hand, had only been established two years before the survey and was far away from even the market opportunities presented by the villages of Tulbagh and Worcester. Thus both men and women had little choice but to work on the local farms.

Most importantly, it is clear that across the Western Cape, freed women did not abandon the public sphere of work. They were involved in income-generating activities such as selling produce, doing people's laundry, and marketing clothes and other goods.[65] While in the decade after 1838 married freed women withdrew from domestic service and regular farm labor where possible, they did not stop working for money. They merely shifted their work to other areas of the economy. Waged work remained as essential for most working-class women at the Cape as it did for their metropolitan peers.[66] Casual labor allowed women to more easily look after their

---

62   ASL, CGH, *Master and Servant. Addenda,* letter from Helm to W. Hope, Clerk of Councils, 25 May 1849.

63   ASL, CGH, *Master and Servant. Addenda,* Table entitled "Missionary Institution at 'Saron,' District of Tulbagh . . . ," 26 February 1849.

64   Ibid., "Tabular Form comprehending Answers to the Queries forwarded by Government Letter of 18th January 1849, relative to the Missionary Institution at Pniel, Groot Drakenstein, Paarl," 28 February 1849.

65   CA, GH 28/35, No. 21, Statement by C. L. Teutsch of Genadendal to SG, 30 December 1846, Enclosure No. a1 to Despatch No. 21 regarding Moravian claims to Hemel and Aarde, 21 January 1847. Teutsch is discussing conditions at Genadendal station.

66   See for example Tilly and Scott, *Women, Work, and Family.*

families in a context in which freed people appear to have seen childcare primarily as a woman's responsibility. In this respect we see some commonality between the gender ideologies being assembled by freed people after emancipation and those promoted by missionaries and accepted in settler society. At Genadendal, "none of the mothers with small children ever" left home to work. The resident magistrate observed that

> whilst the husbands and able-bodied sons and daughters go out to work, they, the wives, have no alternative but to remain at home in charge of their young children, their houses, and gardens which constitute their all. They put the question: "if we abandon our small means, to serve the farmer when he wants it, what are we to resort to when the farmer refuses to support our numerous small children, to him of no use?"[67]

Married women's participation in the economy was possibly also a product of the legal power accorded to men within the freed family under the Masters and Servants Ordinance. Under the clauses which governed most long-term contracts women could be subject to dismissal at the whim of their husband or by the employer if they were pregnant. Working as a washerwoman, or as a casual laborer on the farms in harvest time, gave a woman more control over her time, as well as freedom from the legal power accorded to her husband and employer if she engaged in regular work.

Women's income-producing work often helped to establish and maintain a household's standard of living.[68] At Zuurbraak married women certainly contributed to the economy of the household. In 1849, of the 104 households at Zuurbraak whose means of earning their living was ascertained through interviews by the justice of the peace, 39 depended upon the income of both husband and wife. In the year up to June 1849, for example, the Hartwig family earned a total of £17. The mother, Rozet, contributed £7 by working as a seamstress in the home, and Frederick, the father, earned £10 by working as a woodcutter and laborer. The Jacobs family earned a total of £23.15. Of that, the father, Wilhelm Jacobs, contributed £17 through his work as a woodcutter on the station. Sarah Jacobs, the mother, contributed £4.10 by making mats and their son Jan earned £2.5 by working as a laborer.[69] At Genadendal the tables suggest that fewer married women earned money. Most married women are listed as doing "housework" although a few did bring in money doing washing and sewing for others. However if women did not bring in cash wages they did help support the family. Women listed as doing housework were also in charge of the family garden attached to each house. The existence of garden plots facilitated the entrenchment of a household economy in which women and small children worked on the plots and men worked either in artisanal trades on the stations or, increasingly from the late 1840s, as workers on neighboring farms.

---

67   ASL, CGH, *Master and Servant. Addenda*, Note to Summary B. Trades, Occupations, Stock, Produce, etc., by RM, JP, and the Clerk to the Magistrate, CAL, 24 February 1849, 191.

68   On this point as it refers more widely to women and production in Africa see Margaret Jean Hay, "Luo Women and Economic Change in the Colonial Period," in Nancy J. Hafkin and Edna G. Bay, eds., *Women in Africa: Studies in Social and Economic Change* (Stanford: Stanford University Press, 1976): 87–109, 93.

69   ASL, CGH, *Master and Servant. Addenda*, Supplementary Evidence furnished to the Committee . . . obtained by the Resident Missionary (n.d.), 94–100, 94, 70. Out of the 104 men interviewed, only five were unmarried, while for another seven I was unable to ascertain if they were married or not.

In the course of the 1840s the increase of population on the stations meant that more people had to engage in regular wage labor on the farms. In 1844, for example, the superintendent of Genadendal remarked that people now had to go further to find work and could not "come home every Sunday."[70] The missions became in some respects forerunners of the later rural labor reserves of apartheid South Africa: places predominantly occupied by women, children, and old men. In 1853, the Reverend Helm, of Zuurbraak, lamented that for the

> greater part of the year men are mostly absent from the institution . . . & from the distance they have to travel, some can only visit their families on those occasions at intervals of 3 or 4 weeks. This state of things, it is obvious, is not favourable to improvements of a secular nature connected with the Institution, and is in many ways, hurtful to the morals & detrimental to the religious feelings of the people.[71]

But men tried to come back to the missions when possible so that they remained part of the communities even when they worked off the station. For example, in 1848, three men from Genadendal lived at the farm of a Mr. Swart the whole week long and would travel through Saturday night to reach their homes at Genadendal so that they could spend Sundays with their families.[72]

Laboring Children

The fragility of freed people's economic independence contributed to the formation of a household economy in which each member's contribution was central to the survival of the family. Freed people expected children to contribute to the present or future welfare of the family either through education or a combination of education and labor in peak periods, through work in the home, or through regular waged work, depending on the parents' economic status and locale. In the villages, at least some freed families appear to have depended on children's immediate economic contribution to the household. For example, when Siena, the fourteen-year-old daughter of a Mrs. Achilles of Worcester left home to stay with friends, her mother said, "I gave her a punishment after I got her back. She has also lost her employment so that I must now provide for her."[73]

Parents who wanted to sponsor their children's education had limited options. Most schools which catered to freed people were situated at missions and in the villages; parents living in those places were therefore more likely than resident farm laborers to be able to send their children to school. If they could, parents tried to keep their children away from permanent farm labor. But wages rose during peak periods such as ploughing season or grape harvesting when farmers needed extra labor. Children's school attendance tended to fluctuate with the agricultural calendar and the

---

70 HA, "Letter from Kolbing, 8 July 1844," *PA*, XVII, CLXXXV (December 1844), 125.

71 SOAS, CWM, LMS South Africa, Box 28, Folder A, Report by Daniel Helm of Zuurbraak, for 1853.

72 CA, 1/CAL 1/1/1, Examination in Circuit Court of the Division of Swellendam, Case No. 2, Adolph Adams and others for theft, evidence of Ernst Croze, 29 May 1848.

73 CA, 1/WOC 2/16, Statement by Siena Achilles Sr., in preliminary examination of public prosecutor vs. Saban, Willem et al. for abduction, 28 September 1858.

opportunities to earn relatively good wages. At Zuurbraak, the Reverend Helm stated in 1839 that "this school suffers still much of the hard times we are in; the taller children are often hired out by the parents in order to assist them in bringing up the rest of the family, which proves to be great obstacles to their progress." Ten years later, at Genadendal, school attendance was "indifferent and irregular as is always the case in the ploughing season."[74]

The two decades after emancipation continued to see the prevalence of child indenture. This period, in fact, witnessed a realignment of the meaning of indenture or apprenticeship to fit the more conventional use of the term as a period of practical education. The payment of wages for children's indentures separates this pattern of indentures from the earlier forms of "apprenticeship" in the pre-emancipation Cape in which Khoisan children were indentured without payment in a form akin to slavery.[75] During this period employers paid children a wage even if an inadequate one, and payments, as recorded in the indenture books, were deposited in bank accounts under a parent's name. Particularly from the late 1840s some contracts stipulated that the parents would receive all or part of the child's wage: in this way the child's indenture contributed to the household, and their labor in some cases was exploited entirely to the parents' advantage.

Fortunate parents managed to apprentice their child to an artisan so that the child could learn a skill.[76] More often parents appear to have used indentures to generate income. Parents indentured children to other freed people as well as to farmers, although this was rare.[77] In 1849 Pieter Jan of Worcester indentured his brother-in-law, Abraham Jeptha, aged nine, as a "houseservant" to Phillipus van der Byl. The child received no wages out of this transaction. Jan on the other hand received fifty rix dollars to the beginning of the contract and one hundred rix dollars at the end.[78] By the 1850s some of the districts had savings banks and parents sometimes divided the wage between themselves and the child, putting part of the wage in a savings account for the child when their indenture ended. For example, in 1859 Alexander and Lea McDonald indentured their daughter, Suzie, aged twelve, to Jacob Pieter van Reenen as a domestic servant. The contract stipulated that the father was to received 4s. 6d. per month, while 3s would be deposited into a savings account in Suzie's name.[79]

---

74   SOAS, LMS, Letters Received, South Africa, 1839–1840, Box 16, Folder 4, Jacket D, Letter from Rev. Helm, 1 November 1839. HA, "Letter from D. W. Gysin," PA, XIX, CCI (December 1848), 30 June 1848, 32.

75   I am grateful to Elizabeth Eldredge for this point.

76   For examples see CA, 1/WOC 16/42, Apprenticeship Contract, 3 September 1840, children learning needlework; 1/WOC 16/37, "Indenture of Apprenticeship," 23 July 1849, child learning to be cobbler. CA, 1/STB 18/183, Contract of Apprenticeship, 14 September 1852, child learning baking; and Contract of Apprenticeship, 30 July 1853, child learning harnessmaking.

77   CA, 1/STB 4/1/1/4, No 2085, Criminal Record Book, 17 July 1848; 1/STB 4/1/1/5, No. 45, 12 February 1851. Also see case of the Lamberts below, 1/STB 4/1/1/4, No. 2611, Criminal Record Book, 23 September 1850.

78   CA, 1/WOC 16/37, "Contract of Apprenticeship by Natural Guardian," 30 May 1849. See also "Contract of Hiring and Service," 4 November 1850. Calonie of Worcester town, hired her daughter Treentje, aged eleven, to Michiel Kuys as a domestic servant. The contract stipulated that when Treenjte turned thirteen she would receive wages of 3s per month which would go to her mother.

79   CA, 1/WOC 16/43, Apprenticeship Contract, 26 August 1859. See also 1/STB 10/170, I.G. Gain to RM, 14 June 1865 regarding the wages of a child, Cobus Davidse, which were deposited into the Stellenbosch Savings Bank in 1850–51.

Indentures also seem to have operated as a form of adoption in which the child was indentured to a grandparent or other relative—possibly with greater economic resources. In September 1840, a Khoi man named Jason indentured his two children, Kaatje, aged five, and Griet, aged seven, to their grandmother until they were sixteen so that they could learn "needlework."[80] Given that the father rather than the mother indentured these children one can surmise that Jason was a single parent who decided that the girls' grandmother could better provide for them and teach them skills which would serve them in later years. One can only imagine why he chose the formal route of indenture rather than merely sending them to their grandmother. Perhaps he attempted to insure that they would be well-treated since it was a contract governed by law. This formal contract also guaranteed the girls wages in the latter part of their contract. More formal adoptions also occurred. In 1860 Nicolaas Stynder, the guardian of Thomas Lambert, aged twelve, indentured Thomas to Gert Stynders who was to treat him "as his child."[81] A settler in Worcester also followed this route. In 1859, Pieter Eduard du Toit of Worcester put his son Petrus into apprenticeship with one Jacob Jacobus de Vos. The contract stipulated that De Vos would treat Petrus "like his own child . . . to ensure that he received a proper education . . . and would become a member of the Reformed Church. . . ." Petrus would remain "in service" until 18 May 1863 and would receive 10s per month in the last year.[82]

The indenture system sometimes generated tensions precisely because it aided the economic livelihood of some freed families. In 1849 Willem Wium prosecuted a laboring couple Simon and Maria for withholding their daughter Christina whom they had legally indentured to him. And in Stellenbosch a couple's indenture of their child caused them so much disagreement that the wife brought her husband to court over the issue. Saartje charged Salomon with "having about 2 months ago, wrongfully & unlawfully and against the will of Saartje his lawful wife, taken from the service of Thielman Roos of Moddergat, her son Salomon the younger, whom she has lawfully contracted to him by and with the consent of her said husband."[83]

Another couple also went to court over a similar issue. In 1849 Francina and Jacobus Lamberts took the parents of their apprentice, Simson, to court. The Lamberts were ex-slaves and members of the artisanal elite in Stellenbosch village and had been married in the Dutch Reformed Church in 1839 in terms of the new Marriage Order. He was a shoemaker by trade.[84] Present and Rachel, Simson's parents, do not appear in the marriage records of the Dutch Reformed Church or the Methodist church. Possibly they were a poorer laboring couple who had hoped to secure a better future for their son Simson through indenturing him to learn a skill. The Lam-

---

80 CA, 1/WOC 16/42, Apprenticeship Contract, 3 September 1840. See also 1/STB 4/1/1/5, No. 45, Criminal Record Book, 21 February 1851, Dollie Wanza vs. Hendrik for drunkenness on the job. Hendrik was Wanza's adopted child.

81 CA, 1/WOC 16/43, Apprenticeship Contract, 29 October 1860. See also 1/STB 4/1/1/4, No. 2611, Criminal Record Book, 23 September 1849.

82 CA, 1/WOC 16/43, Handwritten Contract on blue paper, 14 November 1859.

83 CA, 1/STB 4/1/1/4, Criminal Record Book, No. 2217, 29 January 1849. There is no record of the outcome of the case. For a similar instance see No. 2411, 29 November 1849, where Tamar took her daughter Tina away from Mrs. Roos to whom she was apprenticed. CA, 1/STB 4/1/1/5, No. 1182, Criminal Record Book, 16 July 1855.

84 See CA, DRC G2 7/2, 30 June 1839. For more discussion of the Lamberts see Chapter 6.

berts accused the couple of "refusing to allow their child Simson Jacobus Johannes to return to his adopted parents given over previously to the Prosecutors for the purpose of being educated and supported until he attained his majority." The court ordered the parents to return Simson to the Lamberts.[85]

As during the apprenticeship period regional variations occurred in indentures. In Stellenbosch parents seem to have been reluctant to indenture their children although such indentures started to increase in the 1850s. The comparatively small number of apprenticeships in Stellenbosch might be related to the higher wages in that district and the more diversified economy of the district.[86] In the late 1840s increasing numbers of children in Worcester and Swellendam districts were apprenticed both by their parents and by the resident magistrates. Parents were even more likely to indenture their children in the following decade.[87] Swellendam is somewhat distinctive among the districts in that the majority of children were apprenticed on grounds of destitution at the request of their mothers not by the resident magistrate. In the 1850s the overcrowding of the missions and the assault on public land and squatting contributed to the narrowing of the options for poor parents in supporting their families and forced parents to indenture their children more frequently.[88]

A revival of the more explicitly exploitative forms of indenture which had been common in Cape society under slavery accompanied the expansion of more legitimate patterns of child apprenticeship from the 1840s. As we have seen, from the time of apprenticeship through the early emancipation era farmers perceived children as the most vulnerable laborers. It was not without cause that "[t]he view that child-apprentices came closest to bearing 'the traditional badge of slavery' was common among rural labourers."[89]

---

85 CA, 1/STB 4/1/1/4, No. 611, Criminal Record Book, 23 September 1850.

86 Between 1840 and 1853, 24 children were apprenticed out of a total of 163 wage contracts in Stellenbosch District. From the late 1840s apprenticeships of such children are recorded but the numbers never go higher than four in a given year and the majority of these children were apprenticed not by their parents but by the magistrate on the grounds of poverty. Fourteen involved destitute children, and ten were signed by parents. Only one parent apprenticed her children in 1840 and for the next six years no apprenticeships of freed children seems to have occurred. A total of 149 contracts were entered into between employers and people defined as "Khoi and free black" in the period 1843–1846. CA, 1/STB 18/183, Wage Contracts with Khoi and free blacks, and 1/STB 18/189, Indenture Book. CA, 1/STB 18/189, Contract of Apprenticeship by Parent, 14 September 1840. Thirty-eight wage contracts were made in 1843, 34 in 1844, 40 in 1845, and 37 in 1846. 1/STB 18/183, Wage Contract Book.

87 In Swellendam 31 children were apprenticed in the same period and 24 in Worcester. In Swellendam, like Stellenbosch, no apprenticeships were recorded between 1843 and 1848 and the number picked up again in 1848, whereas in Worcester 1843 witnessed the most indentures in the period from 1840 to 1850. See CA, 1/SWM 13/7, Register of Apprenticeship Contracts 1829–53; 1/WOC, Hiring Contracts of "Hottentots and free blacks," 1828–1853. Of the Worcester indentures at least six were deemed illegal-a result of "kidnapping." See below, and 30 September 1843; 1 February 1844; 28 March 1844; and 21 September 1844. Dates refer to illegal indentures.

88 CA, 1/SWM, 13/7. Twenty-five of the 31 apprenticeships involved parents, and of those 25, 24 involved mothers. Since the Masters and Servants Ordinance only permitted mothers to apprentice their children when the father was absent or dead, the Swellendam figures suggest that single mothers were more prevalent in that district and that they possibly faced greater difficulties than their peers in Stellenbosch and Worcester in trying to support their families on their earnings. No records exist as far as I can tell which would provide us with any statistical basis for this argument.

89 PRO, CO 53/104, Civil Commissioner's report, Mossel Bay, 1867, cited in Marincowitz, "Rural Production," 119.

The Colonial Office also worried that children would become the new slaves of the era of wage labor. The fact that so many of the Prize Negroes who were seized from ships of other slave-trading nations and brought to be indentured at the Cape were children points to the importance of child labor to the postemancipation economy. In the late 1840s the British government stipulated that no child Prize Negroes under ten could be indentured without their parents' consent and stated that Prize Negroes under the age of twenty-one had to be employed in skilled trades or as domestic servants—not as farm laborers where conditions most approximated those of slavery. In addition in 1847 the length of the apprenticeship was limited to five years.[90]

Apprenticeship, as a form of indenture, worked to some extent in tandem with the wider processes of redefinition with which British colonialism was so preoccupied in the mid-nineteenth century. From 1834 magistrates could still indenture children if they believed them to be "destitute" or "orphans."[91] Pinning the label of "destitute" on a child clearly facilitated a farmer's claim to labor; it also reinforced the notion that to fit into Cape society one either had to employ others or be employed. Children defined as "Bushmen" remained particularly vulnerable to charges of destitution since farmers successfully argued that their parents did not provide for them since they moved frequently and avoided regular labor: four of the six children who were apprenticed because of supposed destitution in Swellendam between 1842 and 1848 were identified as "Bushmen."[92]

This clause clearly permitted great abuses to take place under the guise of rescuing poverty-stricken children. In 1852 William Mackay, the Caledon magistrate reported that

> It sometimes happens . . . that farmers traveling with their wagons, pick up children—and always boys—on pretence of finding them hungry and naked and in a state of destitution and upon producing such children to the Magistrate teach them, perhaps, how to tell *their* story, or *a* story, and all this because it has been the practice to indenture such children to the *finder* unless on advertizement a relative may claim them.

It appears to me that such practice is calculated to encourage children or apprentices to run away from their parents—or employers. . . .[93]

Settlers also began to look further afield for child labor, and in the process resuscitated both the longer history of depredations against the Khoi and the San, and the close links between dependent labor and slavery which had existed particularly in the interior districts such as Worcester. In the course of the 1840s as various attempts to import labor faltered, settlers in Worcester district, in particular, seized on illegal

90   This information is taken from Christopher Saunders, "Between Slavery and Freedom: The Importation of Prize Negroes to the Cape in the Aftermath of Emancipation," *Kronos* 9 (1984): 36–43, 41.

91   This provision was first established under the Ordinance of 1 March 1841, enacted as an Order in Council of 27 August 1842, and extended by another order of 13 December 1844. This information is contained in CA, GH 28/31, No. 163, Enclosure to Despatch No. 163 of 15 November 1845, "Return of provision made for certain classes of destitute persons, called for by Lord Stanley's Despatch of the 13th August 1845 . . . ," written by Governor Montagu.

92   CA, 1/SWM 13/7, Register of Apprenticeship Contracts, 30 July 1842; 4 August 1848; 4 August 1848; 19 October 1848.

93   CA, 1/CAL 5/1/1/1, RM to AG, 19 April 1852.

means of securing labor—thus participating in the illegal slave trade which had a long history in the northern Cape.[94]

The story of neoslavery emerged in 1843 with a variety of reports surfacing in Worcester, Stellenbosch, and Swellendam districts about the illegal capture of children from across the colony's borders.[95] In August 1843, the clerk of the peace at Worcester reported that a number of African children had been illegally imported into the colony. On 1 August, a boy of about twelve called Veldsman, whom the clerk said belonged to one of the African societies across the border, complained of ill-treatment by his employer, Albertus Adriaan van Wyk, of Tulbagh. Veldsman told the clerk that he had been brought by Van Wyk from Port Natal on the northeast coast of South Africa two years before, along with "three other boys and two female children." Two other African children also worked on the farm. The outraged clerk wrote to the local field cornet, Niehaus, asking him to demand from Van Wyk, "in Her Majesty's name, and forward to Worcester immediately whatever native foreigners he might find in Van Wyk's service. . . ."[96]

Receiving no answer from Niehaus, the clerk wrote again. He reported that on "the day I despatched this letter, Van Wyk himself came to my office, and entreated that the Children might be left in his service." Van Wyk promised to go to the governor himself and account for how the children had come into his employ. The clerk agreed but said that Van Wyk had to send the children to Worcester immediately. A week passed and nothing happened and the clerk despatched a third letter to the field cornet. Finally, four boys aged between twelve and ten, and three girls of twelve, ten, and seven arrived at the clerk's office. He stated that the first two children belonged to the "Mantatee tribe, the 3,4, & 5 to one of the Caffer tribes, and the two last mentioned of the Bushman tribe."[97]

The next day Van Wyk returned saying that he had been in town searching for legal advice. His friends had encouraged him to submit to whatever penalties were necessary in accordance with the law. However, according to the clerk, Van Wyk asked

> that having acted in perfect ignorance of any Law existing on the subject, he hoped this Circumstance would be considered . . . In particular he begged, that I would not bring a Criminal Action against him, for having punished the boy Veldsman, and I agreed to waive the action [Someone, perhaps the Attorney General, wrote in pencil "by what authority?"] should such a course be sanctioned by his Excellency—provided he would forthwith deposit £5 in the Savings Bank for the benefit of the boy.[98]

---

94   See Julian Cobbing, "The Mfecane as Alibi: Thoughts on Dithakong and Mbolompo," *Journal of African History* 29 (1988): 487–519. On depredations against the Khoi and the San in the northern Cape see Penn, "Land, Labour, and Livestock," 13–19. On the Eastern Cape see Crais, *White Supremacy and Black Resistance*, 40–47; Newton-King, "Enemy Within." For an extended examination of the slavery which was not called slavery see Eldredge and Morton, eds., *Slavery in South Africa*.

95   For example see CA, 1/SWM, 16/31, Field Cornet J. W. Smalberger of ValschRivier to CP, 22 November 1843; 1/WOC, 19/69, CP, STB, to CP, WOC, 4 December 1844; AG 2617, Report of AG regarding letter of CP, Paarl, as to the indenturing of two children, 15 December 1843.

96   CA, CO 2814, No. 80, CP, WOC, to SG, 22 August 1843.

97   Ibid.

98   Ibid.

The clerk of the peace did not immediately apprentice the children to the other applicants and placed them among "the respectable inhabitants" of the town until he received orders from the governor. He concluded by remarking that

> I look upon Van Wyk as an improper guardian for such unfortunate beings. . . . I cannot avoid being strongly impressed with the conviction, that these children have in reality been purchased by van Wyk, from the Emigrant Farmers or others. Indeed Veldsman affirms, that he was carried off, while herding his father's calves by a certain "Baas" Christiaan, and that shortly there after he came into the service of Van Wyk, although he cannot say, what consideration was given for this transfer.[99]

Porter, the liberal attorney general, took a particularly jaundiced view of this affair and refused to allow even a provisional suspension of assault charges against Van Wyk which the child Veldsman had brought against him. Porter argued that by employing the ten children Van Wyk had contravened Order No. 49 of 1828 which prohibited the employment of Africans from across the borders of the colony who had no pass to work in the colony. Porter thus asked the clerk of the peace to fine Van Wyk £50. With regard to the children he said:

> If you allow our Colonists who are in the habit of proceeding on Togt beyond the boundary, to obtain servants by bringing in the children of the natives, you will inevitably establish a sort of slave trade on our very Borders. To prevent this you should, I conceive, refuse, under any circumstances to apprentice any child to the party by whom that child has been introduced into the Colony. This is the course which I have on all similar occasions presented to the Clerks of the Peace, by whom I have been consulted on the subject. The children have been invariably removed from the custody of the Persons who brought them hither, and contracted to other parties. . . . These children . . . do not come exactly within the provisions of Or 49 which relate to the apprenticing of destitute children. But they are within the *spirit* of that law, and the Clerk of the Peace may, in my opinion, execute good indentures in the case of the children taken from Van Wyk.[100]

The practice of capturing children from across the borders of the colony continued well into the 1850s and did not just take place in frontier districts.[101] In 1852 Jacobus du Toit, a trader in the interior, went to the resident magistrate of Caledon with a paper he purported to be from the father of an African girl granting Du Toit the right to the child until she attained adulthood. The magistrate wrote to the attorney general saying that Du Toit

> now applies to have the child who appears to be about nine years old, indentured to him at this office. . . . As I am not clear that there might not have been some irregularity in this proceedings I have declined to comply with Du Toit's wishes until I hear from you on the subject.[102]

---

99 Ibid.

100 CA, CO 2814, No. 80, AG to CP, WOC, 1 September 1843. For information on the subsequent indenturing of the children see CA, 1/WOC 16/37, Indentures of 30 September 1843.

101 CA, CO 668, RM, SWM to Colonial Secretary, 23 October 1856, regarding two African children brought from across the border by L. J. Haasbroek of "Uitvlugt" farm in the Tradow area of Swellendam. See also Eldredge and Morton, eds., *Slavery in South Africa*.

102 CA, 1/CAL 5/1/1/1, RM to AG, 17 September 1852.

While Porter's memo of 1843 had acknowledged that such kidnapping was a species of slavery, nearly a decade later he argued that slavery was legally impossible. Porter now framed his thoughts on the subject of "Sales of Kidnapped Children" in very narrow legal terms. In an 1855 memorandum on that topic to the governor, Porter argued that special legislation would have to be enacted at the Cape to deal with this problem. The practice of bringing children into the colony illegally, or even selling their labor to someone, could only be deemed a crime in the "metaphorical sense" since "children acquired in order to be brought into a British Possession where slavery cannot exist, are not acquired in order to their being dealt with as slaves."[103]

In this memorandum Porter implied one solution—later applied in other parts of the empire—to the problem of how to cope with evidence of a continued trade in bonded labor at the very moment that the metropole proclaimed the victory of free wage labor and British colonialism over slavery.[104] By arguing that slavery did not exist legally, Porter claimed solipsistically that slavery therefore did not exist at all—despite all evidence to the contrary.

From the late 1850s the evidence of neoslavery fades from the records. The overcrowding on the missions in the Western Cape drove more freed people into the employ of white farmers. The greater availability of cheap local labor possibly contributed to the decline of illegal labor procurement in the western districts. But white farmers and their representatives complained of the lack of cheap labor well into the century. J. H. Hofmeyr, a leading Cape politician, remarked in 1875 that complaints about labor shortage had stretched from "the beginning of the years until now."[105]

Conclusion

Emancipation liberated slave women into a subordinate place in the wage labor economy, in part because of assumptions about women's proper roles which had guided the abolitionist struggle. And postemancipation labor legislation reaffirmed the limits which marriage and gender placed on women. The social and economic "problem" posed by married women workers particularly exposes the assumptions about men and women's discrete relations to contract which pervaded theories about free wage labor.[106] The framers of Cape postemancipation labor legislation made an exception for married women to make contracts, as otherwise they were prohibited from doing so. This concession indicates the ambivalence among the legislators and reformers in both the metropole and the colonies as to whether working-class women should adopt the gender practices of their middle-class peers, or rather construct a discrete vision of womanhood.

---

103   CA, AG 2621, Memorandum on "Sales of Kidnapped Children," 17 November 1855.

104   See Steven Pierce, "Unseemly Habits: Slavery, Indirect Rule, Islamic Law, and Emancipation in the Sokoto Caliphate" (paper presented to the Postemancipation Societies Conference, University of Michigan, April 30–May 1, 1993).

105   Quoted in Scully, *Bouquet*, 52. For a discussion of labor shortage in the postemancipation Western Cape see Marais, *Cape Coloured People*, Ch. 6; Marincowitz, "Rural Production," Chapter 1; Mason, "Fit for Freedom," Ch. 8; and Van Ryneveld, "Merchants and Missions," Ch. 3.

106   Stanley, "Conjugal Bonds and Wage Labor."

Colonial legislation aimed at freed people also enacted, if only implicitly, racist legislation. At the Cape, freed black women experienced wage labor in the confluence of contradictory demands on their behavior. Labor legislation accommodated settlers' demands that black women work, but at the same time it also circumscribed women's opportunities because of their gender and their race. Yet, while the use of race as a marker of inequality continued to be debated within metropolitan and colonial circles throughout the 1840s and 1850s, legislators seem to have presumed the existence of a gendered hierarchy within both the family and the workplace.

A gendered division of labor appears to have existed in many freed communities. But this did not operate on the axis of private versus public sphere which missionaries in particular advocated to freed people. Freed women contributed to their households either through tending their gardens on the missions or doing washing, or, if working on farms, by sending back wages to their families. But these practices often existed in tension with the cultural patterns some colonial officials imagined would be best suited to the propagation of a responsible freed population. The Colonial Office conceptualized its mission to create a productive and disciplined rural working class out of former slaves as a massive cultural project to mold and reshape the work, leisure habits, and private lives of a whole class of people. Supporters of emancipation wanted to "inculcate the lower classes with various moral and economic virtues, so that workers would want to do what the emerging economy required."[107]

This vast cultural project to create a self-reproducing waged labor force focused particularly upon women's bodies, which through pregnancy or the absence thereof were seen to expose the transgressions and the successes of moral teachings. Part III discusses how the issues of gender, labor, and power, which were exposed by the great experiment which was emancipation, became implicated in larger processes of cultural definition in the rural world of the Western Cape in the years after the ending of slavery.

---

107   Davis, *Problem of Slavery*, 242, quoted in Holt, *Problem of Freedom*, 35.

PART III

―――――――

SEXUALITY, RACE, AND COLONIAL IDENTITIES, 1838–1853

6

Marriage and Family in the Postemancipation Era

Up to the mid-1840s abolitionists and the Colonial Office believed that the inculcation of habits and practices of morality in the slave and later freed population would ensure the success of emancipation. This cultural enterprise would result in the continued refashioning of the moral and self-consciously economic individual. They indicted slavery for having undermined men's sense of responsibility and initiative and pointed to the fact that slavery had proved barren ground for the production of wants which would motivate people to work regularly.[1]

The promotion of those social practices and habits which were believed to reproduce particular kinds of economic relationships become paramount in the postemancipation context at the Cape. While former slaveholders and other settlers looked more to the discipline of labor legislation and the limiting of freed people's economic opportunities to ensure that freed people worked, missionaries and the state were as concerned with issues of culture. They believed, to varying degrees, that the survival of the Cape economy and society would depend as much upon the invisible hand of culture as it would on force. In particular, they looked to marriage to help encode the underlying principles of free labor into civil society.

Both former slaveholders and champions of the ending of slavery shared a perception, however, that having liberated slaves, emancipation would initiate disorder and chaos.[2] Two contradictory ideas coexisted among colonists and colonial officials which paradoxically both reinforced the importance of culture in their plans for the postemancipation world. On the one hand, colonists believed that slaves were without civilization, a group of people on whom ideas could be imposed. On the other, settlers and some government officials both in the colony and in England believed that ex-slaves were potentially rebellious, with ideas that would challenge the premises of

---

1 See *SACA*, "Editorial," 22 January 1840. Dr. John Philip of the London Missionary Society argued in 1828 that raising up the Khoi to "civilization . . . supposes a revolution in the habits of that people, which it requires much time, and the operation of many causes to effect. . . ." Rev. John Philip, *Researches in South Africa; Illustrating the Civil, Moral, and Religious Condition of the Native Tribes . . .* , 2 vols. (London: James Duncan, 1828), 2, 369.

2 See SAL, "Emancipation," *ZA*, 8 April 1831; "Editorial," *ZA*, 22 June 1838; "Zeal and Love," *SACA*, Bound Volume, 7 October 1837; untitled articles, *SACA*, Bound Volume, 8 November 1837 and 20 December 1837.

colonial society. For both these reasons, cultural practice became crucial. If slaves were without civilization, they needed to be taught how to be civilized; if they had alternative ideas of society or civilization, they needed to be reformed.

How freed people imagined family and gender relations, and whether they saw a demarcation of public and private worlds, is difficult to gauge. Certainly the social and geographical landscape of freed people's worlds on the farms and in the villages complicates any evaluation of family within the freed community and skews the neat demarcations of public and private, and the ideas about gender which were being elaborated at the Cape in the course of the nineteenth century. Marriage did not automatically inaugurate the establishment of a nuclear family, and certainly was no guarantee that a couple would live together at the same place in a private domestic sphere.

This chapter examines the debates about marriage and the efforts made by missionaries and officials to promote marriage among freed people from 1839. I argue that freed peoples' lives complicated, although they also sometimes confirmed, the ideologies of family and private life propagated by different colonial groups. Their experiences also force a reexamination of the creation of our evidence. The chapter concludes with an examination of the ways in which the archival record privileges an interpretation of freed peoples' personal lives as being founded in violence and abuse and assesses the extent to which we can use the term patriarchy to describe gender relations within some freed families.

Marriage and Emancipation

In 1838 freed people, colonial officials, and missionaries of various denominations throughout the West Indies and at the Cape, came to agree on one thing: that legal marriage was a rite of emancipation.[3] For the generation of people freed from slavery formal marriage became a central part of their cultural repertoire. Certainly slaves had married during the slave period with such marriages recognized by the community of slaves and unfree laborers long before they received legal recognition.[4] But in a colonial society which generally recognized only legal marriages, freed people married after emancipation in order to secure their relationships and to demonstrate their participation in the world of the free. Ex-slaves also married to create and validate a social world, to signify the freedom to claim a love relationship before a congregation, their community, and God. They married to show their allegiance to a particular church congregation and to show their inclusion in a religious community.[5]

The meanings of marriage and the importance of marriage in conceptualizing freedom arose from very particular gender experiences constituted under slavery. Freed women married in order to help liberate and protect themselves from the pervasive and increasingly racist colonial discourse which represented them as sexually

---

3   See below for contemporary debates as to how to define marriage.

4   I am grateful to Robert Ross for pointing this out.

5   In 1839 a Dutch Reformed Church report on Stellenbosch remarked that "since the abolition of slavery . . . the activities of the missionary in town have increased. Also the religious instruction provided for the heathen is so well attended that too few seats are available. . . ." CA, DRC R1/5, Report on Religion, 1839, 169.

licentious and which therefore reinforced their vulnerability to sexual abuse. Marriage offered slave women a way to gain protection from abuse by securing the legal and social status afforded by being a married and therefore respectable woman. As we shall see in Chapter 8, however, in certain circumstances this mantle of protection could unravel just when a woman might need it most.

Freed men got legally married in part to claim the ties of blood and lineage which had been denied them under slavery. Even if work separated husbands from wives, fathers from children, marriage meant that a man's relationship to his family was recognized by law. And marriage enabled a male laborer to force his employer to recognize the multiple transitions entailed in the abolition of slavery. By being married, a freed man demonstrated his claim to leadership of the familial sphere which lay outside of the master's control, and illustrated his power over his wife and children. For a man, legal marriage helped ratify the masculine rights which had been confirmed by emancipation.

Marriage also had particularly important legal ramifications for fathers. In the immediate postemancipation period, prior to the passing of the Masters and Servants Ordinance of August 1842 which allowed "reputed" parents to have guardianship of their children, marriage was the only way in which men could legalize their paternal rights. In March of 1842, for example, the attorney general argued that a father had no legal right to his illegitimate children and that relatives of a deceased mother had precedence when deciding to whom the children should be given.[6]

In the 1830s and 1840s the Colonial Office generally supported missionaries "in their struggle to build a new society based on the law of God the Father, with marriage and the Christian household at its heart."[7] Reverend W. Robertson of Swellendam, for example, saw marriage as "a powerful stimulus to their acquiring property—binding parents to provide for their children, and being one grand step towards the admission of baptism."[8] The Colonial Office initiated legislation to facilitate marriage, but generally left the active propagation of the institution to the churches. Both missionaries and colonial officials believed that missionaries occupied a crucial place in the postemancipation era as teachers of both morality and hard work to a freed population with little grounding in Christianity.

In 1837 Glenelg, the secretary of state for colonies, sent a circular to the governors of the colonies where slavery was about to be ended saying that reforms should take place to enable ministers to perform marriages. Glenelg stated that

> the great body of Christian Worshippers, are not as in this Kingdom gathered from persons trained from infancy in the profession of Christianity. They are converts from Heathenism and Idolatry. The relation which thus binds the Minister and his people to each other is one of a peculiarly impressive nature and justly gives to the teacher an influence by the right use of which, he can confer the most essential benefits on society at large. To deny to persons occupying such a position the means of promoting a due reverence among

---

6　CA, AG 2616, Report on claim of Job to the guardianship of his reputed wife's children, 14 March 1842. AG stated: "I am of opinion that old Job, as the reputed father of the illegitimate children in question, has, by law, no right to their custody or guardianship. As, by the Dutch law, the mother makes no bastard, the nearest relative by the mother's side is best entitled to the guardianship of the minors."

7　Hall, "In the Name of Which Father?" 23. Also her *White*, Ch. 9.

8　CA, CO 454, No. 81, W. Robertson, Minister at Swellendam, to SG, 15 November 1836.

their converts for the institution of marriage, would be an act, which it would be difficult to say where the impolicy or the irreligion would be the more evident. . . .[9]

However, debates around how to champion marriage in the colony exposed disagreements as to the meaning of marriage and as to whom would most benefit from the institution. The Colonial Office and abolitionists saw marriage as an important civil contract which had moral and religious effects. They supported missionaries' efforts to make marriage more widely available, but framed legislation within the law of secular rather than religious contract.[10] Missionaries primarily perceived marriage as a religious issue and devoted their attention to encouraging marriage among the people on their stations so as to stimulate piety and also increase attendance at their churches. Marriage became a way to bring freed people into the congregation. Some ministers of the Dutch Reformed Church also worried about the Dutch-speaking settlers lack of religious observance and particularly supported efforts to make marriage more freely available to settlers.

At the Cape marriage had been at various times both a religious and a civil ceremony, and, in some respects, predated the trend towards the secularization of marriage which was ratified in Britain in 1837.[11] From 1676 couples had to have their marriages certified as legally valid by a matrimonial court prior to being married in church. In 1804 the Batavian Governor de Mist instituted the civil celebration of marriage by the *landdrost* and two *heemraden* (council members) but this was ended in 1806 when the British permanently took over the Cape. For the next thirty years or so marriages were again solemnized in church.[12] Subsequent legislation in 1818 and 1827 introduced the issuing of special marriage licenses by new matrimonial courts now made up by the magistrate and clerk of the peace on payment of a fee which permitted people to marry without the publication of banns. The matrimonial court registered marriages to ensure that people complied with the civil laws regarding consanguinity. In 1838 ministers of religion remained the only officials who could legally solemnize marriages.[13] Most couples first approached their minister in order to organize the passing of banns and ministers interpreted the law based more on local custom and religious beliefs than legal statute. In the Dutch Reformed

---

9 CA, LCA 8, No. 6, Circular from SSG to Governor, 14 March 1837.

10 Missionaries and other ministers of religion were not merely promoters of the cultural project of imperialism—they brought distinctive perspectives to the colonial experience. Stoler and Cooper, "Tensions of Empire;" Andrew Ross, *John Philip (1775–1851): Missions, Race, and Politics in South Africa* (Aberdeen: Aberdeen University Press, 1986), 34.

11 The 1837 British Marriage and Registration Acts made compulsory the registration of births, deaths, and marriages with a civil authority. Charles, "Name of the Father," 5. For later legal developments see Mary Lyndon Shanley, *Feminism, Marriage, and the Law in Victorian England, 1850–1895* (Princeton: Princeton University Press, 1989).

12 A matrimonial court was established in Cape Town in 1676. Couples had to go the commissioners and demonstrate that they were not contravening any law. After the publishing of banns for three Sundays the couple could be married. Botha, *Collected Works*, Vol. 1, 132–133; R. T. J. Lombaard, *Handbook for Genealogical Research in South Africa* (Pretoria: Human Sciences Research Council, 1977), 87.

13 CA, Government Notice of 20 March 1818, *Cape Town Gazette and African Advertiser*, 21 March 1818. The license allowed a couple to dispense with banns. CA, CCP 6/5/2, Ordinance No. 33 of 1827, "Ordinance for creating Resident Magistrates and Clerks of the Peace in certain Districts and Places in this Colony." For an interpretation of Cape law see CA, A 79, Diary of P. J. Truter, 8 December 1838.

Church ministers generally married people only once they were baptized so that most slaves were excluded from being married in church. In 1834 the synod of the Dutch Reformed Church concluded that ministers should be able to marry unbaptized people provided they had obtained a marriage license through the matrimonial court.[14]

Missionaries in particular worked to make marriage more widely available to the freed population. They generally distinguished between baptized and unbaptized people on their stations, but encouraged people to marry even if it was not legally binding. The regulations of Groenekloof Station in Malmesbury near Cape Town stated that "We consider holy matrimony as an institution of divine origin and of vital importance to the social order. . . ."[15] The Moravians married baptized people in church before the congregation while unbaptized people were married in private by the missionaries. Apart from this distinction, up to 1839, missionaries treated unbaptized couples as if they were legally married. But in 1838 many slaves' and free blacks' relationships were not legally valid and in terms of colonial law their children were illegitimate.

Missionaries therefore petitioned the Colonial Office to rewrite the marriage laws so as to legalize these common-law marriages and to make marriage more widely available to the freed population. In the British West Indies, the Wesleyans worried that while abolition would free people from slavery, it also would emancipate them from relationships which had not had legal sanction. Emancipation might therefore disrupt morality rather than reform it.[16] Cape missionaries received support from ministers in the Dutch Reformed Church who worried about the willingness of some settlers to live outside of marriage. Settlers residing far from magisterial seats, as well as poorer settlers, saw legal marriage as an inconvenience, or too expensive.[17] The Dutch Reformed Churches all over the colony delivered various appeals to the Cape government for reform of the marriage law.[18]

On emancipation, therefore, various colonial officials at the Cape and in the Colonial Office supported revision of the former slave colonies' marriage laws. In 1837 Secretary of State for Colonies Glenelg wrote to the governors of the West Indies and the Cape on the necessity for a "liberal and comprehensive Law, dispelling all doubts respecting the validity of marriages already celebrated by the Missionaries, and removing all obstacles to their solemnizing such contracts hereafter among the

---

14   Various interpretations of colonial marriage law existed even within the Dutch Reformed Church. See CA, CO 485, No. 53, A. Faure to SG, 19 April 1839; CA, CO 454, No. 81, note by AG, 21 November 1836, on back of letter by W. Robertson to SG dated 15 November 1836.

15   "Groenekloof Ordeningen, 1840," I, 23, cited in Ludlow, "Missions and Emancipation," 77; HA, "Diary of Genadendal for 1845," *PA*, XVII, CXCV, (June 1847), 127. Also Raum, "Development," 126, and Ludlow, "Missions and Emancipation," 82. Cape missionaries also encouraged poor people to marry by dispensing with fees to pay for the publishing of banns as was the custom in the Dutch Reformed Church and poor whites in the rural areas therefore tended to marry at the missions. CA, CO 2741, No. 71, Missionary Meyser to CC, George, 18 July 1833.

16   CA, LCA 8, No, 36, Wesleyan Missionary Society, London, to SSC, 24 February 1836.

17   See CA, 1/CAL 21, Eva Dorothea Norman to SG, 29 February 1836; CO 492, No. 45, George Morgan, Minister at Somerset East to SG, 29 April 1840.

18   For example, CA, CO 381, No. 49, Memorial of the Presbytery of Graaff Reinet, 24 April 1830; CO 2471, No. 72, Missionary Meyser to CC, George, 18 July 1833.

Members of their various Congregations."[19] He outlined the concerns which had generated the order in a 1838 letter to Governor Napier:

> On this subject difficulties of the most embarrassing nature have arisen from the ancient Slave Code of the Colonies, and from the low state of Religion and Education which formerly prevailed there. The Negroes were accustomed to form connections which they regarded as matrimonial, although not solemnized according to the Established Rules of Law. The effect is that such ties are sometimes disregarded, and too lightly dissolved—that the parties when religiously observant of them are nevertheless compelled to regard themselves as having lived in Concubinage and that the Offspring . . . are considered as illegitimate. Nor is this all. The paucity of Clergymen in Holy Orders of the Church of England, and the extent to which dissent from the Communion of that Church prevails, render it a matter of great difficulty to contract a legal Marriage. Hence a great comparative disregard of one of the most sacred relations of life, and of the obligations of morality in that respect. The Accompanying Order will be found to provide a remedy for these evils both prospectively and retrospectively.[20]

In September 1838 Glenelg therefore issued a Marriage Order in Council directed at the colonies of British Guiana, Trinidad, St. Lucia, and the Cape and which came into force in the Cape Colony from 1 February 1839.[21] While the impetus for the order came from missionary pressure and this legislation gave missionaries greater powers as regards marriage, it did so, ironically, by making marriage a civil ceremony. At the Cape only ministers of religion had been authorized to solemnize a marriage (except for De Mist's law of 1804). Now, only appointed marriage officers could conduct marriages, and it was as marriage officers that missionaries and ministers were authorized to solemnize marriages. In effect, the Colonial Office made marriage more widely available by enlisting missionaries as part-time civil servants. Marriage officers now had to fill out a form in duplicate detailing for each partner the date of marriage, name, age, status (single or widowed), occupation, whether by banns or special license, and by whom consent was given, keeping the original in the church and sending the copy to the Colonial Office in Cape Town.

The order recognized the de facto marriages of former slaves "which have never been sanctioned by any public ceremony [that is, one sanctioned by settler society] or formally registered," and also allowed children born of those unions to be recognized as legitimate.[22] It explicitly addressed the relationships of former slaves in two ways. It validated any marriage solemnized by a Christian minister prior to emancipation and made specific reference to the marriages of slaves and free blacks. It also provided a grace period of one year whereby slaves who considered themselves married

---

19   CA, LCA 8, No. 36, Circular from SSC to Governor D'Urban with Enclosures, 14 March 1837.

20   CA, GH 1/125, Letter by SSC, 12 September 1838, enclosed in letter to Governor Napier, 31 December 1838.

21   CA, CCP 6/6/1/1, "Marriage Order In Council in force in the Cape from 1 February 1839."

22   Ibid., Sections 35–37. Marriage license fees remained an obstacle to marriage among the poor, and when they did choose to marry, Khoi and free blacks tended to do so in the mission stations rather than the churches where fees put marriage out of their reach. See comments by Missionary Meyser to the civil commissioner of George: "It is an undoubted fact that more marriages take place at our different Stations than at this Village which is chiefly to be attributed to the necessity of paying a sum which they cannot generally afford, and that to a Church with which they have no Connection." CA, CO 2741, No. 72, 18 July 1833.

but had not gone through any formal ceremony, could have their marriage registered and their children legitimated. In this manner, the Colonial Office sought to address the concerns of missionaries to recognize prior relationships, encourage stability, and promote marriage.

The Marriage Order confronted technical difficulties almost immediately since, in asking that people put their Christian names on the form, it implied that the couple were baptized. Reverend Hallbeck came to the conclusion that "as the regards the unbaptized, unless the law be otherwise worded, I see no other way but to postpone their marriage till after baptism."[23] Ludlow suggests that as a result "missionaries followed a conscious policy of not marrying ex-slaves after 1840; or at least of delaying marriage for an extended period."[24] William Robertson of the Dutch Reformed Church in Swellendam complained that many people were cohabiting and that he wanted the law changed so as to allow them to marry also. In 1839 for example he had received an application for marriage

> by the son of a late slave by a Hottentot woman, who therefore was born *free*, and who has been *de facto* married for several years to a free person of color. His Father and two uncles, who were formerly slaves, have been legally married, in accordance with the . . . Article already referred to, and he is anxious to follow their example. I feel a difficulty , however, in consequence of neither of the parties having been in a state of Slavery.[25]

The Cape attorney general defended the specificity of the order saying that the "framers of the order probably conceived that, while the circumstances in which a slave was placed might render him a deserving object of the benefit intended, it would not be possible to place other persons on the same footing, without confounding what, in all probability, was criminal negligence or worse. . . ."[26]

The new Marriage Order encouraged marriages among slaves who had been in permanent unions and made marriage easier in the future for all colonial subjects through the provision of more marriage officers. But the Colonial Office did not seek to redeem those free blacks and settlers who had fallen from grace by living in sin of their own accord. The order also can be seen as being passed in the same spirit as the Masters and Servants Order in Council, issued by the Colonial Office in 1839, which sought to reform the behavior of the working class through coercion and punishment through the medium of contract. While the Marriage Order acknowledged slaves' personal relationships, it distinguished between those deserving indulgence and those deserving punishment. The order only made provision for the legalization of those marriages formed under slavery where at least one member of the couple had been a slave. It did not authorize the legalization of free people's common-law marriages.

---

23   HA, Extracts of letters from Reverend Hallbeck of Genadendal, 24 February 1840, *PA*, XV, CLXVIII (September 1840), 264.

24   Ludlow, "Missions and Emancipation," 83.

25   CA, CO 485, No. 116, Robertson to Colonial Secretary, 20 September 1839. Also see letter by William Robertson to the editor of a newspaper (unnamed), 5 November 1839, in William Porter, *The Porter Speeches: Speeches Delivered by the Hon. William Porter, During the Years 1839–1845 Inclusive* (Cape Town: Trustees Estate and Saul Solomon and Co., 1886), iv–vi.

26   "The New Marriage Law," Opinion of Her Majesty's Attorney General, 25 October 1839, in Porter, *Porter Speeches*, v.

By targeting slaves' personal relationships the order also recalled the moral underpinnings of the antislavery campaigns which had focused on the separation of spouses and the denial of marriage and family as central to the illegitimacy of slavery. In the Marriage Order the Colonial Office authenticated the moral high ground of abolitionism by suggesting implicitly that slaves had had to be rescued from slavery to be enabled to join (European) civilization—signified through marriage, family and wage labor. However, the Khoi, having been rescued by Ordinance No. 50, and other free blacks had had no excuse not to follow the moraland cultural imperatives of European colonialism. They would not be pardoned.[27]

Marriage and Society

The passing of the Cape Marriage Order in February 1839 initiated a great movement of ex-slaves to mission chapels. There, in front of the priest and the congregation couples joined themselves together in freedom.[28] The marriage records of the ex-slaves who were married in the Dutch Reformed Church in Stellenbosch are eloquent testimony to the desires of freed people to legitimate their relationships and their children.[29]

In June of 1839 Jacobus Johannes Lamberts, formerly known as the slave Coridon, married his wife of some twenty years, Francina Catharina de Roos, also formerly a slave of a different owner.[30] The couple had been married already, in the presence of the church elders, in January 1820 and had had nine children. Of those nine, only four were still living at the time of this second marriage: Philda, Sara, Abraham, and Johanna, who was born on 17 January 1839, their first child to be born into freedom. The death of two of the couple's children in April and May of 1839 must have tempered any happiness associated with emancipation and possibly precipitated their marriage in June of 1839. Deborah Johanna Maria Metlzer and Isaac Jacobus Weeber, a former slave, married three months later also under the new marriage order. Like the Lamberts the couple had been married in a religious ceremony in the DRC in 1837 and they seem to have remarried partly to formally legitimate their one child, Magdalena Johanna, who had been born exactly one month after the ending of slavery.[31]

In some areas freed people's desire for nuptial contract was so strong that it had a demonstrable effect on the rural economy. Reverend Hallbeck of Genadendal paradoxically postponed solemnizing marriage "by the consideration that many of these, who are employed on the farms, might have been led to leave their masters at an inconve-

---

27   In the 1840s there was a schism in the LMS in Grahamstown over the issue of whether to marry people who had "lived in sin." I am grateful to Robert Ross for this information.

28   See CL, MS 17 274/1, Register of Marriages, Methodist/Wesleyan Church, Stellenbosch County, 1840–1923. Further research will need to be done on the individual church records in Worcester and Swellendam districts to give further weight to this claim. Marincowitz cites "reports of high marriage-rates among ex-slaves in rural areas" ("Rural Production," 54). Also see Kruger, *Pear Tree*, 197.

29   CA, CO 475, No. 58, Luckhoff, Missionary of Rhenish Society, and Stellenbosch Missionary Society to SG, 12 November 1838.

30   This is the same couple who were involved in the case of the contested adoption discussed in Chapter 5.

31   CA, DRC G2 7/2 30 June 1839; 24 September 1839. See also the following marriages made in terms of the Order in Council of 1838: Martha Elyza Hendriks and Francis Joze, an ex-slave, , 26 October 1839; Benjamin Daniel Alexander and Margritha Francina Abrahamse, 17 December 1839; Hermanus Jacobus Carsten and Florentina Magdalena Jacobse, 26 December 1839; and Robert Charles Griin, a slave, and Jetta Maria Louisa Beer, 22 March 1840.

nient season, if they had been invited to appear here for such a purpose." Nevertheless over a hundred such marriages were performed at Genadendal and at other mission stations up to 1842.[32] It is probable that in the mosques in Cape Town, and in the homes of the Islamic community at the Strand near Somerset West, freed people also solemnized their marriages, though these were not recognized in law until the 1860s.[33]

The marriage records of four congregations in Stellenbosch district provide a case study through which to examine the trends in marriage among the freed population in the aftermath of emancipation.[34] The congregations which form the basis of the study are the Wesleyan mission churches in the villages of Stellenbosch and Somerset West, Raithby mission station in Moddergat, and the freed section of the Dutch Reformed congregation in Stellenbosch village. One of the aims of the Colonial Office and missionaries in passing the Marriage Order had been to make it easier for people to marry. Both individually and together the church records demonstrate that the Marriage Order worked to some extent: the years 1840 and 1841 did witness an increase in marriage over earlier years. However, it is difficult to determine to what extent the Wesleyan and DRC marriage records represent trends in the district as a whole, or in the rural areas of the Western Cape. The *Blue Book* figures suggest much higher marriage numbers than are recorded in the church records I analyzed and do not provide any information on the people who were getting married which makes comparison difficult. In 1840 the *Blue Books* provided figures for divisions rather than districts which were smaller administrative units and in 1840 the tally for Stellenbosch is 404 marriages which constitutes about two-thirds of my total number of marriages for the period 1831–1860. Subsequent *Blue Books* ordered the figures according to "County,

---

32   CA, CO 485, No. 44, Hallbeck to SG, 5 August 1839. Information from the *Periodical Accounts* suggest such a time frame. See also Raum, "Development," 126. At Elim Mission in Caledon between 1839 and 1842 the missionary reported that "fifty couples have been joined in holy matrimony at this settlement, or have had their previous union solemnly confirmed and recognized." Missionaries anticipated "much good from the present regulation, and trust it may be a means of increasing the reverence felt for the marriage bond, as an ordinance of God himself. . . ." HA, "Letter from Brother Genth," *PA*, XVI, CLXXVII (December 1842), 246. At Groenekloof mission station the majority of newcomers who arrived in 1839, most of whom were ex-slaves married shortly after arrival. Ludlow, "Missions and Emancipation," 85.

33   Such evidence was not found in the archives consulted for this book. Act No. 16 of 1860 allowed the government to appoint marriage officers to solemnize Jewish and Moslem marriages. D. Ward, *A Handbook to the Marriage Laws of the Cape Colony, the Bechuanaland Protectorate, and Rhodesia* (Cape Town: Juta, 1906). In the period under review Moslem marriages are not included in the *Blue Books*.

34   For most of the coding I used the classifications indicated on the marriage forms themselves—i.e., whether a person was a widow or single; their age, profession (only men's were recorded), and place of residence and birth. Most of the records did not provide information on birthplace and often residence was ambiguous: e.g., whether a person actually lived in Stellenbosch village or Stellenbosch field cornetcy. I separated both birthplace and place of residence into separate variables coding for country, district, field cornetcy or parish, town or village, and farm, and used the larger geographical area if there was doubt as to whether a person was from Stellenbosch town or Stellenbosch parish. I also coded for racial or ethnic background although at best this can provide only an informed guess. Because I tried to identify those people who were ex-slaves, in this chapter I have used the term "coloured" to indicate people who I could not identify as having been ex-slaves but who belonged to what I have called in other chapters the freed community. I primarily used names as an indicator of race, and coded a number of individuals as unknown if I felt unable to determine the person's race. I used the following values: Khoi; Dutch (Cape); Dutch (Netherlands); English/Scottish/Irish/Welsh; German; coloured (which after 1848 included Khoi, Ex-slave, Prize Negro, and free black unless specifically stated in the record); Prize Negro; Ex-slave where this status was inferred (up to 1848 I guessed this going by name since most of the time people's status was not indicated); Ex-slave where known; African; White; and Children's Friends' Society laborers (where indicated).

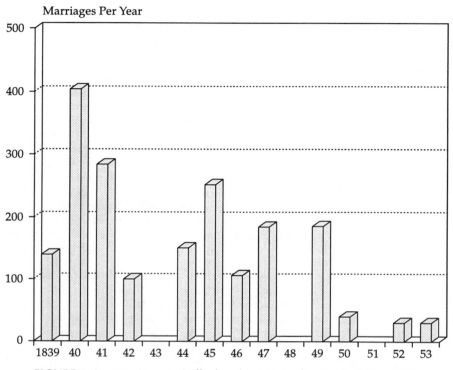

Marriages Per Year

FIGURE 6–1. Marriages in Stellenbosch District, *Blue Books,* 1839–1853

District, or Parish" and while the figures are less startlingly out of line with the numbers of marriages recorded in the Wesleyan and DRC records, discrepancies remain. While some discrepancy could expected given the inaccuracy of nineteenth-century data collection, it does not explain such a wide variation.[35]

Given that in 1838 Stellenbosch district had 5,500 apprentice men, and 4,000 apprentice women, it is clear that many freed people did not marry.[36] Despite the fact

---

35 I did not cover all the churches in Stellenbosch and although I took notes on applications for special licenses I did not include these in the database unless the marriages also were solemnized in the churches I was studying. Some people might have been married in the matrimonial court rather than having their marriage solemnized in church, although cross-referencing suggests that no people of color got married in the matrimonial court, and that the vast majority of Stellenbosch residents who registered their marriage with the matrimonial court also got married in the Dutch Reformed Church. The discrepancy in numbers might arise also from the fact that people from other districts sometimes registered their marriages with the matrimonial court but had their marriage solemnized in another district. The records of the Wesleyan and Dutch Reformed Church should therefore be used with some caution as a baseline for marriage trends in the district and the rural Western Cape as a whole. ASL, CGH, "Return of the Population, and of the Marriages, Births, and Deaths," *Cape Blue Book for 1840,* 229.

36 ASL, CGH, "Return of the Population, and of the Marriages, Births, and Deaths," *Cape Almanack for 1838.* The *Blue Books* do not help one ascertain the relationship between population and marriages in Stellenbosch district since the categories vary between parish, district, and county over the years.

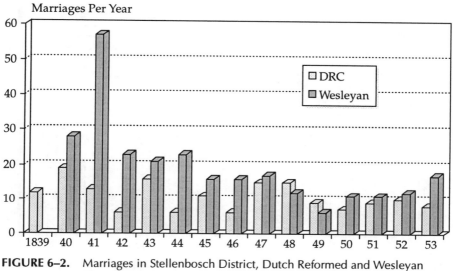

FIGURE 6–2. Marriages in Stellenbosch District, Dutch Reformed and Wesleyan Churches, 1839–1853

that aggregate numbers remained low, substantial data suggests the importance of marriage for the newly free. Freed people who were in relationships not recognized by law married in the aftermath of emancipation; thus people who had children, and who had lived together for many years or had been in a relationship for some time, now married. This accounts in part for the rise in marriages around emancipation since it included both people marrying at the start of a relationship as well as couples well into their forties and fifties.

The records of all the stations demonstrate the stark increase in marriages, particularly in 1840 and 1841, among freed people.[37] At the Wesleyan missions which served the rural working class, marriages in the district increased from just under thirty in 1840 to just under sixty the following year, at the same time that the number of marriages decreased at the Dutch Reformed Church.[38] Emancipation caused an

---

37 Helen Ludlow has shown that at Groenekloof station the number of marriages between newcomers (probable ex-slaves) to the station actually began to fall off as soon as 1840. Possibly people on the established missions were able to take earlier advantage of the Marriage Order, or maybe Ludlow counted religious marriages not sanctioned by law in her figures. Certainly if one breaks down the marriage figures in Stellenbosch district by race and by church it is clear that marriages among the freed population were responsible for this development.

38 The Wesleyan churches made no record of the couple's status, nor did they indicate if the couple were married according to the Order in Council and it is therefore difficult to determine the numbers of ex-slave who might have married there. The Wesleyan records also present a problem in that they only start in 1840 and thus do not document the marriages of freed people who often got married immediately after emancipation. In contrast the Dutch Reformed records indicate when a person had been a slave. Possibly because these records start in 1831 and include 1839, and the year in which ex-slaves were granted the grace period to legitimate their marriages, these records provide us with insight into the slaves who were marrying. However given that the DRC only had a very small free black population in their congregation, the examples of ex-slaves in these records cannot really be taken as representative of all slaves, but they might well be representative of the skilled artisanal class of Stellenbosch village.

Marriages Per Year

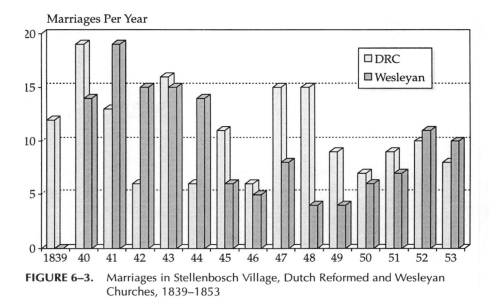

FIGURE 6–3.   Marriages in Stellenbosch Village, Dutch Reformed and Wesleyan
Churches, 1839–1853

unusual number of people to be married in 1840 and 1841. Thereafter the marriages
for the freed population in the district remain above twenty a year until 1848 but do
not reach the high numbers of the early 1840s. The tables for Stellenbosch district
show a decline in marriages among the freed population in the late 1840s.[39] Marriages did pick up again in the early 1850s moving beyond twenty per year among
the "coloured" population.

Marriages possibly declined among freed people off the missions because by the
mid-1840s those ex-slaves who were going to marry had done so, and a new generation was not yet of an age to marry. In the 1840s missionaries in the West Indies and
in the rural Western Cape certainly complained of the supposed moral lapses of their
congregations. Ludlow has suggested that the decrease in marriages in the early
1840s might have resulted from the fact that for those freed people with a "tradition
of unmarried partnerships" many of the meanings of freedom on the mission stations—including gaining access to a house and education for children—could be
increasingly secured without marriage as missionaries realized that they would have
to accommodate freed people's cultural patterns to some extent.[40]

The pattern of marriages at Raithby mission station in Moddergat field cornetcy
illustrates missionaries' influence in encouraging marriage in the early years of a mis-

---

39   For discussion of the British West Indies see Green, *British Slave Emancipation*, 307–308.

40   Ludlow, "Missions and Emancipation," 87. Even so, the Genadendal Diary reported that on 17 August
1845 twelve couples were married who "had already lived together as heathen . . . some of whom were
already grandparents." The records often do not identify if people were ex-slaves, and also often do not say
whether people were being legally married. HA, "Diary of Genadendal for 1845," *PA*, XVII, CXCV (June
1847), 127.

sion's establishment. The station was established in the mid-1840s and marriages were only registered there from 1845.[41] The number of marriages there rose from three in 1845 to six in 1846 and then declined to one in 1847. This substantiates the proposition that people got married both to signify their inclusion in a religious and social community and to enhance their stature in the eyes of the missionaries, so as to receive more benefits, such as access to land. Indeed all the marriages which took place at Raithby in 1845 were of people resident on the station. However, in 1846 people living off the station, but marrying at Raithby, equaled those station residents being married. From then on Raithby marriages of people living on surrounding farms always outnumbered the marriages of station residents.

Clearly the new Marriage Order, however, facilitated marriage among people who had been slaves in Stellenbosch district. Using both the rare instances where the records specified if a person was an ex-slave, and also going by names such as January and February which tended to be slave names (which I used up until 1848 to identify people as probable ex-slaves), a total of thirty-two ex-slaves got married in the period from 1 December 1838 to 31 December 1848.[42] From the end of 1838 through 1848 a total of twenty-one ex-slave men married, while only eleven women did so.[43] The data does not readily suggest who ex-slaves married, since the women's professions are only very rarely provided. There are only three marriages in the records in which both the woman and man were ex-slaves.[44] They all appear in the DRC records in 1839 which suggests that we might find evidence of such marriages in the Wesleyan records from 1838 and 1839.[45] The small number of marriages in which both partners were ex-slaves does confirm the trend under slavery for slaves to form relationships with free blacks and Khoi. Those people whom I guessed were ex-slaves most often married people who I identified as "coloured" although the 131 marriages which took place from emancipation to the end of 1848 where both spouses appear to have been "coloured" probably involved a number of ex-slaves as well.

Where a couple married, and to which congregation they belonged, helped demarcate lines of stratification within the freed population. From 1831 through 1860 298 marriages were solemnized at the DRC in Stellenbosch village involving 523 whites but only 34 people who might have been defined as coloured or free black or ex-slave. In the same period, 341 weddings took place in the Wesleyan congregations but in these cases only 46 people would probably have been defined as White, while 527 probably were "coloured," African, free black, or ex-slaves.

Who were the freed people who married in the DRC? As we have seen during slavery the DRC had a small number of free black members, most of whom artisans. Missionaries regarded baptized free blacks who were already members of the churches as important allies in drawing ex-slaves into the fold. When a man moved

---

41 See Chapter 4 for discussion of the station.

42 The numbers remain the same if one includes the period up to 1860.

43 In the Wesleyan Church 15 freed men got married in comparison with only 8 freed women. In the DRC, 6 freed men married as did 3 women. Until 1848 freed men outnumbered women by about one thousand in the district.

44 CA, DRC, G2 7/2, Jacobus Johannes Lamberts and Francina Catharina de Roos, 30 June 1839; Francis Joze and Martha Elyza Hendriks, 26 October 1839; Hermanus Jacobus Carsten and Florentina Magdelena Jacobse, 26 December 1839.

45 The records I found only started in 1840.

to a new church he would bring with him family members and friends, and if a man had social standing other members of the community might also follow his example and shift their allegiance. In Stellenbosch rather undignified rivalry occurred between the different denominations; for example, between the Stellenbosch Missionary Society and the Wesleyans. In July 1839, Reverend Luckhoff, a Rhenish missionary who worked with the "coloured" chapel of the Stellenbosch Missionary Society complained in his diary that Edward Edwards, the Wesleyan missionary, had lured one "Aleksander" away from the SMS with the offer of a position as sexton at a "good salary."[46] Luckhoff was particularly concerned about the "defection" and the chicanery of Edwards' "agents" because Mr. Alexander had told him that "if my wife and I join the church (the Wesleyan) there are seventeen members of our family who will also join."[47] Luckhoff's concern had some validity: from 1838 through the early 1850s freed people seem to have been more comfortable marrying in the Wesleyan than the Dutch Reformed Church.[48]

The marriage records strikingly demonstrate that freed people from all walks of life got married after 1838. The people who married, and we must remember that many did not, lived on farms in Moddergat, in the field cornetcy between Stellenbosch and Somerset West, at the lower end of Dorp Street and Banhoek Road in Stellenbosch, or in the hamlets such as Alexanderdorp which was probably founded after emancipation.[49] Marriage also did not distinguish between freed men in skilled trades and farm laborers. Over 87 percent of freed men in the marriage records were listed as laborers.[50] Artisans constituted just over 8 percent, while 1.84 percent of freed men who married were farmers. These proportions match the general occupational outline of the freed population who were overwhelmingly engaged in farm labor.

Freed people who married in Stellenbosch district overwhelmingly married people within the same district. Out of the 432 marriages which took place between 1839 and 1853, 373 marriages took place in which both partners lived in the district.[51] Within the district 468 freed people married as compared to only eight who married across district lines. None of the marriages involved freed men from Stellenbosch district, but eight freed women married men from outside Stellenbosch. Five men were from the Cape district and three from Paarl. Three of the women married laborers, while one married a man named Marthinus Andreas—possibly a man of color or maybe an emi-

---

46   The man Luckhoff was referring to was probably either David Fredericus Alexander or Benjamin Alexander, both members of a prominent free black family in the Dutch Reformed Church. CA, DRC G2 6/2, Membership List of 1789–1860, Johannes Alexander, 25 December 1813, and David Pieter Alexander, 4 October 1827. In 1830 Johannes Alexander was an overseer on the farm Klein Ida's Valley. CA, 1/STB 2/31, Testimony of Johannes Alexander in the trial of Adonis for Housebreaking, 28 June 1830. See Chapter 4 for a discussion of the Alexanders with reference to landholding.

47   CA, DRC P 31 1/3, Translation from original Dutch into Afrikaans, of Diary of Luckhoff, 16 July 1839.

48   For example in 1839 45.45 percent of free black artisans married in the DRC, but by the next year that number had fallen to 36.84 percent. Until the end of 1850 the percentage of coloured artisans marrying in the DRC never moved beyond 28.57 percent.

49   D. J. Potgieter, Editor in Chief, *Standard Encyclopaedia of Southern Africa*, Vol. 10 (Cape Town: Nationale Opvoedkundige Uitgewery, 1974), 268, provides information on historic "coloured" areas of Stellenbosch town.

50   After emancipation most freed men in the district continued working as laborers so it is not surprising that unskilled workers constituted the vast majority of freed men who got married.

51   Two hundred fourteen whites married other people within Stellenbosch district as did 426 freed people. I was unable to identify the race of 101 people who were married. Five Africans married also.

grant who farmed in the Cape Flats between Stellenbosch and Cape Town.[52] The other four women married artisans, two of whom lived in nearby Paarl district and two who lived in the Cape district. The presence of artisans in marriages across district boundaries suggests that the social worlds of artisans were larger than those of many farm laborers, but it is striking that no artisans in Stellenbosch married outside of the district.

If freed people and the population in general tended to choose their partners from within the district they also tended to marry within the same local field cornetcy. In 340 marriages out of the 373 involving people who both lived in Stellenbosch district, the couple also came from the same field cornetcy. One hundred sixty-seven whites chose partners from within their field cornetcy and freed people also overwhelmingly married people from the same field cornetcy: 411 did so.[53] This applied whether a man was a laborer or an artisan. Out of the 183 freed men who were laborers in the district 177 married women from their field cornetcy while 16 out of the 18 artisans did so also. The partners whom freed women and men chose to marry were very likely to live in the same small area within Stellenbosch district, even on the same farms.[54]

However, the records do camouflage the mobility between town and countryside and mission and farms that are revealed in other records. It is possible that the marriage records indicate greater homogeneity among residence than might have been the case. When laborers married the missionary possibly noted the place where they worked as their field cornetcy of residence: if a woman or man lived on a farm during the week, or was living in a field cornetcy in harvest time so as to work on the farms, then that would probably have been recorded as her or his permanent place of residence.

If freed people generally married other people who lived or worked in their neighborhood then one can surmise that they probably married people of very much the same status as themselves. This is impossible to chart since the records do not indicate women's occupation. This highlights the pervasive assumption in colonial legislation that men's identity was framed by work, and women's merely by their marital status—the records do indicate if an individual was single or had been widowed. As in colonial labor legislation of this period, race was not mentioned in the marriage records and it is very difficult even to estimate to what extent people married according to notions of racial status and identity, although putative racial categories were clearly crucial in postemancipation society in determining access to jobs and social standing.[55] The following discussion is thus a very faint sketch of the possible relationships between whites and freed people in the postemancipation period.

---

52 CL, MS 17 274/1; Andreas married Aletta Johanna Magdelena Gorridon on 27 October 1840.

53 I did not include in these calculations the five Africans who married within the field cornetcy. For ninety-seven people I could not identify the field cornetcy.

54 The records were very vague for any residence below that of the field cornetcy. For example, the residences of 339 people out of the 373 people resident in Stellenbosch district were unknown at the level of the town. Thirty-two people married other people within the same village or town. Of these 9 were white and 18 were coloured. Of those 10 marriages in which we can identify the farm on which they lived, 8 men were laborers and 2 were farmers.

55 I coded 115 people as being of unknown race when I felt unable to even guess at their possible racial identity.

Using names as index of race, a *very* imprecise marker, in Stellenbosch district the vast majority of people married within racial categories. Eighty-seven percent of the marriages which took place between December 1838 and December 1853 involved people whom I expect in the mid-nineteenth century would probably have been seen as belonging to the same race.[56] Where people married across racial boundaries they were most likely to be white men marrying "coloured" women: seven men did so. I found only one record where a "coloured" woman married someone I could clearly identify as white or African: In December 1846 Sarah Titus of Moddergat married Moravi, also of Moddergat, who most likely had been a Prize Negro, or who had come from Xhosaland to work in the Western Cape.[57]

Interracial marriages generally involved people of the laboring class. Five of the seven men I identified as white who married women who seemed to be "coloured" were laborers.[58] There is some indication in the marriage records that laborers brought out by the Children's Friend Society in the 1830s married "coloured" women and probably became absorbed into the freed community. In 1862 the CFS children "had almost forgotten their language . . . they are mostly associated with the coloured classes."[59] In July 1843, Henry Mullins, "an Apprenticed laborer" and most likely a CFS child, married Styntje Nell. Ms. Nell was illiterate but Mullins was able to write his name.[60] The remaining two white men who married "coloured" women were a farmer and an artisan. William Smith farmed at Hottentots Holland, and in October 1845, aged twenty-two, he married Johanna Zijster, who had to get her parents' permission since she was only nineteen.[61] Edward Sheen, a wagon maker in Stellenbosch married Rozina Elizabeth Hercules on 8 March 1852.[62]

White laborers probably married freed women without too much social cost, particularly as their lives were already so intertwined with those of the freed people with whom they lived and worked. However, marrying a "coloured" woman limited a white man's social and economic mobility. In 1847, for example, the clerk of the peace at Paarl wrote to his Stellenbosch counterpart about one William Allchin, a cooper and wheelwright, who seems to have been applying for a contract in Stellen-

---

56   That is, 376 out of 433 marriages. Fifty-seven marriages involved people who would probably have been seen as being of different races. It must be emphasized that the race of individuals was derived from the names which can only be used as a very rough guide. The observations are therefore very tentative.

57   CL, MS 17 274/1, No. 3, 22 December 1846.

58   CL, MS 17 274/1, No. 133, Henry Mullins married Styntje Nell, 18 July 1843; No. 154, Mark Bryant of Fishhoek married Sophia Eilders of Hottentots Holland, 17 February 1844; No. 140 Patrik Cummings married Eva Leyman, 10 November 1843; No. 190, Henry Binden married Katharina Kavel at Raithby on 8 June 1846; No. 205, John Norman married Julina Afrika at Raithby on 22 August 1847. Another seven marriages involved white men who married women whose race I felt unable to even guess at. Eleven marriages involved coloured men and women of "unknown race." It is possible that these were also interracial marriages.

59   Marincowitz, "Rural Production," 138. In 1858 Robert Blake, a CFS child, married Katryn Jan. Both lived at Stellenbosch Flats. CL, MS 17 274/1, No. 331, 5 January 1858. For information that he was part of the CFS scheme see 1/STB 4/1/1/4, No. 657, Criminal Record Book, 27 March 1840. On the Society see Edna Bradlow, "The Children's Friend Society at the Cape of Good Hope," *Victorian Studies* (Winter 1984): 155–177.

60   CL, MS 17 274/1, No. 133, 18 July 1843. In 1864 another Henry John Mullens [*sic*] aged twenty-one married a Christina Adams in Stellenbosch. Possibly this man was the son of Henry Mullins. MS 17 274/1, No. 411, 10 May 1864.

61   CL, MS 17 274/1, No. 177, 19 October 1845.

62   CL, MS 17 274/1, No. 266, 8 March 1852.

bosch. The clerk of the peace noted that while Allchin was healthy and could earn a good living, he had "unfortunately married a woman of color."[63]

The marriage records from the churches in Stellenbosch district indicate that laboring men married as did their artisanal counterparts, and that freed people tended to marry people who lived in the same field cornetcy as themselves. The marriage records, and the archives in general, are silent on the processes whereby freed people chose to get married, or why they chose thepartners they did, and how that decision was imbedded in wider networks of community approval and sanctions. It is difficult to ascertain to what extent marriage featured in the construction of a household economy. The archives are silent on how people met, or how long freed people tended to know each other before they decided to marry. We also have no real information as to what role parents played in selecting their childrens' spouses. People probably met at work, at the canteens, and on the roads between the farms.

We might imagine that a laborer living in Stellenbosch village met a man on the farm where she was working during February picking grapes. He waited with the wagon at the end of the row of vines while she and other women and children picked the grapes and put them into the baskets on their backs. Maybe they shared the break periods when a laborer came back from the house with the food and the wine in a basket at two ends of a pole. At the end of the season they continued seeing one another and shared Sundays when he would visit her in the room which she shared with other men and women in Stellenbosch village. On Saturday evenings she would meet him at the canteen just outside of Stellenbosch where they would socialize with other laborers. Maybe now and then they would meet at Raithby where sometimes they saw couples married before the congregation. After a few years they decided it would be good to marry—her mother and father had done so when they were freed.

The Geography of Family

The postemancipation landscape did not easily facilitate the establishment of that mythic patriarchal family which the *South African Commercial Advertiser* had invoked in its lecture to freed men on 1 December 1838. Many people continued to live apart from their families and laborers again crisscrossed the Western Cape visiting their children and their loved ones. Even on the missions which promoted nuclear families as the bedrock of society, husbands and wives were separated with women and children remaining on the stations while men worked on the farms.

Even for those people who were able to live permanently with their families their definition of family did not necessarily coincide with that of the missionaries who had propagated marriage so extensively. Many freed people never married, and while their children accepted the idea of marriage perhaps more than their parents, the marriage records suggest that marriage was not very widespread among the rural poor through the mid-nineteenth century. While freed people appear to have distinguished between family members, friends, and community it is unclear whether they perceived the nuclear family as forming an inner circle of family members or whether members of the wider family network all constituted part of this circle. The attorney

---

63   CA, 1/STB 22/43, CP, Paarl to CP, STB, 19 February 1847.

general remarked in 1853 that inhabitants of Genadendal gave a "liberal construction to the term 'family'" which might include nieces, aunts, and other relatives.[64] Freed people privileged kin relationships but these affiliations were constituted within close relations with other members of the working class. Across the Western Cape freed people reshaped their social worlds using materials gleaned from their own histories, as well as from the cultural models offered by missionaries and the state.

The places to which freed people had moved in 1838 helped mold ideologies and practices of gender relations in rural laboring culture. On the missions, missionaries explicitly used architecture and control of access to resources to encourage particular family and gender formations.[65] Missionary societies saw in physical architecture the reflection of an inner morality, and believed that certain spatial arrangements facilitated the development of civilization.[66] The Moravian regulations stated that each inhabitant had to have a house and "the erection of substantial houses" was "strongly recommended."[67] To ensure this, missionaries tried to provide newcomers with materials to build a house and start a garden. Teutsch remarked in 1843 that

> We grant a premium, amounting to £1.17s.6d for every walled house that is erected by a Hottentot inhabitant of our settlements. The encouragement and help afforded, have been of the utmost service, especially since the emancipation of the slaves in 1838. Many of these poor people who flocked to our settlements on obtaining their freedom, and proved themselves by their industry & good conduct to be well worthy of encouragement would have been quite unable to provide for themselves and their families with decent habitations, but for the help afforded them.[68]

At Genadendal missionaries encouraged the building of European-style architecture as opposed to huts made of reed and mud by making only people who lived in walled houses eligible for public office.[69]

Missionaries propagated the benefits of familial structures.[70] They also helped inscribe particular gender relations within the family by giving men authority over women. Single women did not qualify for houses; their access to housing depended upon connection to a man either through being a daughter, or a wife, or widow. A similar philosophy probably guided housing allocation on the London Missionary Society stations. In 1849 J. J. Freeman, the home secretary of the LMS, remarked of

---

64   CA, AG 2620, Report on Genadendal Burgher Levy, 14 March 1853. Freed people did talk of fathers, mothers, grandparents, and aunts, and distinguished them from friends. See for example, CA, 1/SWM, 2/26, No., 6, Documents in the trial of Andries Koller and Anna Koller for Murder and Incest, 14 December 1841; 1/SWM 16/27, CP, Cape Town, to CP, SWM, 23 November 1843. Robert Ross says that Genadendal missionaries made the standard Dutch distinction between *familie* or extended family, and *gezin* which was the nuclear family. Personal communication, 1 February 1994.

65   See J. J. Freeman, *A Tour in South Africa, With Notices of Natal, Mauritius, Madagascar, Ceylon, Egypt, and Palestine* (London: John Snow, 1851), 26; Comaroff and Comaroff, *Of Revelation*; Raum, "Development," Ch. 9.

66   Crais, *White Supremacy and Black Resistance*, 100–104. Philip devoted numerous pages in his polemic *Researches* to the types of houses in which people lived. Sayles, *Coloured Community*, 85.

67   ASL, CGH, S.C. 11., 1854, "Rules and Regulations of the Institution at Genadendal, revised 1827," 38–39.

68   HA, "Letter from Teutsch," *PA*, XVI, CLXXXI (December 1843), 462–63.

69   Van Ryneveld, "Merchants and Missions," 49.

70   Raum argues that on the Moravian stations the family was one of the most significant elements of the community. "Development," 125.

Zuurbraak that "no females live in houses by themselves; all the houses are occupied by married couples and their families."[71] The mission communities did provide much greater support for family life than many people had experienced under slavery. In 1849 those newcomers who were still at Groenekloof mission in Malmesbury averaged 2.8 children per couple thus "producing larger families than slave women at any time prior to emancipation."[72] It is unclear to what extent the Moravians' hopes of facilitating nuclear families through the provision of a house for each household head worked in practice. Glimpses from the archival records suggest that in general nuclear families lived in individual houses but that other relatives were welcomed for lengthy stays.[73]

But even where nuclear families existed the ideal of the patriarchal unit existed more in theory than practice. The Moravians would have preferred people on the stations not to work for farmers because that exposed them to alcohol which was prohibited on the stations, and because people had to share rooms which the Moravians felt led to immorality.[74] Especially from the 1840s when men increasingly had to work on the farms in order to generate income, women headed many of the mission households in practice and husbands visited only on the weekends.[75]

Off the stations people could not easily create a private domain of the nuclear family even if they wanted to do so. Particularly on the farms architecture did not often operate as a boundary between work and home, or between family and community. Most farm laborers lived on the place where they worked, their rooms in sight of the main house. Workers lived in extremely close proximity to their fellow workers and their peers, frequently sharing rooms with others. Klara Bantom, who worked on the farm Koelenhof in Bottelary field cornetcy near Stellenbosch shared a room—which served as a place to sleep, eat, and rest—with a number of other laborers.[76] On some farms workers did not have any room they could call their own: the Holms of Frenchhoek made their servant Eva sleep in the pantry.[77] And sometimes laborers were segregated by sex even if they were married or involved with other people. Samuel, who was employed on the farm of a J. I. de Villiers of Koelenhof (probably a relation of Klara Bantom's employer), lived in the "men's apartment" even though his wife worked on the same farm.[78]

---

71 Freeman, *Tour in South Africa*, 26.

72 HA, *PA*, XVI, CLXXV (June 1842), 134; *PA*, XVI, CLXXXII (March 1844), 518; Ludlow, "Missions and Emancipation," 99–100; see also Kruger, *Pear Tree*, 298.

73 For example, in 1842 Wilhelmina Nooman and her husband Librecht Valentyn shared their house with, among others, her nephew Wilhelm Nooman who had lived with them for some time. CA, 1/CAL 1/1/1, Preliminary examination into charges that Librecht Valentyn assaulted Wilhelmina his wife, 16 March 1842.

74 Raum, "Development," 79.

75 Reverend Kuhn visited Genadendal to investigate outbreaks of typhoid and his investigations indicate the ongoing presence of extended family arrangements some thirty years after emancipation. CA, 1/CAL 4/1/1/1, Kuhn to RM, 18 August 1865.

76 CA, 1/STB 22/37 Statement of Klara Bantom before Justice of the Peace, 19 September 1839. See also 1/STB 22/38, Statement of Rachel to Clerk of the Peace, 1 April 1842; CSC 1/1/1/15, No. 7, Preliminary statement of Dina Jacobs, 6 March 1855, in Trial of Steyn for concealing the birth of her child, 1 May 1855.

77 CA, CO 503, No. 53, Justice Kekewich to Governor Napier regarding the trial of Galant for murder, 14 June 1841.

78 CA, 1/STB 2/37, Preliminary statement of Samuel, 15 April 1840, in documents in the trial of Josephus and Alie for cellar breaking and theft . . . , 1 July 1840.

In the records, freed people mention sharing beds (or more often sacks on the ground) very casually which suggests that this too was a common phenomenon. Bella Agulutz of Genadendal mission station, who worked on farms in Worcester district, recalled that at Rietfontein farm the laborers sometimes shared beds, while in Swellendam, Zetje October, aged fourteen, said that she always shared a bed with her aunt. An African laborer in Goudini near Worcester town stated that he shared a room with a married couple as well as two other laborers.[79] On some farms employers continued to reproduce the living patterns of slavery as well as, perhaps, the sexual exploitation. In 1842, Dirk Cornelis Laurens, a farmer in Swellendam, made an eight-year-old servant girl sleep in his bedroom at night.[80]

People who were employed by wealthier farmers secured greater degrees of privacy and separation of home from work. Adriaan Cloete of Schoongezicht farm outside Stellenbosch rented out rooms in the back of his house in Stellenbosch to his former male slaves and their families—probably as a way of inducing the men at least to remain in his employ. The women appear to have stayed in town while the men worked on the farm.[81] In the villages families also might have their own room: in these cases, walls and doors, formal architecture, demarcated the limits of family and the community. Laborers renting rooms at the back of whites' houses might secure a room for one family but living conditions were still cramped and people shared meals, washing places, and social space.[82] For most laborers the villages did not offer much more privacy than the farms.

Postemancipation Patriarchy?

By 1838 all members of Cape society had participated in the creation of a colonial world in which gender relations were a key constituent. The belief that men had ultimate power in the family and in society at large was widespread and legally enforced in most societies in the Atlantic world, and certainly at the Cape in the nineteenth

---

79 "One night we were all sleeping in one bed, I at one end and Kronenberg at the other, and Rosetta . . . and her mother in the middle." CA, 1/CAL 1/1/3, Statement of Bella Agultz, 28 March 1857 in Documents regarding the preliminary examination in the case of David Kronenberg for assault, 28 March 1857. CA, CO 708, No. 86, Preliminary statement of Klaas, 6 November 1857, in letter from Justice Cloete to Governor Napier, enclosing documents in the trial of Bymen Toontjes for murder, 18 December 1857. See also CA, 1/STB 2/37, No. 11, Preliminary Statement of Jan Roos, 3 October 1840, in documents in the trial of Damon and Piet Arries . . . 1 July 1840. See 1/SWM 16/27 Testimony of District Surgeon, 27 October 1843, CP, Cape Town, to CP, SWM, 23 November 1843.

80 CA, 1/SWM 2/26, No. 17, Preliminary examination of Franscina Louw for murder, 26 April 1842. See also 1/SWM 2/29, Statement of Johanna Susanna Kannemeyer, 15 April 1846, in letter from CP, Cape Town, to CP, SWM, 31 August 1846.

81 It is unclear if the men lived on the farm and returned to town on weekends or if they traveled from the village to the farm each day. CA, 1/STB 22/37, Statements by Dina, and Adriaan Cloete, 7 March 1840, in preliminary examination regarding Dirk alias Vogel . . . for theft of Stretcher.

82 The Laubin family for example lived on Mr. Philip Haupt's premises in Stellenbosch village with the parents and a number of children sharing one room in a complex with another worker who "was in the habit of coming into" their room. CA, CSC 1/1/1/15, Documents relating to the Trial of Willem Africa for Rape in Bills of Indictment presented to the Grand Jury on the Criminal Session of the Supreme Court on 1 November 1855. See also 1/WOC 2/16, Preliminary examination of October and Regina Johanna Hendrietta for assault on Doortje October, 13 January 1858; CA, 1/STB 22/45, CP to J. N. de Villiers of Paarl, 13 October 1838.

century. It is not surprising that most freed men and many women shared this assumption to some extent. For women freedom from slavery did not necessarily entail liberation from violent assault on their persons, either by the men they married or lived with or by men in colonial society in general. Freedom did not necessarily erase personal and social demons.[83]

But talking of patriarchy within the culture of the rural poor perhaps misrepresents the sense of powerlessness which could lead to murder of a spouse. Emancipation also liberated freed people into a society in which the power of representation, the power to generate wealth, and the power to incarcerate, was heavily laden on the side of settlers including members of the former master class. Any story of gender relations within freed families therefore is also a story of how the archives themselves delineate a patriarchal and gendered narrative of emancipation which represents groups of people as differently located within the colonial moral economy of the nineteenth-century Western Cape.[84]

In daily life people on the farms and the missions spent a great deal of time in the company of others. Precisely because freed people lived in such close proximity to one another—sharing houses, rooms, and beds—they staked claims to personal relationships through particular patterns of social interaction. How could one show that one was married, how could one signify special intimacy in a situation in which rooms, beds, utensils were shared by so many? The records suggest that the exclusive bonds between husbands and wives in rural laboring culture in the Western Cape were defined and made evident both to the partners and outsiders by language, the cooking of meals, the serving of food, and sexual relations. A wife's subordination to her husband also appears to have served as a crucial marker of the boundary between a married couple and other laborers in some farm communities.[85] If a woman cooked food especially for her partner or served him before others, or if she made his bed, she indicated the importance of her relationship with him. If he called her 'wife' he too signified its importance. Exclusive sexual relations between a man and woman also signified to members of the community the importance of that relationship.[86]

In the era of legal freedom, it is through the criminal records of domestic abuse, assault, and murder that we gain access to relations between husbands and wives. These archives give eloquent testimony to the success of the former master class in

---

83   For gender relations at the Cape see Bradlow, "Women at the Cape." On freed families in the U.S. South see Jones, *Labor of Love*, 103–105, and particularly Nell Irvin Painter, "Soul Murder and Slavery: Toward a Fully-Loaded Cost Accounting," in Linda Kerber et al., eds., *U.S History as Women's History: New Feminist Essays* (Chapel Hill: University of North Carolina Press, 1995).

84   See below. Also Spivak, "Can the Subaltern Speak"; and Scott, "Evidence of Experience."

85   Hans Medick and David Warren Sabean, "Interest and Emotion in Family and Kinship Studies: A Critique of Social History and Anthropology," in *Interest and Emotion*, 9–29.

86   CA, CO 537, Chief Justice Wylde of the Circuit Court of Swellendam to Governor Napier regarding the trial of Noortje for culpable homicide, 7 September 1844. In 1841, a woman named Delie was killed by her husband, Galant, a laborer in Frenchhoek, when she refused to make his bed. His employer, a Mrs. Holm, said that he and "Delie had been in our service for about two months, she appeared to be about 19 years of age, she and Prisoner appeared to live well together, I never heard them quarrel." CA, CO 503, No. 53, Testimony of Mrs. Johanna Catharina Holm in the report on the trial of Galant for murder held at the Circuit Court, Stellenbosch, 14 June 1841, sent by Judge Kekewich to Governor Napier, 14 June 1841. See also 1/STB 2/35, Documents in the trial of Robert McClane, laborer for assault with intent to murder his wife, 15 May 1837.

using the rule of law to continue the subordination of the freed communities of the Western Cape.[87] Our knowledge of the life of freed people in general, and particularly of relations between husbands and wives, lovers, grandparents and grandchildren, is gleaned through those cases where relationships were rendered problematic, their flaws and instability exposed.

Like the records on rape which are examined in the final chapter, the records documenting violence among the rural poor produce their own history of colonial rule. Violence was endemic in Cape society and was a key social language in the postemancipation era. The criminal record books for Caledon and Stellenbosch list numerous incidents of violence by employers against servants, and between various members of the rural poor.[88] However, violence within the family was not equally surveilled: the criminal records document abuse and all levels of violence within the working-class family and are almost totally silent as regards tensions within wealthier white families. The criminal records produce and reproduce the "fact" of violence and degeneracy within poor families and the "fact" of harmony and support within settler families. The archives also suggest how social space demarcated areas of acceptable and unacceptable activity.

Examples of domestic violence among settler families emerge almost solely in civil cases for divorce or separation.[89] The fact that magistrates documented numerous cases of domestic abuse (termed assault) involving members of the rural poor in the Western Cape but recorded none involving members of the settler elite suggests that officials consented that such behavior only required regulation when it involved members of the working class (in this case both whites and blacks) or perhaps when it occurred in the public domain.[90] The very notion of privacy within the household was always rather ambiguous at the Cape where Cape Dutch architecture with rooms leading into one another challenged the strict separation of public and private areas marked off by corridors and sealed rooms in English houses, for example.[91] In other respects, however, the architectural landscapes of emancipation effectively helped produce and criminalize certain kinds of behavior. The key division that applied was between incidents which happened within a house or dwelling and those which occurred in public urban or rural space. The fact that so many freed people did not have a domestic space exposed them to the regulation by the state in the public sphere: many of the domestic abuse cases arose precisely

---

87   Scully, "Criminality and Conflict."

88   Between 1843 and 1849 the magistrate of Caledon recorded 608 criminal cases ranging from drunkenness to murder. Of those, 110 involved drunkenness and 159 involved some sort of assault. 98 men were charged with assaulting other men, and 38 involved men assaulting women. Only 6 were clearly cases involving spouses. CA 1/CAL 1/2/1, Criminal Record Book. See also 1/STB 4/1/1/4, Criminal Record Book.

89   Domestic abuse within white families is not documented in the criminal records of the Cape archives. One has to read between the lines of civil suits for divorce and separation to learn that white middle-class men hit their wives. Tensions within middle-class families also emerge in suits over property, wills, and breaches of promise to marry. The volumes of civil cases in the Cape Supreme Court are filled with such suits. See especially CSC 2/1/1/9–86.

90   CA, CSC 2/1/1/60, No. 21, Agnes Barrow born Osmond vs. Thomas Pownall Pellew Barrow, 8 June 1848; CSC 2/1/1/64, Maria Elsje Aletta Pretorius vs. Johannes Lodewicus Pretorius, 28 February 1850.

91   I am grateful to Robert Ross for helping me with this discussion of social spheres.

because a couple had been fighting in public and a constable charged the man with assault.[92]

Women rarely initiated a complaint and most often retracted the charge. But women did also use the law as a means of restraining violent men. In 1845 Sarah Paulson, who was about four months pregnant, complained about her husband after he hit her on the road to Stellenbosch on their return from work on the farm of Willem Adriaan van der Byl in Paardeberg. Ms. Paulson stated that

> Prisoner has often beaten and ill-treated me before during the 2 years I have lived with him, but I tried to keep him in check by threatening to complain . . . when he would promise to behave more kindly to me . . . and this morning he begged me to withdraw the complaint against him which I was willing to do.[93]

By prosecuting domestic abuse only when it occurred in public judicial officials maintained the fiction that freed people could participate in the creation of a domestic domain where abuse was a private affair. Officials therefore made legitimate the notion of a dichotomy between private and public. In 1848 the attorney general stated that "a man may be committed for assaulting his wife; but it will be discreet in the Justice not to resort to such a step, unless in of some enormity."[94] The concept of a domestic sphere also justified intervention into the lives of those people whose behavior seemed inappropriate (e.g., people should not fight in public, but in private where such outbursts belong) thus perpetuating stereotypes of the unruly underclass which led to more interference and monitoring, and added legislation governing other parts of their lives.

A history of abuse and brutality under slavery did reproduce itself to some degree in social violence after 1838, perhaps most particularly among people on the farms whose lives had changed the least of all after emancipation.[95] Living conditions in which many people shared a room if not a bed, were constantly around one another either at work or in the room, and rarely had a moment to themselves probably exacerbated tensions between spouses. The widespread practice of the tot system—giving wine as part of the wage—which increased with the ending of slavery as a means of keeping laborers on the farms also probably contributed to the level of violence in underclass society. Tensions between husbands and wives in laboring culture arose precisely in those symbolic practices which identified people's intimate relations with one another. Willem Noortje of Swellendam, for example, had "desired his wife—two or three times—to find his hat—and after her not readily attending to

---

92 For example, CA, 1/STB 4/1/1/4, No. 920, 13 June 1842; No. 960, 6 October 1842; 1/STB 22/41, Preliminary statements to the CP in the case of Dirk Hartzenburg for assault, 25 December 1845; 1/STB 4/1/1/1/4, No. 1547, 5 February 1846.

93 CA, 1/STB 22/41, Preliminary statement to the CP in the case of Dirk Hartzenberg for assault, 25 December 1845. For another case in which a woman brings the charge see 1/STB 4/1/1/4, No. 2347, 13 August 1849.

94 CA, AG 2618, AG to JP, Wellington, 9 November 1848.

95 For a discussion of violence in the slave family and the need to historicize family violence see Mason, "Fit for Freedom," Ch. 7; and Painter, "Soul Murder." See also CA, 1/CAL 21, Letterbook of JP, 26 May 1834; 19 February 1835; 27 August 1835; 1/WOC 19/28, Draft of Proceedings in Slave Cases, Amelia vs. Nicolaas Smit for assault, 14 April 1835; 1/STB 2/35, Documents in the trial of Robert McClane, laborer for assault to murder his wife, 15 May 1837. Certainly farmers continued to be brought to court for inflicting violence against their servants. CA, 1/STB 4/1/1/4–5, Criminal Record Books 1838–1865.

his request, had taken up a stick . . . and had given his wife 2 or 3 strokes with it. . . ." Willem T'Gontinie also beat his wife. He beat her with a quince stick after she had given him food which was not to his satisfaction and she died of her injuries.[96] Husbands' jealousy and suspicion of their wives' infidelity appears frequently in the documents of domestic abuse. This suggests both that sexual relations were regarded as an important element of a relationship between a couple and that freed men possibly shared in and contributed to the characterization of black women as sexually licentious. Women frequently bore the brunt of the anger even if they had been subject to unwanted sexual advances. One Galant tried to have sex with a married woman, but it was her husband who ended up beating her, not Galant.[97]

A case from Tulbagh painfully illustrates relations within one freed family shortly after emancipation and is a cautionary tale to the historian who might romanticize freedom only as a triumph. Too many women and too many men found themselves in painful situations framed by poverty, emotional fragility, and few of the blessings which emancipators had envisioned so optimistically for slaves. In 1841 Dirk Frederik was sentenced to death for the murder of his wife, Fyjte. The couple had lived at Pienaar's Kloof in the Achterste Omtrek of the Cold Bokkeveld, one of the more remote regions of what had been a part of Worcester district. Fytje and Dirk Frederik had worked as a cook and a shepherd for Sina Harmse and her husband Jacobus Marthinus Piel.[98] The Piels also owned another farm called Vaal Fontyn. At the trial Miggel Strydom, a laborer who had been working at Vaal Fontyn recalled that in the beginning of the previous winter he had been working for Piel at the farm Vaal Fontyn. On his way back from an errand at Pienaar's Kloof, where Mrs. Piel and her daughter were residing, he had met Dirk Frederik who asked her where his wife had slept when she had last been at the farm. Strydom told Frederik that the first night Fytje had slept with his wife, but that on the second night she had slept at a different house where three men also slept. He had visited there late that night, and found that she had fainted. Strydom said that he had helped her to recover. On hearing this, Frederik became angry and said he "knew what kind of fainting it was, and that if I came to Pienaar's Kloof again I would not see him nor his wife . . .[99]

Once he had gone to that farm, Frederik did try to shoot his wife. Mrs. Piel sent her daughter on horseback to Vaal Fontyn to collect Mr. Piel, while their son Carl wrestled the gun away from Frederik. The testimony continued, "Prisoner then went to the round house, & brought from there his *keerie* [stick] and his horse whip. The *keerie* was a bamboo, about the length of his arm, and as thick as my waist. . . ."[100] Frederik started to hit Fytje, and on Mrs. Piel begging him to stop, he said, "Mistress

---

96   CA, CO 537, Chief Justice Wylde of the Circuit Court of Swellendam to Governor Napier regarding the trial of Noortje for culpable homicide, 7 September 1844; 1/SWM 2/26, Documents in the trial of Willem T'Gontinie for murder of his wife, or reputed wife Mietje, 21 April 1841.

97   CA, CO 589, Written report of proceedings in trial of Johannes alias Johannes Galant, convicted of murder at Circuit Court held at Swellendam on 15 May 1849, enclosed in letter from Justice Menzies to Governor Harry Smith, 22 May 1849.

98   Ms. Harmse's names suggest that she was possibly of Khoi or slave descent.

99   CA, CO 503, Justice Menzies to Governor George Napier submitting report in Writing of all proceedings of Trial of Dirk Herdy, alias Dirk Fredrik, held at Circuit Court 1 November 1841 at Tulbagh for murder of Reputed Wife Fytje on 29 April 1841 at FC of Achterste Omtrek of Cold Bokkeveld, 1 November 1841.

100   Ibid.

go away, or if I hurt you, you must not complain of my hurting you; She was his wife, and he would beat her until she was dead. . . ." A little while later Mrs. Piel said she had seen Dirk Frederik go to the water and fetch some in an old pot. He washed Fytje, who was now lying on the ground, with water. Mrs. Piel said, "[He] wet a handkerchief and placed it over her face. I went into the house, & then I came out again. Prisoner was gone. . . . I went up to her and called Fytje! Fytje! but received no answer. . . ." Mrs. Piel said that on the day before he had beaten his wife she had heard Frederik say that he was going to kill his wife and would go to Port Natal.

About a week afterwards Frederik came to the kitchen at Pienaar's Kloof where Miggel was sitting with his wife. He was carrying a gun and asked for something to drink. Miggel Strydom recalled that Frederik "said that he felt very sorry he had killed his wife—that he had no night's rest—and that even the birds persecuted him, so that he could not get a night's rest."[101]

Conclusion

In the decade from 1838, many stories can be written of the lives that freed women and men constructed after the ending of slavery. Some people lived on mission stations with strict regulation of relationships and sexuality. Others lived out freedom on the same farms on which they had been slaves, and in conditions which did not easily facilitate the creation of a "private sphere." Yet whether married or unmarried, living on missions or villages, or on farms, freed people rendered freedom an intensely personal experience.

For many ex-slaves family and liberty were embedded in community relationships in which friends and fellow workers shared rooms, living space, and social activities. As we have seen emancipation also inaugurated an era of attention by colonial authorities to social relations within the ex-slave community. For many colonial actors caught up in emancipation, legal freedom entailed a redefinition of the relationship between individuals, and between individuals, society and the state.

Missionaries and state officials concentrated on promoting the social structures which would supposedly facilitate an interior moral revolution among the freed population. This focus on morality had particularly important ramifications for freed women's lives after emancipation. Freed women had to negotiate various currents of colonial opinion and state intervention which sought to place limits on both their working and their sexual lives. The next chapter analyzes, through a study of infanticide in the 1840s, the ways in which ideas about motherhood, morality, race, and labor converged to become one pillar of a controversy about the place of missions in Cape society.

---

101   Ibid.

7

Rituals of Rule:
Infanticide and the
Humanitarian Sentiment

In the decade immediately following the final abolition of Cape slavery in 1838, a cluster of ostensible infanticide cases occurred in three rural districts. In the 1840s, six women with connections to mission stations in Caledon, Swellendam, and the Cape districts were charged with the crime of infanticide or concealment of birth. These infanticides were not remarkable; between 1843 and 1870 at least thirty-seven such cases are recorded in the criminal records of the Western Cape.[1] This cluster of cases involving mission stations is, however, unusual: for the following two decades only two infanticides by women connected with mission stations were found in the records of the Cape Supreme Court.[2]

As distant onlookers of these events we are left with many questions. Was there anything particularly significant about the 1840s that might have caused women connected to mission stations to kill their newborn infants? Why did the colonial state pay such close attention to these events? And why did the judge in two cases seem to be at odds with the sentence passed and appeal on the women's behalf for clemency

---

1   This is a tentative figure based on a survey of the criminal records of the Cape Supreme Court from 1843 to 1870, and also on local criminal records for Stellenbosch, Caledon, Swellendam, Paarl, and Worcester. Edna Bradlow states that there are many cases of infanticide in the Cape criminal records. Bradlow, "Women at the Cape," 73. Fifteen cases of concealing the birth of a child were brought before the Supreme Court between 1860 and 1879. Patricia van der Spuy, "The Involvement of Women in Violent Crime as Processed by the Institutions of Justice in Cape Town, 1860–1879" (B.A. Hons. diss., History Department, University of Cape Town, 1989), Table 3, p. 47. Andrew Bank documents fifteen cases between 1890 and 1900. Andrew Bank, "Crime in Cape Town, 1890 to 1900" (BA. Hons. diss., History Department, University of Cape Town, 1988), Table 4.1, p. 82. Ordinance No. 10 of 1845 allowed the state to prosecute women for concealment of birth if there was not clear evidence of infanticide. This cast the net of identification much wider than had been the case under the infanticide legislation. See CA, CCP 6/3/1/6.

2   CA, CSC, 1/1/1/14, Case of Betje Blankenberg, 15 January 1850. She was found guilty of concealment of birth, the jury being unable to tell if the child was born dead or alive. She received a "recommendation to mercy" owing to the good account of her character given by J. Stegmann, a missionary from the station. Also CA, CSC, 1/1/1/19, 2 February 1863, Margaretha Roubyn of Pniel, who received twelve months hard labor for concealing the birth of her child. She did not receive a recommendation to mercy.

from the English justice system?[3] These cases in rural areas of the Western Cape warrant the attention of history if only because they underscore the profound repercussions of engaging in a social act which lay at the intersection of important social processes unfolding in the Western Cape in the mid-nineteenth century.

Infanticide implicated various colonial actors in contestations over definitions of freedom, motherhood, sexuality, and authority; it lay at one juncture of competing moral and legal economies of power.[4] The trials of Elizabeth August, Franscina Louw, Lea, Anna Sebastian, Wilhelmina Alexanders, and Dorothea Gideon were in part ritual procedures through which the British colonial state sought to demonstrate legitimacy against, and hegemony over, competing colonial actors when the balance of power between freed people, missionaries, former slaveholders, and the state was clearly contested and equivocal. The cases of Franscina Louw and Elizabeth August in particular became the basis for discussions between various branches of colonial society regarding the nature of justice, punishment, and the production of a respectable colonial working class.

In 1838 the missions and the Colonial Office had been in general agreement as to the need to propagate marriage and family among people newly freed from slavery. But from the 1840s it became clear that colonial officials and missionaries had rather different ideas both as to how to promote respectability and also how to accommodate freed people in colonial society. The cases of infanticides on the missions in the 1840s exposed a wider set of anxieties over labor, the place of the missions, and the nature of colonial rule.

The killing of infants in the rural Western Cape surely happened before the 1840s, yet the records are mostly silent on this action.[5] The apparent increase of crimes such as infanticide and prostitution reflects in part the penetration of British legal discourse into new terrains of social life in the empire. In the course of the nineteenth century, marriages, deaths, family relationships, and sexual activities all came under the legal spotlight in both the metropole and the colonies.[6] Thus, even as the private sphere became conceived of as a domain separate from a place called "the public sphere," relations there became ever more analyzed, codified, and intervened upon.

Thomas Laqueur has argued that the late eighteenth and early nineteenth century witnessed the elaboration of a humanitarian sentiment which sought to "declare epistemological sovereignty over the bodies and minds of others" by locating and describing suffering and offering a "model for precise social action." Narratives

---

3 Particularly in the light of judicial attitudes to the rape of black women, which we will examine in Chapter 8.

4 See Nancy Scheper-Hughes, "Culture, Society, and Maternal Thinking: Maternal Detachment and Infant Survival in a Brazilian Shantytown," *Ethnos* 13 (1985): 291–317, 292, for a discussion of the cultural construction of maternal feeling. Also Carolyn Steedman, *Landscape for a Good Woman: A Story of Two Lives* (New Brunswick, NJ: Rutgers University Press, 1987).

5 An analysis of the records of the Cape Supreme Court from its inception in 1828, and of local criminal records from 1828 to 1838 revealed only three cases of infanticide, including one in Cape Town. I am grateful to Helen Bradford for sharing her data with me. See Van der Spuy, "Collection," Paper 4, 152–98, for an analysis of an infanticide in the amelioration period.

6 See Kenneth Ballhatchet, *Race, Sex, and Class under the Raj: Imperial Attitudes and Policies and Their Critics 1793–1905* (New York: St. Martin's Press, 1980); Michel Foucault, *History of Sexuality: An Introduction*, Vol. 1 (New York: Vintage Books, 1990); Judith Walkowitz, *Prostitution and Victorian Society: Women, Class, and the State* (Cambridge: Cambridge University Press, 1980); and Weeks, *Sex and Sexuality*.

focused on the diseased, wounded, or dead body—such as the autopsy and infanticide—were the locus for this union between "facts, compassion, and action."[7] The emphasis on searching out, and then pardoning, perpetrators of infanticide enabled the dual and ambiguous project of humanitarianism to be elaborated in practice—blame in order to pardon, mark the person in order to demonstrate how much they need our help.[8] Scientific and medical discourse was central to the reclamation of the diseased or fallen body. "The new consciousness of infanticide was not unconnected with the enhanced self-image of the medical profession."[9] Infanticides and autopsies become a stage on which the medical profession demonstrated knowledge in detailed examinations of the body, in order to reach moral conclusions as to the guilt or innocence of the defendant: knowledge of the individual body legitimated intervention and power over the individual soul.

If a broader humanitarian discourse was developing in the nineteenth century, it was clearly contested and far from hegemonic, particularly in the colonial setting. This cluster of ideologies dominated British imperial life in the nineteenth century and had particular resonance at the Cape in the 1840s as various colonial actors sought to control the terms of postemancipation society. At the Cape, tensions between Dutch-speaking farmers, local district officials, mission stations, and the British colonial state recast the dynamics of the humanitarian struggle. The 1840s were particularly important in framing the terms of British rule and intervention. Former slaveholders still smarted from the loss of their slaves and had not yet fully come to appreciate how much the British shared their belief in deference and hierarchy. For slaves too, the 1840s were a period in which they demonstrated some independence from both missionaries' and colonial officials' understandings of the meanings of freedom and respectability.

In order to hear the multiple meanings of the infanticide cases, we have to bear witness to the tensions and cracks in the various actors' conceptions of law and power and to women's accounts of their actions. We need to locate the "discovery of infanticides" on the rural missions within the broader transformations occurring in the rural Western Cape in the postemancipation period.

Missions and Morality

In 1838 many freed people had looked to the missions as places which could provide them with a plot of land to call their own. Missions also promised some freedom from farm labor, a future for their children who would be educated in the ways of the colonizers' world, and inclusion in a community of the saved. Missionaries stipulated that access to these opportunities depended upon acceptance of the moral discipline of the

---

7   Thomas Laqueur, "Bodies, Details, and the Humanitarian Narrative," in Lynn Hunt, ed., *The New Cultural History* (Ithaca: Cornell University Press, 1989), 188, 178, 179.

8   See Douglas Hay et al., *Albion's Fatal Tree: Crime and Society in Eighteenth-Century England* (New York: Pantheon Books, 1975) for discussion of the use of pardon as a means of exercising power. For application in the South African context see Scully, "Criminality and Conflict." Of course this narrative is very much a part of the humanitarian discourse of abolitionist ideology.

9   Lionel Rose, *Massacre of the Innocents: Infanticide in Britain, 1800–1939* (London: Routledge and Keegan Paul, 1986), 41.

mission. For many freed women and men this offer, and the kinds of social behavior upon which it was contingent, seemed a worthwhile bargain. The influence of the mission spread beyond its boundaries in part because of the constant flow of men to and fro from work on the farms. The boundaries of mission and farm life were very permeable: indeed, some people who considered themselves members of a mission station often lived nearly as many days on a farm as did people who resided permanently on a farm. The mission community was as important as a symbolic space, as a frame of mind, as it was a physical location of community and independence.

The religious teachings of the missions provided one language through which former slaves could evaluate their lives. Community help and community censure underpinned much of the activities of individuals on the stations. The missionaries encouraged people to follow religion through kind words; they also cowed and intimidated members of the community by threats of expulsion. Missionaries took more seriously than their peers in government the need to ensure that people on their stations lived according to strict rules of sexual propriety and monogamy. These rules became even more important after emancipation as farmers began to complain about the stations, often framing their complaints through an attack on the lax standards of the missions.[10] The Moravians blended Pietist, Lutheran, and Calvinist beliefs, stressing both the spiritual inner life and the dignity of work. They policed social interaction between members of the community to prevent what they perceived as immoral and inappropriate behavior.

Both the London Missionary Society and the Moravians had strict moral requirements for inhabitants of their stations. Apart from murder, the greatest sins were extramarital sex and illegitimacy, and mission regulations were designed to prevent such moral lapses. At the LMS stations "matters of sexual morality and drunkenness were the most common reasons for exclusion" from church membership.[11] Section 29 of the Rules and Regulations of Genadendal explicitly stated that anyone who "cohabits in an irregular manner, or is guilty of adultery cannot remain a member of the institution, and deviations from the rules of virtue and chastity are subject to church discipline. . . ."[12] Indeed, in 1842 a missionary at Groenekloof stated that "there is a regulation of our Institution with respect to unmarried women having illegitimate children. If we find they are in such a state . . . we then desire them to leave this place."[13] Sexuality was policed by making people return to their "dwelling, and none is allowed to walk about the establishment" after church each night. Parents had to ensure that their children only stayed overnight in other people's houses with their permission and all "intercourse between the sexes" had to be "according to the rules of morality."[14]

In the early years after the ending of slavery the missionaries rejoiced that "[we] have no reason to complain of the conduct of the former slaves, who have lived

---

10 See below.

11 Sayles, *Mission Stations*, 39.

12 ASL, CGH, Select Committee, *Granting Lands in Freehold to Hottentots*, S.C. 11, 1854, 38.

13 Ibid.

14 Ibid., p. 42. The *Periodical Accounts* of the Moravian Church provide the best archival sources for internal mission politics. The correspondence of the London Missionary Society does not provide quite the same degree of detail about issues relating to family and gender.

among us only one year and a half. They go out to their work, and return quietly, and behave themselves very peaceably and orderly; they frequent the Church diligently, & shew great devotion."[15] A Wesleyan missionary reported in 1842: "During the past year considerable improvement in the religious advancement of our members has taken place; many of them now appear to better understand their duty to God and each other, and they often weep and lament that so many years of their lives have passed away in sin, and in ignorance of God and his salvation. . . ."[16]

However, by the early 1840s missionaries across the Cape and the West Indies lamented that the people under their charge were falling into sinful ways.[17] In the Western Cape, the Moravian missionaries were most vocal about the moral degeneration at their stations. Teutsch of Genadendal despondently noted in 1843 that there were "too many nominal members of our flock, who are in a state of lukewarmness or indifference to spiritual things." His colleague Kolbing wrote: "During the last months, we have had to complain . . . of many deviations from the way of holiness, many instances of individuals yielding to temptation, and fulfilling the appetites and lusts of the flesh. . . ."[18] In 1842 H. Helm of Zuurbraak rejoiced that a religious revival was taking place at the station but in 1843 while he said the revival continued he also remarked that the year had "been a time of trial . . . a few cases occurred in which not only were involved some of the new converts, but also such as had been members of the church for some years, which caused us much grief." By the next year Helm now lamented that the

> revival of our young people have [sic] not realized the hopes which I did entertain of them 3 years ago. The making of the road and bridges in this colony, in which they are employed, has been the occasion to bring them in contact with labourers of bad habits, and some of the young people . . . became worldly minded and were enticed to commence drinking again. . . .[19]

The Wesleyan reports are much more opaque. Missionaries only made references as to how much their congregants still needed to learn or to the fact that at Raithby station near Stellenbosch, for example, there had been "a marked improvement in their general conduct." Possibly the fact that the Wesleyans preached to the community at large rather than on a relatively self-contained station made them less hopeful of bringing about an immediate revolution in social and moral habits.[20]

---

15 HA, "Diary of Genadendal, 1840," *PA*, XVI, CLXXIII (December 1841), 30.

16 SOAS, "Notes by Rev. Joseph Jackson after a visit to KhamiesBerg Station in Little Namaqualand after a visit to Cape Town; Extract from Stellenbosch District Report," in *Report of the Wesleyan-Methodist Missionary Society for the Year Ending April 1842* (London: Wesleyan Missionary Society, 1842), 79.

17 Green, *British Slave Emancipation*, Ch. 11, 341. For an excellent discussion of missionary discourse in Jamaica see Sean Buffington, "After the Riot: Social Relations and Ideologies in Metcalfe Parish, Jamaica, 1866-1871" (paper presented to the Conference on Postemancipation Societies and Race, University of Michigan, April 1993).

18 HA, Letter from Teutsch, *PA*, XVI CLXXXI (December 1843), 462; Letter from Kolbing, *PA*, XVI, CLXXXII (March 1844), 518.

19 CA, LMS ZL 1/3/15, Box 18, Folder 5, Jacket A, Report for 1842 by H. Helm, 2 August 1842; ZL 1/3/16, Box 19, Folder 3, Jacket C, Report for 1843 by H. Helm, 1 November 1843; ZL 1/3/17, Box 21, Folder 4, Jacket B, Report for 1844 by H. Helm, 1 November 1844.

20 SOAS, *Report of the Wesleyan-Methodist Missionary Society for the year ending April 1846* (London: Wesleyan Missionary Society, 1846), 62; *Report of Wesleyan-Methodist Society for the year ending April 1853* (London: Wesleyan Missionary Society, 1853), 43.

The growing concern about morality on the missions in the early 1840s arose partly because of missionaries' ambivalence about the movement of thousands of emancipated slaves onto their stations. Missionaries worried that the freed people would bring sinful ways to the stations which had previously ministered mainly to the indigenous Khoisan. After 1838 missionaries explicitly targeted sexual and gender relations as areas needing reform and intervention. In 1840 missionaries at Groenekloof mission signaled a new emphasis on the importance of legal marriage by deleting the clause from the 1827 regulations which allowed people who had cohabited before they arrived on the mission to be treated as married people.[21] In addition, the expulsion of women from the station for extramarital sex only started in the 1840s at Zuurbraak mission station.[22] This is one reason for the proliferation of ostensible infanticide cases in the 1840s involving women with connections to mission stations.

In the 1840s, the battle for virtue on the Moravian and LMS missions in the Western Cape took place particularly through the regulation of women's sexuality.[23] Single women in particular were seen as posing special challenges to the morality of the community. Missionaries attempted to control women's sexuality because through pregnancy their bodies testified to supposed immoral behavior on the part of the entire mission community. One missionary stated that if a single woman "had brought forth a child at Zuurbraak I would have called upon her and questioned her in the presence of the overseers and told her she had forfeited the Institution that is that she must quit."[24]

The stress on women's morality also owed much to the notion, common in Europe in the nineteenth century, that women were the repository of moral virtues and able to control their sexual desire, if it was acknowledged at all, far better than men. This concern with women's morality arose partly because women played such an important role on the missions. Women formed the backbone of the religious community at the missions, attending church and school more regularly, and more likely to have been baptized than the men who were so frequently off the station.[25] Women at the missions bore the responsibility of maintaining the virtue of both themselves and men. It is therefore not surprising that missionaries primarily blamed women for perceived lapses in morality among the mission community as a whole.

Former slaveholders also focused on black women's sexuality. As we have seen, gender was always implicated in the complex struggles over labor. White farmers identified the missions as the root of their difficulties in finding cheap labor and

---

21 Ludlow, "Missions and Emancipation," 82. Raum suggests, however, that the Moravians were fairly accommodating to customs as long as they did not conflict with Christian ideas. People were permitted to live together without legal marriage as long as they adhered to the general moral principles of the station. I have relied heavily on Raum for my understanding of the Moravians and Genadendal history. Raum, "Development." See also Isaac Balie, *Die Geskiedenis van Genadendal 1738–1988* (Cape Town: Perskor, 1988).

22 CA, GH 28/19, No. 3, Statement by CP, Trial of Franscina Louw, 23 July 1842.

23 Raum, "Development," 31.

24 CA, GH 28/19, No. 3, Enclosure No. 3, Deposition of H. C. J. Helm, 23 July 1842.

25 HA, Letter from Genth, Elim, *PA*, XVI, CLXXV (June 1842), 134; Letter from Kolbing, Genadendal, *PA*, XVIII, CC (September 1848), 389. Raum, "Development," 42, argues that women were "more susceptible to the teachings of the missionaries than the men. One reason for this was, as the missionaries realised themselves, that the men left the settlement in order to work."

especially female domestic servants. These farmers argued that missions encouraged women not to engage in waged work, promoted education which took children and women out of the labor market (at least in theory), and provided families with a haven from farm labor. They framed their complaints about the new gendering of labor relations through a specific attack on freed women's sexuality and their supposedly immoral habits. White farmers argued that the missions encouraged debauchery and licentiousness.[26] In 1845, for example, T. B. Bayley, a farmer in Caledon district, blamed the lack of labor in the district on the support given to families by the missions in the form of houses and gardens. Bayley stated that Moravian missions were "directly injurious to the Farmer & indirectly to the Labourer" and he illustrated this by pointing to the supposed immorality of the "Hottentots" from Genadendal. Bayley specifically targeted women's supposed sexual habits, notably including all women in his description of the "Hottentots" from the stationincluding ex-slave women who had come to Genadendal after emancipation: "Again whenever I have employed some particular women, they have always been attended by certain men. not [sic] husbands . . . I believe *conjugality* and female chastity are of no great consequence . . . and this is the result of so much idleness, & so little superintendance. . . ."[27]

Settlers' sexualization of freed women was framed in part by the ubiquitous belief in Cape settler society that Khoi and slave women were predisposed to immorality. Such a representation assumed greater importance in the postemancipation period. The ending of slavery allowed freed women to redefine sexual relations by rejecting the passivity often forced upon them in sexual relations under slavery. Freed women exercised choice both through patterns of sexuality and reproduction, and by refusing to be mothers. Those choices, to the extent that women were in a position to choose, were circumscribed by law which rendered them dependent on men, by the economy which made it difficult to secure personal autonomy with economic independence, and by pervasive male notions that women should be sexually available.

Narratives of Infanticide

On 18 May 1840, James Barnes, the resident magistrate of Caledon district, made a preparatory examination of a case of possible infanticide perpetrated by a woman named Lea. Lea never speaks in the records of this case; we only hear the testimony of Adonis, a freed man, and Michael Daniel Otto, the field cornet of Diep River. Otto told the magistrate that Lea had come to his house some ten days before on her way from Genadendal. His wife had asked Lea if she had a husband as Lea looked preg-

---

26   This discourse was pervasive in the mid-nineteenth century. See Crais, "Vacant Land." See also ASL, CGH, *Master and Servant*, JP, Zwartkop's River, question 11, 70. He argued that women rarely stayed in employment for longer than three months "In ten years, I have had but one adult female servant who was not a drunkard, or vicious character of a worse description." D. Buchanan, JP, SWM, complained that "the institution swarms with idle women and naked children." *Master and Servant*, Question 11, 82.

27   Bayley argued that "a more dissipated, immoral, and dishonest race of people than the Hottentots of Genadendal cannot be found in any civilized quarter of the globe." CA, CO 4024, No. 26, T. B. Bayley to SG, 24 February 1845.

nant but Lea denied carrying a child. Adonis stated that the previous morning he had followed a fellow laborer into a neighbor's garden. On seeing something under a fig tree they had gone to examine it and found the body of a baby. Adonis said that "stones and part of a brick were laying near the child." No other records of the case were found.[28]

Two years later two women connected to mission stations were convicted of infanticide. These cases became the center of a discussion about missions and morality between the governor, judges, and the attorney general. Franscina Louw of Zuurbraak was convicted of the murder of her baby on 26 April 1842. Franscina Louw, who like Lea also worked on a farm, admitted to burying her baby but said that the child had been born dead. Apparently she was not given the opportunity to defend herself in the magistrate's court. The court heard the testimony of Anna Christina Laurens, Franscina's employer. Anna Laurens testified that Franscina had said "she was sickly, and that her courses had remained away in consequence of her having got wet by rain." However on 26 April Franscina went to the river for water and then told Mrs. Laurens that "her courses which had remained away so long had appeared." Franscina said she had washed her body because it was "troublesome" but her employer thought that she was pregnant. Do not "deny it any longer," Mrs. Laurens said, "you must bring forth a child. You had better tell me now so that I may send for my mother."[29]

Anna Laurens's mother examined Franscina and saw that her breasts were full of milk. Finally Franscina told Mrs. Laurens that she would confess as her breasts were so

> full of milk she was obliged to milk them out. She complained also that there was something in her private parts; and at last she told me she had had a child and been delivered of it on the Tuesday Morning when she had gone to the river for water. I asked her what she had done with it. She moved her hand to shew how she had dug a hole, and she said she had put it in the hole. She said the child had been born dead and that its head was swollen. I asked why she had not told me of it and she said she was afraid I would be frightened.[30]

Franscina's mother also testified. Delie Louw said that she had known that her daughter was pregnant before Franscina went to the farm and that she had scolded her about it. Apparently her daughter had been terrified of being expelled from Zuurbraak, which she "knew would be the case if she got a child without being married."[31]

The case of Elizabeth August arose out of similar circumstances. On 14 June 14 1842, Elizabeth came to the missionary at Groenekloof, and according to him said that he must forgive her: "She came in clasping her hands together and saying you must forgive me! it [*sic*] was not yet a child—it was not yet a child—it was only a

---

28 CA, 1/CAL 1/1/1, 18 May 1840. The case is brief and sparse. The RM wrote in the margins that the case was sent to the CP in Cape Town. For conclusion of the case see CA, CO 503, No. 39, Justice Menzies to Governor Napier, 5 April 1841.

29 CA, GH 28/19, No. 1, Enclosure No. 1 for Despatch 150, 1842. Records of Proceedings in the Case of Franscina Louw, Statement of Anna Laurens, 28 July 1842.

30 Ibid.

31 CA, GH 28/19, No. 3, Enclosure No. 3, Deposition of H. C. J. Helm, 23 July 1842, enclosing letter and memorandums, Deposition of Delie Louw, n.d.

bladder and if you will not believe me I will go and shew you. . . ." The next morning the missionary saw Elizabeth at her parents' house. Elizabeth August said she had had a child on the Sunday afternoon and had twisted its neck and then rolled it up in a sheepskin and put it under her bed till 7 p.m. when everyone was at service. She had then buried it near the river.[32]

In 1848, Wilhelmina Alexanders, also a member of a Moravian station, but this time of Elim in Caledon, was brought to trial for concealing the birth of a child. She had been a widow for about four years when the incident occurred. Two children found the body of a baby girl wrapped up in a petticoat and covered with the skin of a merino sheep buried in the ground about two hundred yards from Wilhelmina's home. The missionary asked Elizabeth Smals, a midwife at Elim, to go and investigate the different houses of the station to see who had had a child. On coming to Mrs. Alexanders' house, Mrs. Smals examined her.

> I could smell the smell women have when they are in childbed, I then examined her breasts both of which were full of milk, and when rubbing it the milk ran out of it in my hands, I asked the prisoner "Wilhelmina what have you done" on which she voluntarily confessed that on the Saturday night before she was delivered of a child the one which was found, in a fowl house. . . . I know the prisoner a long time she lives in a state of widowship . . . I never heard before that she was in a state of pregnancy . . . It appeared that the child was born alive . . . the prisoner denied it, and said that after the birth she tried to put her fingers in the mouth.

The doctor who was called to examine the body said that he found the child's lungs in "perfect state, filling the whole of the inside of the thorax and . . . filled with air, as proof that the child must not only have breathed, but also cried." In the preliminary exam Wilhelmina Alexanders herself said:

> I admit to having been delivered of a female child . . . I wrapped it up in an old petticoat, and concealed it there to shew to our Superintendent Elizabeth, but on Sunday . . . I got weak, and it was found before I could put my intention into action.[33]

The following year, Anna Sebastian, who lived at Genadendal, was tried at Swellendam on 12 May on the charge of concealment of birth. According to the special verdict which the jury delivered, "she proceeded to the bushes near the bridge, where she was delivered of the child, without being aware that she was about to be delivered of the child . . . she left the child . . . at the spot where it was born, and . . . she afterwards gave no information to any person that she had been so delivered. . . ." The jury stated that it could not say if the facts added up to a charge of concealing the birth of the child. In a letter dated 22 May 1849 the attorney general ordered her to be released and a verdict of not guilty entered on the record.[34]

---

32 CA, GH, 28/20, No.1, Enclosures to Despatch No. 209; Proceedings of the Trial of Elizabeth August, testimony by Joseph Lehman, 20 October 1842.

33 CA, 1/CAL 1/1/1, Preliminary examination into the case of Wilhelmina Alexanders, for concealing the birth of child, 16 February 1848.

34 No preliminary examination could be found for her trial. We know of her case only through the printed indictment which is lodged in the criminal records of the Circuit Court. CA, CSC 1/2/1/43, No.13, Circuit Court Swellendam, 22 May 1849.

The final mission-related infanticide for which I have records in the 1840s concerns Dorothea Gideon. In 1848 she had been at Elim for some nine to ten years. This suggests that she probably had been a slave, and had participated in the great movement to the missions of the late 1830s. In 1849 she was charged with the crime of concealment of birth, the court not being able to determine if her child was born dead or alive. Dorothea was married and a formal member of Elim mission station. She worked, however, at the farm Eland's Kloof in the service of the Moolman family. Apparently the Elim community was alive with gossip that Dorothea had had a baby while at Eland's Kloof. On her return from the farm, therefore, Dorothea was brought before the four missionaries and questioned. She confessed to having buried her baby alive. A missionary reflected that Dorothea and her husband often went to work together and he could not understand what had made her kill her child. Perhaps, he said, it might have been

> the trouble of rearing the child. . . . it struck us that she might perhaps have had connection with another person or the trouble of rearing the child which induced her to commit the crime on a former occasion about six years ago there was a report at Elim that this person had a miscarriage she admitted to me that it was so, but that the child not being full grown or alive she buried it. . . .[35]

Dorothea said only, "My husband is the cause of all this it is true that I was delivered of a child and after it died, I buried it."[36]

Interpreting Infanticide

What do we do with these tales of desperation? All the women were connected in some way to mission stations. And it was precisely their ties to missions, and their status as women who could be reclaimed into respectable working-class society, which generated the interest of the state.[37] Lea had come from Genadendal to join her father on the farm where he worked. Franscina lived on Zuurbraak and worked on the Laurens's farm. Elizabeth August lived on Groenekloof; Wilhelmina and Dorothea lived on Elim.

We hear little from these women as to their reasons for hiding their pregnancies, concealing the birth of their babies, and/or killing their children. The court narratives are constructed using answers by doctors, lawyers, members of the mission communities, and farmers and their wives to questions posed by the magistrate. We enter the events through the interpretations of onlookers, and through a linear narrative constructed by colonial officials operating within a historically specific ideology regarding the relationship between law, medical discourse, and state power. How do we avoid replicating the structures of power illuminated so eloquently in the records?

---

35   CA, 1/CAL 1/1/2, Documents in the Circuit Court trial of Dorothea Gideon for Concealing the Birth of her Child on 1 May 1849 at Eland's Kloof, 4 October 1849. Preliminary Examination conducted by RM, statement by August Lemerts, n.d.

36   Ibid, Statement of Dorothea, n.d.

37   The working-class background of these women is consistent with every other infanticide case I have found in the Supreme Court Criminal Records.

And to what extent do we participate in colonial discourse in labeling the events "infanticide"?

The "facts" of the cases suggest that the women had hidden their pregnancies, and then in one way or another either actively killed their children or left them to die of exposure. The court narratives give no hint that the women abandoned their babies in the hope that they would be rescued by members of the community.[38] It seems indeed that we are dealing with infanticide—or at least the European definition thereof. Infanticide was conceptualized as a crime in which a mother killed her infant of under one year.[39] But did the women in the cases share this criminal definition of infanticide?

As members of the rural poor they participated in a complex and heterogeneous cultural life with origins in slave culture, Khoi and San societies, and the societies of East and Central Africa. As such they possibly brought to the killing of infants a different cultural perspective than that of the British or the Dutch. Many pre-capitalist African societies had a variety of codes regarding infanticide.[40] Isaac Schapera argues that San and Khoi societies of the Northern Cape also practiced infanticide as a means of child spacing—killing a baby born while another was still at the breast by burying it alive or leaving it to be eaten by wild animals. Schapera states that the Khoisan communities of the southern Cape did not follow this practice, but the similarity in the practices of the six women involved in the 1840s cases to those he describes suggests possible cultural continuities.[41]

Dorothea Gideon "dug a hole in the ground and buried it [the baby] alive."[42] It is not clear if Wilhelmina Alexanders intended to kill her child, but she left it in the cold overnight. Franscina Louw claimed that her child had been born dead—she buried the infant in a hole near the river.[43] We should be wary of overstating such a possibility, however, since the rural context of these infanticides meant that burial or exposure might have been the only means of committing the crime in any event.

If the form of infanticide in the mid-nineteenth century retained some similarity to earlier practices, the meaning of and the reasons for the practice were not necessarily the same. Schapera, writing in 1935, used sources from the eighteenth and nineteenth centuries as evidence for his comments on contemporary Khoisan societies. He provides an ahistoric ethnography which portrays a society supposedly living in

---

38   Compare John Boswell, *The Kindness of Strangers: The Abandonment of Children in Western Europe from Late Antiquity to the Renaissance* (New York: Pantheon Books, 1988).

39   Van der Linden, *Institutes*, Section 12; Rose, *Massacre of the Innocents*.

40   In Zulu society, for example, one twin was often left out to die so as to enable the mother to give all her milk to only one baby and thus strengthen its chances of survival. See Marianne Brindley, "Old Women in Zulu Culture: The Old Woman and Childbirth," *South African Journal of Ethnology* 8 (1985): 98–108. I am grateful to Keletso Atkins and members of the South African seminar at the University of Michigan for highlighting this concern. Nancy Scheper-Hughes argues that maternal bonding is culturally and historically specific and that in communities where infant mortality is high, parents distance themselves from their children in order to see if the infants will survive. Scheper-Hughes, "Culture, Scarcity, and Maternal Thinking."

41   Isaac Schapera, *The Khoisan Peoples of South Africa* (Reprint, London: Routledge and Keegan Paul, 1960), 116.

42   CA, 1/CAL 1/1/2, Testimony of Johannes Albertus Moolman, missionary, 4 October 1849.

43   1/CA, GH 28/19, No. 1, Testimony of Anna Christina Laurens, 21 July 1841. I cannot tell if Franscina Louw killed her baby or not although she had concealed her pregnancy. The jury found her guilty of infanticide.

the 1930s as it might have in the eighteenth century—and suggests that the eighteenth-century picture is pristine in its "authenticity" and lack of contact with European influence. But Khoisan societies of the eighteenth century had already been in long contact with European settlement: infanticide as birth-spacing might well have been a culturally specific response to colonial disruption of previous birth-spacing practices.[44] In giving weight to a culturalist interpretation we have to accord that infanticide as we encounter it in these cases is embedded in a colonial context of material and ideological domination.

It is striking that all six women hid the fact that they were pregnant—which suggests that they had always intended to somehow get rid of the babies at birth.[45] Wilhelmina Alexanders was a widow of four years when she gave birth. She kept her pregnancy secret from the community. Four women were apparently so frightened of the consequences of having illegitimate children that they hid their pregnancies and buried their children. In all the cases, fear of being abandoned by the community and of being banished from the station seems to have governed their actions. This fear was a real one. Lehman, a missionary at Groenekloof Moravian mission stated that

> We have poeple [*sic*] who have been there a long time, who tell it to the younger ones—when new people come to the institution we tell them, if you do not behave like a Christian x [*sic*] according to the Word of God—you will be turned out. I am as certain that it is as well known that young women will be turned out if they have bastard children—as they know it is wrong to have bastard children.[46]

The women were brought before the missionary of their station where they confessed to the sin of killing their child, but this did not necessarily absolve them of having contravened the laws of the community.[47] Moravians, in particular, put much emphasis on confession as a means of cleansing the soul, but it did not always translate into redemption. The community was a source of strength and love, but also of intervention. The need to belong to the mission community seems to be one reason why these women concealed the births and deaths of their illegitimate children, but those very communities were also the instruments of their undoing. In the trial of Dorothea Gideon, for example, August Lemerts of the station stated that there was "a talk at Elim that the Prisoner Dorothea . . . has been delivered of a Child." Female neighbors turned in Wilhelmina Alexanders to the Superintendent of Elim.[48] As the backbone of the religious life at the stations, women were, perhaps, particularly protective of moral and religious standards. Jealousy over the sexual lives of women who chose not to follow the strict injunctions against premarital and extramarital sex might also have fueled women's complaints against their peers. Fellow women often

---

44 See Nancy Rose Hunt, "'Le Bébé en Brousse': European Women, African Birth-Spacing, and Colonial Intervention in the Belgian Congo," *International Journal of African Historical Studies* 21 (1988): 401–432, for a similar argument.

45 Abortion might have been attempted, but we have no way of knowing. Helen Bradford is currently working on a history of abortion in South Africa.

46 CA, GH, 28/20, No.1, Enclosures to Despatch No. 209; Proceedings of the Trial of Elizabeth August, testimony by Joseph Lehman, 20 October 1842.

47 See Vicente Rafael, "Confession, Conversion, and Reciprocity in Early Tagalog Colonial Society," *Comparative Studies in Society and History* 29, 2, (April 1987): 320–39.

48 CA, 1/CAL 1/1/2, 4 October 1849; CA 1/CAL 1/1/1, 16 February 1848.

turned in the perpetrators of infanticide. Lea was turned in by Keyter's wife, while both Wilhelmina and Dorothea were exposed by women.

Dorothea Gideon, the only married woman of the six, situated her case within a very specific context of blame. She stated "my husband is the cause of all this." Was she blaming her husband for having made her pregnant? Was she condemning him for making her work and therefore making it difficult for her to rear a child? Was she indeed blaming him for making her kill her child? On the missions, a sexual division of labor in which women worked in the gardens at the missions and men worked either in artisanal crafts or on the farms might have created resentment among those women who had to work on the farms. Did the fact that at least three of the five women were employed outside the home factor into their actions? Did they compare their situation unfavorably to other women who were able to reside on the missions?

Lea, Franscina Louw, and Dorothea Gideon were farm workers. It is possible that one reason for their actions arose from their status as women workers whose employment could be terminated by her employer if they became pregnant.[49] However, in their subsequent investigations into these cases, neither the missionaries nor the state considered that the women might have been forced to kill their children precisely because of their incorporation into the wage labor economy as subordinates to men.[50] The moral codes of the stations regarding illegitimacy and the permanent casting out of perceived miscreants become the causal factor in the narrative of infanticide.

Without knowing the exact histories of Lea, Franscina Louw, Wilhelmina Alexanders, Anna Sebastian, Elizabeth August, and Dorothea Gideon, it is difficult to write of their longings and feelings, of their cultural perceptions of the world around them. In the court narratives the women and the witnesses make much of the dishonor and humiliation which accompanied illegitimacy on the mission stations. We must be wary of attributing such feelings to the women whom we meet thirdhand, and in a very structured judicial context. Yet people were caught up in the regulatory world of the mission regardless of whether its moral precepts helped them in daily life. Infanticide was imbricated in colonial definitions of right and wrong, and official scripts of justice and power. As such we must place these cases into other contexts at the Cape and in the international moral economies in the decade after slavery.

Moral Reclamation and the Humanitarian Sentiment

Infanticide at the Cape became, for a moment, a site of the elaboration of a new conception of power by officials in the emerging colonial state. The Cape infanticide narratives can be interpreted as forming part of a wider cluster of discrete and overlapping dis-

---

49 Employers did terminate women's employment on these grounds. For example in 1867 Mary Ann Chappel, aged sixteen, who was apprenticed to J. G. Faure of Stellenbosch became pregnant as the result of a relationship with another laborer on the farm and Faure fired her in terms of the Masters and Servants Act of 1856. The attorney general adjudicated that this dismissal was legal. However, Mary Ann having been originally apprenticed when she was under ten years of age, the indenture itself was illegal. CA, 1/STB, 10/160, Henry Baas to RM, 11 February 1867; AG to Acting CP, STB, 15 February 1867.

50 For more analysis of the context of labor in these cases of infanticide see Pamela Scully, "Narratives of Infanticide in the Aftermath of Slave Emancipation in the Nineteenth-Century Cape Colony, South Africa," *Canadian Journal of African Studies* 30, 1 (1996) (Special Issue on Wicked Women and the Reconfiguration of Gender in Africa, edited by Dorothy Hodgson and Sheryl McCurdy), 88–105.

courses regarding upliftment of the "worthy" poor, the inculcation of morality, and the institution of new forms of rule based on a capillary conception of power emanating from the sovereignty of the state.[51]

The British and Cape impulses behind infanticide/concealment of birth prosecutions rested on slightly different foundations. The colonial Ordinance of 1845, which allowed for criminal prosecution for concealment of birth, prefigured its British counterpart by sixteen years.[52] The ordinance allowed juries to award an alternative sentence if infanticide could not be proven. Rose argues that this alternate sentence was part of a move in the British justice system towards leniency regarding conviction of women for cases of infanticide.[53] At the Cape this ruling was more ambivalent. The ordinance widened and deepened state power with more coercive intentions, at least with regard to the prosecution of black women.[54] Indeed the governor stated as much in May 1845. He said the ordinance had been submitted to the Legislative Council, it "having appeared to the Attorney-General, that the criminal law of this Colony was defective in not constituting the concealment of the birth of a child a crime, inasmuch as facilities were hereby afforded for the commission of infanticide without detection."[55]

The colonial state focused on infanticide precisely because it was in many ways an act which was situated at the heart of different cultural understandings of morality and autonomy. In killing her child, a woman declared sovereign power over both her body and the body of her child. Possibly through infanticides these women also refused "maternity" and the "maternal instinct." They thus rejected the constructions of motherhood promoted, for example, in the amelioration legislation and on the mission stations.[56] These infanticide proceedings became symbolic trials serving as platforms from which colonial officials described what behavior was not acceptable, legitimated state legislation on the sphere defined as "private," and sought to inculcate practices and values conducive to the reproduction of a self-reproducing rural elite and stable working class needing minimal state intervention.

In the humanitarian discourse we witness the rise of "the expert" who comes to know more about the individual than the person herself. Under Roman Dutch law the doctor's decision was central to the determination of guilt. The decision as to whether a child was born dead or alive rested on medical testimony as to whether the lungs floated when thrown in water. If they did, the child was deemed to have been

---

51   See Michel Foucault, *Discipline and Punish: The Birth of the Prison* (New York: Pantheon Books, 1977) for a discussion of how the industrializing state (not his terms) reconfigured relations of power based on the sovereignty of the state and the displacement of sovereignty located in the individual. On discourses of upliftment see Elaine Hadley, "Natives in a Strange Land: The Philanthropic Discourse of Juvenile Emigration in Mid-Nineteenth-Century England," *Victorian Studies* 33 (1990): 411–37.

52   For a similar observation see Sandra Burman and Margaret Naude, "Bearing a Bastard: The Social Consequences of Illegitimacy in Cape Town, 1896–1939," *Journal of Southern African Studies* 17 (September 1991): 373–413, 387. Rose, *Massacre of the Innocents*, 71, gives information on the metropolitan chronology.

53   Rose, *Massacre of the Innocents*, 70.

54   From a brief perusal of verdicts it appears that the perceived race of the victim played a large part in the type of verdict delivered. White women were more likely to be found to have extenuating circumstances for infanticide, although juries appear to have become more lenient in general in the course of the nineteenth century.

55   CA, GH 23/15, No.86, Governor to SSC, 14 May 1845.

56   I am grateful to Philippa Levine for alerting me to this point.

born alive.[57] Ordinance No. 10 of 1845 gave the medical expert a larger stage on which to jostle for authority with the legal profession. Physical exams involved issues of power and state intervention in a very private sphere. The court narratives are constructed in such a way that the doctor's testimony is cited last: as the reader we turn to him for resolution of the case. In the case of Elizabeth August, Dr. William Daly's testimony contradicts her claim to having strangled the child: "[T]he baby might have been smothered either by the placenta itself or by being under the bed-clothes or by the actual process of childbirth." Daly stated that he might have missed the damage to the child's neck if the clerk of the court had not told him of Elizabeth August's confession.[58]

Attending to the struggle between new conceptions of power allows us to account for what at first appears to be an anomaly in these cases when compared to others in England in the same period. Lionel Rose states that there was enormous public sympathy for mothers who were believed to have killed their babies and that juries were generally loath to return "a criminally culpable verdict against a female witness."[59] At the Cape juries were more ambivalent than their British peers and this period generally passed a verdict of guilty.

Until the late nineteenth century juries in the rural areas came only from the white community. The Cape law "relating to juries contained no colour bar . . . but in practice juries tended to be dominated by whites." Only qualified voters, of whom the vast majority were white, and always male, were allowed to sit on juries. In Cape Town juries were mixed, although still dominated by whites, but in the rural areas it was only after 1874 that juries were made up of both white and "coloured" men.[60] Possibly the unsympathetic verdicts rendered by many rural juries in infanticide cases stemmed from an ill-disguised resentment against former slaves and dependent laborers who now in freedom were seen to be confirming a long-held belief that they were immoral and untrustworthy. Racism no doubt played a part since white juries probably found it easy to convict an African woman. That many of these women seem to have had sexual relations out of marriage might also have contributed to the juries' willingness to convict the women of infanticide. Juries used the weight of the law to sentence members of their former slave class to death. Lea was sentenced to death and was hanged after a trial in the Circuit Court at Swellendam.[61] Both Franscina Louw and Elizabeth August were also condemned to death, but the chief justice asked that their sentences be commuted. It was through a revocation of the verdicts on these latter two cases that the colonial state challenged missionary notions of authority and sought to establish the hegemony of the colonial state over the missions.

---

57 Van der Linden, *Institutes*, 218.

58 See CA, GH 28/20, No. 1, Case of Elizabeth August. Testimony of Dr. William Daly, 20 October 1842. Also CA 1/CAL 1/1/1, Case of Wilhelmina Alexanders. Testimony of Abraham Albertyn, doctor, 16 February 1848. Laqueur cites a case of infanticide in which the medical testimony contradicts the woman's confession of having killed her child. Laqueur, "Humanitarian Narrative," 188.

59 Rose, *Massacre of the Innocents*, 43.

60 Albie Sachs, *Justice in South Africa* (Berkeley: University of California Press, 1973), 60, 59–70.

61 CA, CO 503, No. 39, Justice Menzies to Governor Napier, 5 April 1841. Wilhelmina Alexanders received twelve months hard labor in 1848 for concealment of birth. CA, CO 575, High Sheriff to SG, 3 March 1848. I have the circuit court trial records, but no verdict for Dorothea Gideon's case. CA, 1/CAL 1/1/2, Circuit Court trial of Dorothea Gideon for Concealing the Birth of her Child, 4 October 1849.

Rituals of Rule

The humanitarian discourse of the colonial state was multifocused and practiced with discrete effects on different colonial actors. Colonial officials sought to reclaim rural women into the respectable working-class community through pardoning their sins and laying a foundation for action. They also targeted the missionaries who had caused the pain. *Naming* the women as deviant established the moral superiority of the British colonial state vis-à-vis both those women who had killed their children, and the missionaries, who it was argued had caused the women to take that action. In summing up the trial of Elizabeth August, the attorney general praised the Moravians for helping "their disciples learn to combine active performance of the duties of this life with the most fervent aspirations after another and a better." However, he also argued that the crucial problem on the mission stations was that the rule regarding women's morality was imposed by the missionaries instead of coming from the community itself.

> If that rule were the natural growth of moral and religious feeling amongst the coloured class itself . . . it would in all probability, be attended with comparatively few dangers . . . it will be strongly fortified by sentiment and principle against the original temptation, and even if she chance to fall, her mind and moral feeling are too well disciplined to allow her to incur the sin of murder rather than the shame of exposure. . . . But . . . does it not come to pass that females of infirm principles and half formed notions of right and wrong, confound all the boundaries of criminality, and, in their darkened imaginations, are found to fear the frown of the missionary and expulsion from the institution more than the guilt of murdering their offspring?[62]

This targeting of the missionaries played into wider tensions between state and missions over control of the laboring population. This tension became increasingly evident in the 1850s with the constitution of commissions investigating landholding on the missions and addressing the white farmers' concerns about their inability to secure cheap sources of labor.[63]

The attack by members of the Cape government on infanticide on the mission stations invoked and legitimated Victorian gender standards. Women were blamed for killing their children, but not held responsible for their actions.[64] The implicit assumption was that "infanticide was male-instigated, and women left to their own devices, would never kill their children. . . ."[65] Laying blame on the missionaries removed agency from the women and again resolved the issue within the parameters

---

62 Porter, *Porter Speeches*, 132–36.

63 For example, see GB, Parliament, House, Minute by SG on Representative Institution for the Cape, dated 14 January 1851, in "Further Papers Relative to the Establishment of a Representative Assembly," *Parliamentary Papers* 1851 (1362), p. 165; SAL, CGH, Parliament, "Debate on Missionary Lands, 3 August 1854," *The Advertiser and Mail's Parliamentary Debates in the First Session of the First Parliament of the Cape of Good Hope, Appointed to meet 30th June 1854*, State Library Reprints, 33, 1 (Pretoria: State Library, 1968); ASL, CGH, Select Committee, *Minutes of Evidence taken before the Select Committee of the House of Assembly on Granting Lands in Freehold to Hottentots*, S.C. 13 (Cape Town: Saul Solomon and Co., 1856).

64 See Ruth Harris, "Melodrama, Hysteria, and Feminine Crimes of Passion in the Fin de Siecle," *History Workshop* (1988): 31–63, for a discussion of how women manipulated this perception to their advantage in murder trials.

65 Rose, *Massacre of the Innocents*, 26, with reference to England and the leniency of infanticide convictions.

acceptable to the colonial state by legitimating state intervention into the lives of the rural poor.

Once the infanticides on the mission stations came to their attention the attorney general and other high-ranking colonial officials were appalled at the rigidity of mission station regulations towards lapsed members of the community. The judicial documents in the infanticide cases of Franscina Louw and Elizabeth August present a particularly vivid example of how colonial officials characterized the difference between civil society and the mission stations. The governor stated with regard to Franscina Louw:

> I agree with the judge that the crime of which she is convicted is to be attributed to their dread of the consequences of being expelled from the Missionary Institution of Zuurbraak, and therefore taking into consideration the favourable circumstances mentioned in the Judge's letter, together with his opinion that it would not be prejudicial to the ends of justice that the sentence of death should be suspended until her case shall have been submitted to the Gracious consideration of Her Majesty the Queen, I have granted her a Reprieve. . . .[66]

Three months later the chief justice of the colony sent a similar letter to the governor regarding the case of Elizabeth August and asking for clemency. He hoped that the observations of the presiding judges in the two cases

> will produce a relaxation in a rule which was made for the encouragement of morality, but which from its undue severity leads unfortunate females to the commission of the most unnatural Crimes. . . . however it would be a delicate task for the Govt to interfere further with those institutions than has been done on these two occasions, leaving it to time and experience to shew that *rigorous discipline will not supply the place of morality, and that Missionaries to effect their object must appeal to other and higher sources for checks to the evil which they wish to eradicate by public expulsion and excommunication* [my emphasis].[67]

In the interpretation of these cases by high government officials the missionaries' conception of power did not allow for reclamation of women who had fallen from grace through contravention of sexual and family norms. The chief justice argued that discipline could not prevail over habit. He implied, instead, that the cultural transformation of freed people would be more successfully accomplished in the realm of civil society where the state would help inculcate habits and values which would be shared by all.

But were the moral projects of the British colonial state and the Moravian missionaries so very different? For most of their residence in the Cape since 1792 the Moravians had enjoyed good relations with the government, especially in comparison to the stormy relations between the London Missionary Society and colonial officials and farmers. As we have seen, the Moravian community was rooted in respect for authority, hierarchy, and the word of God as interpreted by the missionaries. This had served the stations well in the immediate postemancipation period. In addition,

---

66 CA, GH 23/14, Vol. 1, No. 152, Governor to SSC, enclosing the report of the proceedings on the case of Francina [sic] Louw, 10 August 1842.

67 CA, GH 23/14, No. 209, Chief Justice to Governor, 31 October 1842.

both the Moravians and the London Missionary Society subscribed to many of the sentiments outlined by Chief Justice Wylde and William Porter. One of the main aims of Philip's reforms on LMS stations in the 1820s was precisely to lead by example, to instill morality through the inculcation of habit.[68]

Indeed the colonial authorities caricatured missionary authority and judicial practice. Procedures existed to allow the reentry to the mission community of people who had been expelled. Reverend Helm of Zuurbraak stated that if she "had shown any signs which led me to think that she really repented of her conduct I would have told her she could remain."[69] By the mid-nineteenth century the numbers of expulsions at Genadendal had increased, but expulsion had also become more difficult to enforce. This was partly in response to community pressure: relatives simply kept the person at the station. This speaks too to tensions within the community itself as to the means of inculcating morality. Significantly, in 1857, the Cape government added a section to the Rules and Regulations of Genadendal which made expulsion subject to the consent of the magistrate.[70] The government wrote into law the desire for firmer civic control over missionary life for which the attorney general, the governor, and the chief justice had implicitly appealed in their analysis of the mission infanticide trials of the 1840s.

Conclusion

The extensive prosecution and scrutiny of cases of infanticide relating to mission stations in the 1840s can be regarded as examples of competing theaters of colonial hegemonic practice. The Moravians and the LMS shared to some extent the Dutch farmers' conception of power as being located in theatrical demonstrations of power over the body of the individual. Missionaries and state alike exploited the occasion of infanticide to invoke rituals of rule. Colonial officials, I have argued, used these cases as practices to illustrate simultaneously both the immorality of the crime of infanticide, the wrongheadedness of the missionaries, and the beneficence of British justice. Similarly the missionaries exploited the occasion of infanticide to invoke rituals of religious observance—such as confession, which at once bound the mission station together through religious practice and targeted as "other" the woman who had stepped outside the boundaries of convention.[71]

The difference between the colonial state and the missionaries revolved around the proper arena of demonstrating power and the ultimate means whereby to fashion a colonial community. For the missionaries, and the mission community, the sphere of articulation remained the mission station and the mission court. For the colonial state, theaters of rule were to be located in the public space of the colonial legal system. The 1840s produced a convergence of factors which helped privilege the articulation of

---

68 Richard Lovett, *A History of the London Missionary Society, 1795–1895*, 2 vols. (London: Oxford University Press, 1899).

69 CA, GH 28/19, No.3, Trial of Franscina Louw, 23 July 1842.

70 Raum, "Development," 56–59.

71 At Groenekloof, "the expulsion of young women is public. I first intimate it privately to the party and afterwards publish it from the Pulpit, the name of the cause of her expulsion." CA, GH 28/20, No. 1, Trial of Elizabeth August, Testimony of Joseph Lehman, 20 October 1842.

some colonial tensions within a discourse on infanticide. The "discovery" of infanticides on mission stations in the 1840s is a product and a reflection of a moment of acute struggle between different colonial actors to define the contours of colonial rule.

The cases of infanticide also uncover the ways in which ideas of race, gender, and sexuality helped to define both the worlds which freed women had to negotiate after 1838 and the laws which were put into place in the new era of freedom. In the early 1850s, the period at which this book ends, the confluence of race, sexuality, and the elaboration of colonial identities were very clearly exposed in discussions about rape, and particularly through those cases which involved the rape of freed women. The narratives of rape examined in the final chapter demonstrate the centrality of sexuality to the constitution of various colonial identities and reveal the often implicit assumptions about race, gender, and class which so often guided colonial rule.

8

Rape, Race, and the Sexual Politics of Colonial Identities

If infanticide literally and figuratively explored the contested cultural terrains of civility and the nature of authority, rape raised questions of race and respectability. Freed women's actions in bringing men to court for rape challenged the assumptions that their bodies were fields upon which men of both races could play with impunity. Analysis of these cases is important, because, paradoxically, they hint at freed women's constructions of their world and identities.

Emancipation freed slaves into a world in which at least some colonial officials and missionaries believed in the possibility of "civilizing" each individual. No laws existed in the mid-nineteenth century Cape prohibiting interracial marriage and sexual relations such as one finds in the postemancipation legislation of the U.S. South, for example, where slavery ended in the 1860s.[1] This arose partly because Cape slave emancipation occurred in an era of particularly marked competing definitions of race. Race was seen to derive as much from culture as from biology. At the Cape the legacy of Dutch colonialism also facilitated a rather a hazy elaboration of racial differences.[2] The Booysen rape case which is examined below is particularly enlightening because it uncovers the legal suppositions, even in this more optimistic moment, as to how equality before the law could be mediated by race, and more particularly overdetermined by the intersection of properties of femaleness and blackness.

In addition, a study of various cases of rape in the aftermath of emancipation shows an important limit on freed women's experience of freedom. Historians of

---

1   See Eva Saks, "Representing Miscegenation Law," *Raritan* VII (1988): 39–69, for an excellent discussion of the U.S. legal framework.

2   Thus the tensions around race which surfaced in the debates over postemancipation labor legislation; see Chapter 5. See also Bank, "Liberals," and William F. Freund, "The Cape Under Transitional Governments, 1795–1814" in Elphick and Giliomee, eds., *Shaping*, 324–57, esp. 336. For a comparison of Dutch and British racial and sexual practices and laws in one setting, see Taylor, *Social World*.

colonial life have tended to analyze sexual violence primarily as a metaphor for or index of tension within colonial societies rather than examining rape as a fact of violence.[3] This is a curious feature of the historiography: that authors have in general been more concerned with the elusive myths concerning white women as victims of black rapists, than with the ways in which colonialism created conditions which authorized the pervasive rape of black women by white men.[4] Indeed there are relatively few studies which examine cases in which black women were raped either by black or white men.[5]

The narratives of rape with which this chapter is concerned suggest the centrality of sexuality to the making of various colonial identities and expose the often implicit assumptions about race, gender, and class which frequently informed colonial rule. Below I analyze the ways in which various communities and individuals received and interpreted rape cases (that is, the cultural narratives constructed about any given case); the degree of power accorded rape as a metaphor for a more amorphous or general crisis; and the ways in which the categories of race, gender, and sexuality informed and were themselves constituted through discussions about morality, law, and the social order.

The Booysen Case

On 2 April 1850, a rape occurred in the rural district of George about two hundred miles from Cape Town. Anna Simpson, the wife of a laborer, told the local justice of the peace that Damon Booysen, aged eighteen, had raped her "about a month" after he had started working for her husband. Mrs. Simpson stated that one day when her husband had gone to town, Booysen came to her house. "He asked me to go with

---

3   For a discussion and critique of analyzing sexual violence purely metaphorically see Stoler, "Carnal Knowledge"; also Jenny Sharpe, "The Unspeakable Limits of Rape: Colonial Violence and Counter-Insurgency," *Genders* 10 (Spring 1991): 25–46. For a study of rape, race, and gender in contemporary cases of sexual violence see Sherene Razack, "What is to Be Gained by Looking White People in the Eye? Culture, Race, and Gender in Cases of Sexual Violence," *Signs* (Summer 1994): 894–923.

4   For example, see Norman Etherington, "Natal's Black Rape Scare of the 1870s," *Journal of Southern African Studies* 15 (1988): 2–53; and Amirah Inglis, *The White Women's Protection Ordinance: Sexual Anxiety and Politics in Papua* (London: Sussex University Press, 1975).

5   The exceptions lie in the literature on slavery and emancipation. Historians have argued that at the Cape the rape of slave women by their owners operated both as a field of sexual and social power and, whether intentionally or not, as a means of reproducing the Cape slave population. Mason "Fit for Freedom," Ch. 3, 202–225, discusses rape as a form of patriarchal control, as does Van der Spuy, "Collection." For an early study of slavery and sexuality at the Cape see Ross, "Oppression, Sexuality and Slavery." For the U.S. South see Laura F. Edwards, "Sexual Violence, Gender, Reconstruction, and the Extension of Patriarchy in Granville County, North Carolina," *The North Carolina Historical Review* 68 (July 1991): 237–60; and Deborah Gray White, *Ar'n't I a Woman?: Female Slaves in the Plantation South* (New York: W. W. Norton & Co., 1985). Histories of lynching in the U.S. South have also provided compelling studies regarding the implications of the reinscription of older discourses about the need to protect white women from rape by black men: Hazel V. Carby, "'On the Threshold of Woman's Era': Lynching, Empire, and Sexuality in Black Feminist Theory," *Critical Enquiry* 12 (Autumn 1985): 262–77; Jacquelyn Dowd Hall, "'The Mind That Burns in Each Body': Women, Rape, and Racial Violence," in Ann Snitow, Christine Stansell, and Sharon Thompson, eds., *Powers of Desire: The Politics of Sexuality* (New York: Monthly Review Press, 1983).

him I refused; suddenly he seized me from behind and threw me to the ground. . . ." Booysen threatened to stab Mrs. Simpson and then raped her. On her husband's return from Mossel Bay Mrs. Simpson told him of the rape.[6] Booysen was brought to the town of George for a preliminary examination at the office of the clerk of the peace and on 4 April 1850 Booysen confessed to the charge of rape. He confirmed, "It is true that I committed the crime . . . true that I forced Annie Simpson. I was half drunk. I fully accomplished my lust."[7]

At the Supreme Court's circuit court trial on 16 September 1850, the presiding judge, Justice Menzies, stated that at the preliminary examination "the prisoner fully confessed having committed the crime . . . and . . . he neither cross-examined the witnesses nor stated anything in mitigation of his guilt." Menzies therefore found Booysen guilty of raping Anna Simpson and sentenced him to death.[8] Nowhere in the records is any mention made of the race of Damon Booysen. However, remarks by the judge, the names of Damon Booysen, his mother, and friends, and his occupation as a day laborer working for another laborer in the poorest section of rural society, all suggest that in terms of the racial and social taxonomies of the mid-nineteenth-century Cape he probably identified himself and was identified by the various communities of George as being a man of color.[9] In 1850, Damon Booysen had good reason to expect that his life was about to end.

At the end of September, however, Justice Menzies wrote to the governor saying that he, Menzies, had made a terrible mistake in sentencing Booysen to death. The victim, Anna Simpson, a woman Menzies had thought was white, had turned out to be of a different racial identity. A deputation of "eight or ten most respectable Inhabitants [read white] of George" having called on the judge and told him that "the woman and her husband are Bastard coloured persons, and that instead of her being a respectable woman, her character for chastity was very indifferent and that it was

---

6   CA, CO 599, Justice Menzies to Governor Harry Smith, 27 September 1850, enclosing Preliminary Examination held at Schoonberg Lange Kloof, before JP, George Division, 2 April 1850. Anna Simpson's name is spelled differently in each of the documents, ranging from Anna to Ann to Annie. I use the name cited in the legal document of the Circuit Court trial. In 1830 George had a population of 8,022. Of that number 5,962 were listed as "free persons" and 2,060 as slaves. Twenty years later the district occupied the same area of 4,032 square miles with a white population of 7,964 and a now undifferentiated coloured population of 7,369. CA, *Cape Almanack for 1830*, 77. ASL, CGH, "Return of the Population and of the Marriages, Births, and Deaths," *Blue Book 1850*, 308–309. George Simpson lived on the farm Brak River and presumably had sufficient money to hire another laborer to help him work on the farm. It is unclear if Simpson was sharecropping or if he was a waged laborer on the farm.

7   CA, CO 599, Justice Menzies to Governor, 27 September 1850, enclosure, Declaration of Damon Booysen to the CP, George, 4 April 1850.

8   CA, CO 599, Justice Menzies to Governor, enclosing the "Report in Writing of all the proceedings of the trial of Damon Booysen, at Circuit Court held at George on 16 September 1850 for rape of Anna Simpson, guilty, to be hanged," 27 September 1850.

9   Damon was a name common to people of Khoi and slave descent in the Western Cape. For example see CA, 1/STB, 2/37, No. 11, Documents in the trial of Damon and Piet Arries for theft of sheep, 1 July 1840; CL, MS, 15 099, Register of Baptisms (in a church in Stellenbosch catering to freed people), Damon Salmon baptized, 10 March 1844. Damon Booysen's mother's name was Maria Platjes, another name which connoted some heritage linking her to the indigenous Khoi pastoralists of the Western Cape. Damon Booysen identified his friend J. Botha as "a man of color." See CA, CO 599, Justice Menzies to Governor, 27 September 1850, enclosing Statements in Inquiry, Statement by Maria Platjes, 16 October 1850; and Petition of Damon Booysen, made in George jail, 21 September 1850.

strongly suspected that she had on several occasions previously voluntarily had connection with the Prisoner."[10] In the light of this development the judge agreed with the deputation in urging the governor to commute Booysen's death sentence to a term of imprisonment with hard labor. The last records available of the case show that the death sentence was indeed commuted. Importantly, while the governor instituted an enquiry into the respectability of Anna Simpson in order to determine the severity of punishment required, the enquiry investigated only her status as a respectable woman; the charge of Anna Simpson being "black" was now undisputed.[11]

The events described took place some twelve years after the ending of slavery. George was a predominantly agricultural district located to the west of Swellendam. As elsewhere in the rural Cape the legal freedom gained for the Khoi by Ordinance No. 50 of 1828 and for slaves by the emancipation of 1838 did not usher in great economic and social opportunity. Both freed people, Khoi, and other members of the free black community continued to work mostly in farm employment.[12]

In the course of the nineteenth century freed people, people of color who had been free under slavery, and some working-class whites and their descendants came to be seen as falling under the racial classification of coloured.[13] This rearrangement of various previously distinct racial status groups into a new racial classification had multiple origins. Into the nineteenth century freed people seem to have continued to construct ethnic sensibilities distinguishing between people of Khoi, Mozambican, and slave descent.[14] However such identities were not mutually exclusive and through the experiences of slavery and freedom a wider rural culture of the poor emerged in the postemancipation Cape. Recent historiography has suggested that identification with a "coloured" ethnic identity arose both from the imposed ascriptions of governmental discourse and from the self-identification of some members of the freed population. It is certainly difficult to pinpoint when in the nineteenth century, and to what extent, the rural poor began to define themselves as coloured . But, as a number of authors have shown, coloured identity emerged among members of the freed population in the rural areas, as well as from "members of the skilled and educated" class, who, in the 1880s, began to validate the term coloured using it as a

---

10   CA, CO 599, Justice Menzies to Governor, 27 September 1850.

11   CA, CO 599, SG to Justice Menzies, 21 October 1850, enclosing letter from RM, George to SG, "containing the result of the inquiry respecting Ann Simpson," 17 October 1850.

12   In 1830 George had a population of 8,022. Of that number 5,962 were listed as "free persons" and 2,060 as slaves. In 1840 George had a white population of 5,561 and a "coloured" population of 5,694, making a total population of 11,185. The overwhelming majority of people (9,000) were employed in agriculture, with 900 involved in manufacturing and 400 in commerce. A decade later an even greater proportion of people were involved in farming, with only 39 engaged in manufacturing and 270 in commerce. CA, "Population of the Cape of Good Hope," *Cape Almanack for 1830*, 77. ASL, CGH, "Return of the Population, and of the Marriages, Births, and Deaths," *Blue Book 1840*, 228–29, and *Blue Book 1850*, 308–309.

13   Mason cites *De Zuid Afrikaan* 7 December 1838 as using the term "gekleurde." Mason, "Fit for Freedom," 589. This is a translation of the English word for "coloured." In later Afrikaans usage, the noun "kleurling" predominated, describing a person who "possessed" the "property" of "colouredness."

14   Adhikari argues that the "distinction between ex-slaves and Khoisan remained fairly clear-cut for the generation that experienced bondage." Mohammed Adhikari, "The Sons of Ham: The Making of coloured Identity," *South African Historical Journal* 27 (1992): 95–112, 109.

platform for political action.[15] In part the rise of the category coloured also arose from what Eva Saks has called, in the context of the postbellum U.S. South, a new "property in race."[16] At the Cape, the possession of legal and/or customary title to whiteness became more important to former slaveholders who could no longer justify claims to authority because of their status as slaveholders. The struggles by Dutch and British settlers to realign domination and status along the axis of a putative white superiority thus influenced their articulation of a racial sensibility about "colouredness."

If the use of the term coloured became increasingly widespread from the mid-nineteenth century it was not necessarily accompanied by great certainty regarding exactly who fell under designation. The "recognition" of "colouredness" depended upon an almost unconscious invocation of "common sense" derived from local association with the norms of domination, status, and somatic recognition upon which so much racial consciousness depends. Settlers seem to have been more certain than British officials of their ability to determine the racial origins or status group to which a person belonged: in the Booysen case, for example, it was the local white inhabitants of George who confidently asserted that Anna Simpson was a "Bastard coloured"—a term probably synonymous in colloquial speech with "Bastard Hottentot." The ambiguity of the term suggests the shifting meanings of racial categories as well as the way in which local claims to knowledge about a person's background helped secure racial identity. Ironically, while British bureaucrats invoked race as a category free of moral or cultural assumptions, it was often their invocation of racial categories which exposed the cultural construction of race as a category of social life.

The term coloured was generally employed by settlers and bureaucrats with much more certainty in terms of including who was *not* a part of the "coloured population." "colouredness" most clearly marked people in the Western Cape who were "not white." The coloured category evolved from the mid-nineteenth century in part to enable whites to distinguish the people of "colour" native to the Western Cape, who had absorbed many of the cultural practices of the colonizers, from the increasing influx of Africans from Xhosaland and other parts of the Eastern Cape. As such, many whites' relationships with people they saw as coloured rested on a profound ambivalence. Whites "recognized" the freed people of the Western Cape as having at least a cultural kinship with whites, but at the same time preserved the notion of whiteness as untainted by relationships with slaves, Khoi, and other Africans. This ambivalence is but one of the strands which came to so complicate the outcome of the Booysen case.

---

15 For an early mention of the term coloured by freed people see, for example, CA, LCA 6, No 46, "Petition of the coloured Inhabitants of the Caledon Missionary Institution," 11 August 1834. For an analysis of the emergence of coloured identity in the Western Cape see Ian Goldin, "The Reconstruction of coloured Identity in the Western Cape," in Shula Marks and Stanley Trapido, eds., *The Politics of Race, Class, and Nationalism in Twentieth Century South Africa* (London: Longman, 1987), 156–81, 160. Mohammed Adhikari suggests that coloured identity "crystallized in the 1880s." Adhikari, "Sons of Ham," 99. Also see Vivian Bickford-Smith, "A 'Special Tradition of Multiracialism'? Segregation in Cape Town in the Nineteenth and Early Twentieth Centuries," in James and Simons, eds., *Angry Divide*.

16 Saks, "Representing Miscegenation Law," 41.

Another feature of racial identification in the nineteenth century was the its location at the intersection of ideas about gender, sexuality, and class identity. In the Booysen case, for example, Justice Menzies' ascription of coloured identity to Anna Simpson, and the meanings which collected around that identity in the context of her rape, can only be understood by analyzing the multilayered colonial and metropolitan histories whereby sexuality, race, gender, and class became referents for one another, as well as being discrete categories of everyday life and of historical analysis. Paradoxically, while the process of classifying an individual's racial identity arose out of a complex identification of class, sexual, and racial markers, once that person had been identified as belonging to any given racial and status group, the ambiguity as to how to deal with that individual often evaporated in the face of the logic of colonial categorization. Once Anna Simpson's race had been proclaimed with certainty by members of the settler elite of George, Judge Menzies confidently proceeded along a different route of sentencing in accordance with the logic of how to deal with the rape of a black woman. Slippery conceptual and social categories could result in unambiguous social and political consequences.

Rape, Race, and Law

The nineteenth-century Cape offers a rather interesting, and sometimes baffling, conjuncture of different legal systems juggling for authority. The legal system was premised upon Roman Dutch law, lawyers and judges were trained in England, and juries were predominantly made up of settlers who drew on local Roman Dutch legal customs. The two legal systems were not so much antithetical as placed at different ends of a continuum. Roman Dutch law placed the individual more firmly within a community than did English law which treated people as individuals before the law. Roman Dutch law continued to be the dominant legal system at the Cape through the nineteenth century although new laws brought the Cape increasingly in line with English legal tenets. The British retained Roman Dutch law in part because it was so deeply entrenched at the Cape, but also because the total elimination of Roman Dutch law in favor of English law would have entailed more effort and expense than the British were willing to invest in this far-flung colony. The establishment of the Supreme Court in 1828 and the reorganization of the judiciary involved the introduction of British legal procedures including the use of preliminary examinations and indictments, the establishment of juries to try serious criminal cases, and the use of English rules of evidence.[17] Abolished in the reshuffle were the centuries-old office of *landdrost* (replaced by magistrates) and the citizen boards called *heemraden* which had controlled district government. The British also eliminated the judicial responsibilities of the field cornets, often farmers themselves, who were notoriously biased in favor of settlers.

The discrepancy between the written laws and the cultural assumptions which informed judges and juries led to a tension between the letter and the interpretation of the law in evaluation and sentencing. While legal precedent did not operate very

---

17 Sachs, *Justice in South Africa*, 38. For an argument as to the importance of British legal views for the Cape see Martin Chanock, "Writing South African Legal History: A Prospectus," *JAH* 30, 2 (1989): 265–88.

forcibly in Roman Dutch law, which was guided more by the original writings on legal issues, British-trained judges and lawyers used precedent nonetheless as a way of arguing for or against certain kinds of punishment. More importantly, since the Charter of Justice explicitly dictated that Roman Dutch law be accommodated to English law, judges and lawyers were given much leeway in bringing their own interpretations to the adjudication of cases. British legal and cultural perceptions particularly influenced crimes located in discourses on sexuality and race. These categories became highly charged in British imperial life in part because of the proliferation of concerns about sexuality in Britain itself in the Victorian era, but also precisely because sex in the colonies was a political act with repercussions as to which children would be included in the category of colonized and which in settler society. "Colonial control was predicated on identifying who was 'white,' who was 'native,' and which children could become citizens rather than subjects, designating who were legitimate progeny and who were not."[18]

In Cape Roman Dutch law rape was understood to be "both the *forcible ravishing* and the *forcible carrying off* of a woman or *maid against her will*."[19] While it is difficult to chart the changing Cape laws relating to rape, at least up to 1845 a man could only be convicted of rape if the prosecution could show that ejaculation had occurred: "that there was emission as well as penetration."[20] The significance of ejaculation in determining rape made the prosecution of rape more difficult at the Cape than in England where after 1828 rape victims no longer had to demonstrate that the rapist had ejaculated.[21] The discrepancy between the Colony and the metropole suggests the ways in which racial hierarchy depended upon the control of sexual relations: illegal reproduction, particularly when it involved a black man and a white woman, threatened the foundations of colonial life.

Cape rape law in the nineteenth century allowed for the death penalty in cases of great severity such as the rape of "a girl still unmarriageable," married women, and rape by men in positions of authority—the latter possibly serving as a racial marker for whiteness.[22] In Cape Dutch settler society a woman's honor referred as much to the men of her family as to the woman herself. Honor and status crucially determined rape cases, influencing whether the rape was reported, how it was evaluated, and the degree of punishment dealt to the rapist. Under Roman Dutch law possibly marriage functioned in this instance, as a potential social marker, dividing women deserving respect and status from the undeserving.[23]

If one can only surmise that such social plots functioned in the actual legislation regarding rape in the Cape Colony, they do seem to have operated very clearly at the level of judicial interpretation. Lawyers appear to have read the terms "married

---

18 Stoler, "Carnal Knowledge," 53.

19 Van der Linden, *Institutes*, 232.

20 Porter, "On the Judicial System," in *Porter Speeches*, 478. Speech made on 15 December 1845.

21 Anna Clark, *Women's Silence, Men's Violence: Sexual Assault in England 1770–1845* (London: Pandora Press, 1987), 60.

22 Van der Linden, *Institutes*, 232.

23 In those cases where marriage did not work as a racial signifier, race was exposed as the final logic operating in sentencing for rape cases. Thus when an unmarried white woman was raped by a black man in 1837, he still received the death sentence. CA, 1/STB 2/36, No. 15, Documents in the case of Regina vs. Adam alias Willem Patience . . . for rape, 5 January 1838.

women" and girls "not yet of marriageable age" as marking those women who deserved the full protection of the law. By being married, women signified publicly that they held to the Christian moral and religious principles of colonial society, and those young girls who had not yet menstruated had the potential to be respectable married women. On the other hand young unmarried women latently violated the sexual code of colonial society. Since they were already of marriageable age, their single state refused, if only symbolically, the married condition. The absence of a death penalty in cases of the rape of an unmarried woman possibly allowed lawyers to dismiss the significance of rape as regards working-class women and, possibly more specifically, black women who were less likely to be married than their settler counterparts. Cape slaveholders' practice of not allowing slaves to marry and the movement of many free blacks into the Muslim community meant that up to the mid to late nineteenth century most young women who were not formally married in the Christian church would have been slaves, free blacks, and other black women. "Married women" came to mean settler women, or certainly women of a certain socioeconomic status. Colonial officials, settlers, and indigenous people understood (although they did not of course necessarily agree with the fact) that race functioned albeit silently dividing beneficiaries of colonial rule from people more explicitly subject to it.

Cultural definitions and redefinitions of rape and sexuality gained prominence in the mid-nineteenth-century Western Cape because the legal system was imbedded both in the cultural assumption of Roman Dutch law, and in the various cultural perceptions of rape and sexuality which judges, lawyers, and juries brought to their interpretations and deliberations. In deliberations regarding the severity of rape and the appropriate punishment both juries and judges at the Cape, like their peers in England and in the U.S. South, fell back upon "common sense" notions of female honor and sexuality derived from local colonial constructions of women and mens' sexuality under slavery, and from the elaboration, both in colonial and metropolitan arenas, of ideologies of female domesticity and chastity.[24] The Supreme Court judges interpreted the law through a perspective on sexuality which saw male sexuality as a result of "uncontrollable passions" and enticement by women. They viewed any evidence of a woman's sexual history outside of marriage to come to conclusions that the woman was a "strumpet" in the words of one judge.[25]

For a woman to show evidence that she had had previous sexual experience was sufficient evidence to dismiss the charges. In a case of rape at Genadendal mission station in 1855, Wilhelmina Johannes lost her case since, according to the clerk of the peace, she said that "had the Prisoner before he committed the Rape civilly asked her consent to have connexion with her, she would have allowed him."[26] Miss Johannes asserted her right to accept or reject a man's advances. In this respect she violated the sexual code which judges demanded of single women: that they reject all sexual advances as a matter of principle. Miss Johannes' charge of rape was further under-

---

24 Bradlow, "Women at the Cape." Also see Edwards, "Sexual Violence," 243.

25 CA, CO 686, Justice Sydney Bell to Governor, 2 October 1856.

26 CA, 1/SWM 16/36, CP, SWM, to AG, 1 March 1855. On the case see CA, 1/CAL 1/1/3, Preliminary Examination in the case of Johannes Stompies for rape, 12 February 1855. For another reference to the case see CA, CSC 1/2/1/54, Records in the Criminal Cases tried at the Circuit Court for the Division of Caledon on 3 March 1855, Printed Indictments.

mined in the opinion of the clerk of the peace by the fact that she stated that she had had sex with other men before this.[27]

Justice Menzies, the Scottish Supreme Court judge who adjudicated the Booysen case, was a most articulate defender and proponent of an interpretation of rape premised upon an emerging discourse about the seemingly unproblematic connections between sexuality, race, and respectability. Menzies also faithfully upheld Roman-Dutch law.[28] He combined his loyalty to legal tenets with a noticeably jaundiced interpretation of the morality of working-class women. In the 1840s, a period which also saw the tenure of liberal Attorney General William Porter, government officials continued to advocate the notion of equality before the law and Menzies appears to have been quite a lone voice in legal circles at this time. George Napier, governor of the colony in the 1840s, regarded Menzies as somewhat dim and pedantic, and does not appear to have shared Menzies' views on the gender and class limits of equality.

In 1843, seven years prior to the Booysen trial, Governor George Napier asked Menzies to give his opinion on whether the Cape Colony should follow Britain which had abolished the death penalty for rape cases in 1841. Menzies suggested that the Cape should not. He argued that the motion had passed in England only because the juries had "of late years shown such an aversion to the infliction of the Punishment of death for such cases of Rape as were brought for trial before them, as, in violation of their oaths as Jurymen, to acquit all persons tried before them for that crime . . . rather than by convictions to put them to the hazard of suffering a Capital Punishment." Menzies stated that the juries must have decided that the cases were not serious given

> the number of chaste & virtuous women in England who would prefer death to being dishonored—and the intense horror which every right-minded man . . . must regard even the idea of . . . Rape being committed on any woman nearly or dearly related to or connected with him. . . . in other words that the injury inflicted on the women in the cases . . . had not been to those women of the same character, class, or station in life, to punish capitally those by whom the crime had been committed.[29]

Menzies believed that the key issue in deciding on appropriate punishment was the "degree of injury which has been occasioned to the woman." In this regard he followed the precepts of Roman Dutch law, which, as we have seen, allowed for the death penalty in aggravated circumstances. Yet Menzies evaluated this injury through his own assumptions of what constituted such circumstances and insisted that class provided an evidentiary and experiential category whereby a woman's honor could be ascertained, an argument with which Governor Napier apparently did not concur.

Menzies stated that "the degree of injury" could only be determined by the victim's feelings of "self-abasement" as a result of the crime, and by "her degradation in the opinions of the class with which she associates." He argued that "it is certain that

---

27 CA, 1/SWM 16/36, CP, SWM, to AG, 1 March 1855. For an example of a similar assessment of a woman's previous sexual history see Clark, *Women's Silence*, 33, the case of Mary Hunt, a prostitute who charged a man with rape.

28 Sachs, *Justice in South Africa*, 41.

29 CA, CO 521, No. 16, Menzies to Governor, 10 February 1843.

women in the lowest ranks on whom rape has been committed suffer much less injury from degradation in the opinions of their associates, than would be occasioned to women in a higher rank of life." And, he concluded, "the injury occasioned to them by their being ravished is not so great as to make it expedient to endeavour to prevent its occurrence by taking the life of the offender." At this point the governor appears to have written in the margin "I cannot agree in this Doctrine. Why, because a woman is poor, she is not to be as securely protected as a rich one, I do not understand."[30]

In talking of women "of the lowest ranks" Menzies spoke in the language of class, but invoked also the colonial knowledge of the almost perfect dovetailing of race and class in the Western Cape in which Africans and freed people occupied the lowest rungs of society. Menzies thus managed to exclude most African and freed women from the circle of honor while permitting the possibility that class might triumph over race in those cases where freed women had moved into respectability. He did allow that at the Cape

> there is a very large proportion of virtuous women in this Colony, principally of pure or nearly pure European Blood but including also in it women of mixed Blood, many of whom would prefer death to being dishonored, on all of whom the commission of Rape on their person would inflict the most poignant & permanent mental anguish & grief [In the margin, George Napier wrote, "I dare say there are"] & whom in many cases, especially if committed by a colored man, it would so degrade in the estimation of their associates, as to drive them from the Society of those with whom they had associated, & mar all their prospects of happiness in life.[31]

In a colony as sparsely populated as the Cape, where men had to travel and leave their wives alone on farms and where, Menzies felt, "a large proportion of the male population of this colony consists of half-civilized & uneducated persons of colour whose passions & appetites are under no restraint except what arises from fear of punishment. . . . I am of opinion that the fear of Punishment of death at present affords to . . . virtuous females of this colony, particularly in the Country districts, their only protection against violence of Lust. . . ." Again, Napier wrote, "I am not prepared to concur in this sweeping clause."[32]

The 1850s, however, witnessed a move away from the liberal humanitarianism of the immediate postemancipation period. While representative government in 1854 introduced a qualified non-racial male franchise, settlers pursued a conservative legislative agenda which had lasting implications for the political economy of the Cape, and later, South Africa as a whole. Legislation passed in this decade criminalized "laziness," desertion, and collective action on the part of workers (who were understood to be mainly black or "coloured"), expanded the powers of field cornets, and introduced divisional councils, dominated by settlers, which controlled access to land. These measures all limited freed people's access to the notion of equality before the law promised by emancipation. A sign of the shift in public life is demonstrated

---

30 Ibid., marginal notes. I cannot be certain as to the author of the comments, but the initials appear to be GN: that is, George Napier.

31 Ibid.

32 Ibid.

in the Booysen case. While Governor Napier had frowned on Menzies' sentiments in the 1840s, in 1850, Governor Harry Smith followed Menzies' interpretation.

Black Women and Rape

Throughout the nineteenth century black women in the Western Cape took men to court for rape: no legal statutes precluded black women from bringing men to court on rape charges.[33] The majority of the rape cases are only accessible through the abstracts of cases which came before the Cape Supreme Court. These tell us the name of the accused and the victim, the place where they resided, and give a brief history of the alleged crime. We encounter the voices of poor rural women through linguistic, colonial, and gendered translations. We can only guess at the many nuances of the witnesses' and victims' original declarations which were lost in translation. They spoke probably in creole Dutch, which was translated by a court translator (who would be most familiar with High Dutch) into English, and then transcribed by a clerk. The few initial preliminary examinations, which are located in the criminal records of the resident magistrates, do provide at least some information into the women and men involved in rape cases. Most often, however, the records on rape are very brief and allow the historian considerable latitude in interpretation. The analysis below is thus offered as one which seems the most plausible given both the evidence and our knowledge of Cape history in the mid-nineteenth century.

No systematic analysis of rape in the nineteenth century Cape has yet been undertaken. The outline below sketches a broad trend derived from different archives covering the period 1831 to 1865.[34] The majority of women bringing men to court for rape at the Cape were members of the working class; indeed the records identified 77 percent of the victims in prosecutions as domestic servants or laborers.[35] Race played a part in determining who was most likely to appear in court as a victim of rape, and who was most likely to be charged with the crime. The majority of the women involved in the cases of rape or attempted appear to have been black. Black

---

33 See CA, 1/STB 22/159, complaint by Theresa to APS, 26 Jan., 1833; CA, 1/STB 2/34, Documents in the trial of Jan Hermanus (Khoi) for rape of Anna (Khoi), 4 March 1834; CA, CSC 1/2/1/15, No. 7, Circuit Court for the District of Swellendam, Case of Jacob Oranje (Bastard Hottentot) for attempted rape of Silvia, a slave, 19 January 1835; CA, 1/STB 2/35, Documents in the trial of Andries Bantom, 19 March 1835; CA, 1/WOC 3/9, Preliminary Examination in case of Pass Platjes for rape of Dina Koeberg, 6 February 1843.

34 These figures are very difficult to gauge correctly. My records from each archive overlap in terms of period, but not all the records cover the entire period 1831 to 1865. In addition, it was hard to determine if rapes listed in one archive are also cross-listed, in different form, in another. The sources used for the following discussion include records of proceedings in criminal trials from the archives of the Stellenbosch, Swellendam, Worcester, and Cape Town magisterial districts. The Cape Town criminal records include cases from Paarl, Stellenbosch, and other country locales close to the town. I also draw on records from the Cape Supreme Court circuit court, and the reports of the High Sheriff on cases to be tried in the Supreme Court. For a brief comparison between Yorkshire rape figures and those of the Cape see Scully, "Rape, Race, and Colonial Culture," 348–353.

35 I have had to collapse the categories of domestic servant and laborer since it was not possible in most cases to be more precise than to say that the woman was working in some sort of unskilled work. Only two of the cases involved slave women (both of whom were raped by laborers), while six involved women who were identified as the wives of sawyers, coachmen, and fishermen. Only three cases involved the rape of farmers' daughters.

men also made up the overwhelming number of the men charged with rape or attempted rape.[36]

The class and racial profile of rape victims arose in part because of the near perfect dovetailing of race and class status in the nineteenth-century Cape, although a stratum of white laborers is evident in the records. Despite inadequate precision and different ways of categorizing information, the censuses of 1865 and 1875 reveal that black women "predominated among those who can unequivocally be designated pauper and working-class women." Black women were also prevalent among "the lowest unskilled but 'respectable' group of working-class women—washerwomen and laundresses."[37] White women do appear as rape victims, but it is striking that these women were largely members of the working class, being domestic servants, laborers, or wives of laborers.[38]

Working-class women were most likely to be victims of assault defined as rape since they often worked late at night and had to walk long distances by themselves.[39] For example, one evening in 1835 a laborer, Andries Bantom, raped Jannetje, the daughter of an ex-slave of Carel Petrus Theron at Klein Drakenstein outside Stellenbosch when she was sent by her "mother Philida with some curtains which she had washed" to a Mrs. Mellet who resided nearby. Bantom received thirty-six lashes and twelve months hard labor.[40] Eight years later Mentor Klouters raped Rozet, a fellow worker on a farm in the Worcester district, when she was working in a garden "fully a mile from the house." Rozet's mother testified that her daughter was a virgin at the time of the rape, which was probably the reason why Mentor Klouters initially received a sentence of death.[41]

Like domestic abuse, forced sexual relations tended to be labeled as rape in the mid-nineteenth century when it occurred outside the family and domestic circle. The

---

36 Of the 67 rapes in which the women were identified, 43 of these cases appear to have involved black women while in 12 cases white women were the victims. The remaining 12 cases constitute those in which the race of the woman was difficult to gauge. Black men were involved in 65 out of 90 cases of rape. Only 12 white men were brought to trial on rape or attempted rape charges. In the remaining 13 cases I was unable to ascribe a racial identity to the defendant. In all these cases, however, it must be stressed that the tally of rapes is very tentative, and very imprecise markers such as name and occupation were used to determine the race of the woman since race was rarely indicated on the forms summarizing the cases. Edwards' analysis of rape in Granville county shows that about half of the twenty-four cases there involved black women. Edwards, "Sexual Violence," 242.

37 Bradlow, "Women at the Cape," 68, 69. The immigration of children under the auspices of the Children's Friends Society in the 1830s added to the white laboring population, as did those sailors who decided to remain at the Cape.

38 For example on 30 July 1861, Ellen Pearson, wife of William Pearson, a bricklayer, was raped by one Jessie Ruth, a laborer, at Bennetsville in the division of Paarl. Ruth was found guilty and given two years hard labor. CA, CSC 1/1/1/18, "Calendar of the Names of Parties . . . .against whom Bills of Indictment will be presented to the Grand Jury," Criminal Session of Supreme Court [hereafter "Calendar of Names"], 1 November 1861. Edwards, "Sexual Violence," 242, finds a similar pattern.

39 Anna Clark suggests that poor women in England were similarly preyed upon by men who saw women walking alone as legitimate quarry. Clark, Women's Silence, 38.

40 CA, 1/STB 2/35, Documents in the trial of Andries Bantom, 19 March 1835.

41 CA, CO 521, No. 105, Justice Menzies to Governor, enclosing a report on the Proceedings and Evidence at the Trial of Mentor Klouters, at the Circuit Court at Worcester on 13 November 1843, 18 November 1843. Klouters' sentence was subsequently commuted. For another example of such vulnerability see 1/STB 22/43, Statement of Silvia to JP, 18 March 1847.

fact that women of the middle and farming classes are so absent in the records as victims of rape in the Western Cape might also have arisen from the way that rape was popularly and legally defined in the nineteenth century. Forced sexual attention by a man against a woman was most likely to be defined as rape if the man was not the husband or a close friend of the woman.[42] Women were more likely to have success prosecuting rape, and were possibly themselves more likely to have defined sexual abuse as rape, if it involved someone outside their immediate family. White women in the towns lived increasingly circumscribed lives; they did not leave their houses unaccompanied very often.[43] The men to whom they were probably most vulnerable regarding rape, such as their husbands and other male relatives and peers, were protected by their positions in society. In addition, social pressure from families not to appear in court and dishonor the family, and the use of civil measures such as bringing men to court for seduction might be reasons why so few middle-class women appeared in the records as victims of rape.[44]

Working class women appear to have been much more willing to prosecute men for rape or attempted rape. Under slavery slaveholders literally had owned women's bodies. In the postemancipation setting freed women possibly sought to stress their ownership and control of their person. The consolidation of the tradition of legal appeal during amelioration in the 1820s and 1830s, and apprenticeship from 1834 to 1838, provided impetus in the postemancipation period for rural women's actions against what they perceived as infringements of their rights.[45]

In 1836, Anna, a woman defined as Khoi in the record, in the service of a widow in Stellenbosch, complained that she had been attacked by Dienaar de Vries, a Khoi hawker. Anna said the widow Van der Byl had ordered her to collect wood and she left the house in order to do so at about 6 p.m. De Vries followed her on to the property of Pieter Edward Hamman and then approached her. Anna testified that she had stated that she was not acquainted with him to which "he replied that did not signify . . . that he had long been on the lookout for such a one as I was. . . ." Dienaar

---

42   No cases of incestual rape within white middle-class or farming families appear in the records. I found only a handful of cases relating to incest and they involved only men of the laboring or skilled working class. For example CA, CSC 1/1/1/20, "Calendar of Names," 1 November 1865; and CA, CSC 1/1/1/21, "Calendar of Names," 15 January 1867.

43   For the history of Victorian gender ideology at the Cape, see Bradlow, "Women at the Cape," who suggests that among rural Dutch families, women were not encouraged even to engage in charity work. The records of the Dutch Reformed Church in Stellenbosch however do indicate that women were prominent in the missionary activities of the Stellenbosch Missionary Society. See CA, DRC, P 31 1/3, Diary of P. D. Luckhoff, of the SMS, 4 December 1838.

44   It is virtually impossible to determine if any of these civil cases originated in rape, but it does suggest that women's honor was crucial in determining eligibility for marriage, and so bringing a man to court on a charge of rape, in a situation where the victim was on trial as much as the accused, might very well have acted as a deterrent. See for example CA, CSC 2/1/1/5, No. 49, 12 October 1828; CSC 2/1/1/16, No. 21, 21 June 1831; CSC 2/1/1/20, No. 16, 26 June 1832; CSC 2/1/1/25, No. 28, 8 August 1833; and CSC, 2/1/1/67, No. 19, 3 June 1851.

45   CA 1/STB 22/19, Complaint to the Assistant Protector of Slaves, Stellenbosch, by Theresa, a slave, against a slave man for raping a fellow slave woman, 26 January 1833; CA, CSC 1/2/1/15, No. 7, Circuit Court for the District of Swellendam, case of Jacob Oranje, for attempted rape of Silvia, trial held 1 January 1835. For discussion of the importance of amelioration for validating legal procedures see Wayne Dooling, "Slaves, Slaveholders, and Amelioration in Graaff Reinet, 1823–1830" (Honors diss., Department of History, University of Cape Town, 1989), Ch. 2, 32.

took her behind a bush and said he wanted "to have connection with me . . . I told him I could not allow it, that I had a husband . . . I was not used to remain in the bushes that I had a young child at home and that my mistress would be angry." De Vries took her to a threshing room where, after putting a brick to her head "with which he threatened to knock out my brains," he tried to rape her, being prevented from doing so when a laborer came into the room.[46]

In her testimony Anna raised a number of reasons as to why she "could not allow" Dienaar to have sex with her, invoking her status as a married woman and a mother of a child, and referring too to the possible anger of her mistress should she, Anna, return late. Anna employed respectability as a way of staking her claim to the protection and understanding of the court; she also alluded to her position as a dutiful servant. Anna might have used these rhetorical strategies "to acquire status not as a mute, colonized object, but as a voiced individual with a socially condoned moral . . . life. . . ."[47] By raising her marital status in court, Anna possibly attempted to alert the magistrate to her status as a "respectable married woman" thus emphasizing her claim to honor and protection. By saying that she "was not used to remain in the bushes" Anna perhaps also sought to set herself off from contemporary stereotypes of Khoi women and men which represented them as living "wandering" lives and preferring the "bush" of barbarism to the community of civilization.[48]

As a last resort she appealed to her and De Vries' shared experience as subalterns in a colonial system which privileged the rights of masters over those of servants. Anna invoked her "special status" as a married woman who did not live in the bush to try to obtain respect from De Vries and from the magistrate. She thus employed a variety of rhetorical strategies to prevent being raped, and also used this rhetoric in subsequent testimony possibly to invoke a sympathetic response from the resident magistrate, but these tactics did not work: the judge acquitted Dienaar de Vries. While the records of rape cases in the rural Western Cape rarely tell us much about the motivations of the rapists or the reactions of the victims, this case suggests that one woman perceived unwanted sexual attention as an infringement of her rights and on her body, and rape as a heinous crime against her person.[49] Freed women might well have defined honor in terms of getting public redress for infringement upon their persons. Honor and shame thus were configured differently perhaps for women of the former slaveholding class and women who had been slaves or dependent laborers, but not in the way that Menzies envisioned. Freed women at the Cape saw rape as a violent act and attempted to seek redress for this crime.

Of the men who were identified as rapists, out of the sixty-nine cases in which the occupation of the assailant is known, fully 81 percent of the alleged rapists were

---

46 CA, 1/STB 2/35, Documents in the Trial of Dienaar de Vries . . . for intention to commit rape on Anna," 15 December 1836. On the back of the trial documents it is written that Dienaar was a "Hottentot." Anna's last name is not provided.

47 Ferguson, *Subject to Others*, 289.

48 The dichotomy of the bush and the town as metaphors for barbarism and civilization played out both in British colonial rhetoric and in some indigenous symbolic systems. For archival references by Dutch farmers and officials to the Khoi see for example, CA, 1/STB 18/188, Statement by Widow Spykerman, 5 August 1836; CA, GH 23/12, Governor to SSC, enclosing Opinion of the Attorney General regarding the proposed Vagrancy Law, 22 June 1838. For the British see Crais, "Vacant Land."

49 See also the case of Wilhelmina Johannes mentioned above, as well as that of Rosie Dryden, below.

identified as laborers. The man most likely to be charged with rape at the Cape was a working-class man, and particularly a man involved in unskilled labor. Of the fifty cases in which I was able to identify the occupation of both the victim and the alleged assailant, 66 percent involved laborers, 1 percent involved laborers raping wives or daughters of skilled workers, and only one case involved a farmer who was alleged to have raped a servant woman, a case which never came to trial.[50]

Black men were much more likely to be charged with rape than white men.[51] The majority of the cases in which white men were charged with rape involved laborers, or sailors: that is, men of the working class who enjoyed little status in Cape society. Most of the rapes which came to court in the Western Cape in the mid-nineteenth century therefore were perpetrated by men of the laboring class against women of the same class, and in those records in which we are given sufficient detail to make an analysis, it seems that the women knew the men concerned. In 1835, Willem, a so-called "Bastard Hottentot" of Caledon district, attempted to rape a Khoi woman, Amelia Hartenbeeste, with whom he seems to have had a relationship. Ms. Hartenbeeste stated in her testimony that on the 22 August, a Saturday night, at

> about nine o'clock. Willem, a bastard Hottentot, in the service of the field cornet PAR Otto, came to the pondok where I reside at Caledon. I was in my bed . . . he laid hold of me and said he would *druk it too*, that he would have me for his wife, that I had drank with him, and if I would not have him for a husband, he would murder me & that no other man would have me.[52]

Willem seems to have thought that Ms Hartenbeeste's willingness to socialize with him in another context gave him the right to have sex with her when he chose.

Rape, Race, and Colonial Culture

Very few insights into sexual exploitation or sexual relations between white farmers and their female employees or other women of the rural poor appear in the local records of Stellenbosch, Swellendam, or Worcester districts. This silence on the question of possible sexual relations across putative racial categories echoes the larger silence on these issues in the wider archival record. In the cases involving men whom I guessed would have been thought of as white, only two involved farmers, or men who would have had some social standing in the community, and even then

---

50 CA, 1/SWM 16/35, CP to AG, 15 February 1855. A complaint was made against Charles Barry but it was not followed up. Possibly this is because six months elapsed between the alleged rape and the woman's complaint.

51 Of the seventy-seven cases in which the race of the assailant can be identified, 84 percent of the cases involved black men. The close correlation between the 81 percent of laborers charged with rape, and the 84 percent of black men, points again to the association between race and class status which continued through the nineteenth century. "By the early 1860s, there were around twenty-three thousand 'agricultural workers' in the Western Cape. Of these, approximately three thousand, or nearly 13 percent, were 'European'. Only 10 percent, or 1,416 out of 13,712, farmers in the western Cape were 'coloured.'" Marincowitz, "Rural Production," 116.

52 CA, 1/SWM 16/29, JP, CAL, to CP, SWM, 29 August 1835, Preliminary Examination, 27 August1835. As far as I can ascertain the charge was not followed up. For other examples see CA, 1/STB 2/35, Documents in trial of Andries Bantom, 19 March 1835. Also see CA, 1/WOC 3/9, Preliminary Examination in the case of Pass Platjes for rape, 6 February 1843.

it is difficult to measure whether they were wealthy farmers or farmers working on the share. These two cases were for rapes of white women.[53] The demographics of rape suggest that a black woman could more easily bring a black man to court for rape or attempted rape than a "respectable" white farmer: the archive does not easily reveal the sexual exploitation by farmers and men of social standing of working-class women. The annals of sexual exploitation at the Cape say perhaps more about the suppression involved in the creation of identities and histories, than the elaboration of "facts." We hear more of the echoes of what might have been than a record of the past.

A case from Swellendam district illuminates the location of sexuality within an intricate pattern of racial ascription, status, and power. In 1852, the child of Clara, a laborer on the farm of Johannes Zacharias Moolman of Swellendam, was murdered and buried in a ditch. The defendants were Zamonie, identified in the documents as a "female negro about 17 years of age," and Marthinus and Joppie Roodman, fellow laborers on the farm. It seems from the evidence that these men were white and that Joppie Roodman was the father of the child that he was accused of killing.[54] In the ensuing case Zamonie was cleared of all charges of murdering the child but in return was called to make a statement to Resident Magistrate Clarence Thomas Wylde.

Zamonie stated in her first testimony in November 1851 that Joppie Roodman had frequently stated that he wanted to "destroy the child." Zamonie declared that Joppie had wanted to sleep with her but that she had "told him he had a child by a Hottentot what would he do with me. . . ."[55] In a statement on the previous day, Charl Willem Jooste, who was not identified, said that it "was the general conversation in the neighborhood that Joppie's relations were angry about his having a Hottentot child."[56]

Joppie seems to have killed his child since the social censure within the white community was so great against him having had a child with a Khoi woman. If he was a member of the white sharecropping class, which became particularly prevalent in Swellendam and Caledon districts from the 1860s, then the only barrier which raised him above his fellow laborers was his race: no wonder his family was so incensed that he had had relations with a Khoi woman.[57] It seems though that Joppie himself, while eager to abolish evidence of a sexual relationship with a black woman, was nonetheless very enthusiastic about having a sexual relationship with Zamonie.

---

53   CA, CO 578, Chief Justice to Governor, enclosing a report of the proceedings in the trial of Cornelis Volschenk for rape of Anna Eliza de Vos, daughter of Wouter Abraham de Vos, held at the circuit court at Swellendam, 13 March 1848, 20 March 1848; CA, CSC 1/1/1/20, "Calendar of Names,"1 May 1866. Benjamin Smit Altree, tried on 7 May 1866 for rape.

54   CA, 1/SWM 2/31, Documents in the trial of Zamonie for murder of child of Clara, 18 February 1852. Different sets of evidence refer to Joppie as Joppie, Joppy, and Toppie. I have used the name which emerges most often. The handwriting in the records was sometimes difficult to read, so this name is still only a good guess.

55   Ibid., Loose-leaf statement, 12 November 1851. Zamonie said further that "I told him if he looked to the child which he had by Clara—he could then sleep with me. I meant that he was to make away with the child. I know that Mrs. Moolman [her employer] wanted the child—and Clara would not give up the child. Toppie wanted her to do so and they quarreled about it."

56   Ibid., Statement by Charl Willem Jooste, 11 November 1851.

57   Marincowitz, "Rural Production," 123.

On 17 July 1852 the resident magistrate asked Zamonie about her child. Zamonie stated that on an earlier occasion she had said the child was Cheko's, an African laborer on the farm,

> and if my child that I have now in my arms were a black child I would have said still that the child was his, but now seeing my child is white I say that the child is Pieter Moolman's. The son of my master. I would not say so before because I feared my master and mistress. Cheko slept with me first and afterwards Peter [sic] Moolman. The child is not Joppie's as Joppie has brown eyes and my child has blue eyes like Pieter Moolman.

Pieter Moolman had no connection with me in Swellendam. But at Roespes Weg in the Mill [unclear]. He may deny it but I swear that the child is his.

Joppie never had any connection with me. . . .[58]

It is unclear from Zamonie's statement whether she perceived her child as white when it was born, or whether under the questioning of the resident magistrate she was led to the conclusion that the child was white. In July, the district surgeon wrote to the clerk of the peace at Swellendam saying that he had looked at Zamonie's child.

> How far forensic practice likeness to parents, or color may be admitted to prove criminality—I am no judge, but physiologically speaking I should have no hesitation in fathering the child to Joppie—I admit having seen light colored children from Mozambique parents—but invariably with the short woolly hair peculiar to Africans—This child is particularly light colored with silky soft hair and if I may use the terms Caucasian.[59]

Given the fact that Zamonie had stated that Pieter Moolman, her employer's son, had had sex with her not Joppie Roodman it is striking that the doctor linked the child directly to Roodman. He seems to have wanted to move the case away from considering the evidence of a sexual relationship between Moolman and Zamonie. It would be helpful to know more of Joppie Roodman's background. If he was poor white, the doctor's projection of paternity for Zamonie's child onto Joppie might also be an indication of the power that wealthier farmers possessed to steer evidence of sexual impropriety away from themselves onto men who were less respectable, in this case Joppie Roodman who had already demonstrated his degeneracy by having a child with a Khoi woman. In this tantalizing case in which so many of the pieces are missing we still have dramatic evidence of the various costs and implications of engaging in sex across acceptable boundaries of status and race. It appears that Joppie Roodman was prepared to kill his own child in order to destroy connection to the Khoi woman Clara.

The records suggest that black laborers and their employers shared some attitudes regarding the rape of black women and that a tenuous bridge of masculinity could be momentarily constructed around a joint perception of the sexual availability of women. In 1839 a laborer called Charles who worked on the farm of Jacob de Villiers in Franschehoek was charged with the rape of Rosie Dryden, a domestic servant from Cape Town. Miss Dryden and her aunt and cousin had been visiting her relatives in "the interior" and stopped on their return to Cape Town at De Villiers' farm

---

58 CA, 1/SWM, 2/31, Documents in the trial of Zamonie for murder of child Clara, 18 February 1852, Statement of Zamonie, 17 July 1852.

59 Ibid., District Surgeon to CP, SWM, 8 July 1852.

so that they could visit their relatives who were in his employ and who were ill with measles. De Villiers threw her off the farm charging that she had brought the disease. As Rosie Dryden and her cousin were on their way to a neighboring farm where her aunt had found employment, Charles came up to Rosie Dryden and asked where they were going.

> I replied "to my Aunts at Mrs. Roux"—when he told me "that my Aunt said I was not to come as she slept in the kitchen and there was no place for me, but that I should return to his master's and sleep in his room. . . . I told him that I would not go back to his room . . . I said "I don't like to sleep with all black boys" he then said "why not" "It was not proper for girls to do so"—I said—"and the smell in your room is too disagreeable."[60]

Charles tried to rape Rosie but Savonie, her cousin, got help from two laborers who brought Charles and the women back to De Villiers. When De Villiers had heard the story, Miss Dryden said "he replied, if Charles had cut off my head, it would have served me right . . ." Charles subsequently asked Rosie's forgiveness, but, finding his apology unacceptable, she proceeded to lay a complaint against him at the local magistrate's office. According to Rosie Dryden, Charles said "he did not intend to murder me but to have connexion with my body—I replied he should ask his God to forgive him, and not ask me. . . ."[61]

Rosie Dryden did not say merely that she did not want to have sex with Charles, but identified Charles' putative skin color and living habits as reasons why she had no wish to sleep with him. She identified him as "all black" thereby invoking the boundary between herself and a man who seems to have fallen in her mind outside of the coloured category. While in the early nineteenth century the slaveholding community and travelers had represented slaves of Mozambican descent as being most inferior to Malay and Cape-born slaves, this instance suggests that some free black women shared this perception in the mid-nineteenth century.[62] Charles and Mr. de Villiers seem to have shared an opinion that a woman had no right to refuse sex when a man demanded it, or at least that a working-class woman did not have that right: Mr. de Villiers clearly saw Miss Dryden's charge of rape as inconsequential, while Charles perceived her objections as arising from her understanding that he had wanted to kill her, not from objections to his attempted rape.

Rape, Whiteness, and Masculinity

Returning to the case of the rape of Anna Simpson, at first it seems astonishing that in 1850, a group of men, who were very likely to have been white settlers, should petition the government on behalf of a lowly black laborer. After all, only twelve years before the Cape had been a racially stratified slaveholding society dragged into an

---

60 Very little evidence exists about the thoughts of the men who were charged with rape. CA, 1/STB 2/36, No. 7, Documents in the case of Charles . . . for rape . . . , 19 July 1839.

61 Ibid.

62 See William Bird, *State of the Cape in 1822* (Facsimile reprint edition, Cape Town, 1966), 74, where he asserts that "The Africander [sic] slave girl would consider herself disgraced by connection with the Negro, or the production of a black infant."

era of free wage labor by the impulse of the antislavery movement in Britain and a resigned Colonial Office. The actions of settlers in the aftermath of emancipation only heightens the strangeness of this gesture of empathy: in 1834 farmers throughout the Cape called for a Vagrancy Act which would have forced freed people and other free blacks to work, subsequently helped draft stringent labor laws which severely impeded the rights of servants as against those of employers, and complained incessantly to the Colonial Office about the unwillingness of freed people and other people of color to work on the farms. If anything a reader of the Cape mid-nineteenth-century archival record might expect that white settlers would have been rather happy to see a black rural laborer lose his life at the gallows. However in the light of what we have learned from the Dryden case perhaps it is not so surprising that in 1850 white men of George could find commonality with a black laborer over the rape of a rural working-class woman.

In fact, additional incidents occurred in the aftermath of emancipation in 1838 in which white men petitioned the government on behalf of a black man accused of rape. In 1852 seventy-four men of George again petitioned the Governor to commute the death sentence of Kobus Goliath, stating that Kobus had had no intention of killing the woman he had raped and that the "offence did not seem to be premeditated, and that the complainant was not deprived of her life."[63] As in the case of Anna Simpson (once her racial status had been "clarified") the woman raped was a black woman.

The petitions written predominantly or exclusively by white men on behalf of black men accused of rape indeed have one feature in common: that the woman who had been raped was black, or at least perceived as being so in the white community. As one might recall, the petitioners for Damon Booysen insisted on labeling Anna Simpson and her husband "Bastard coloured." The fact that the petitioners perceived Anna Simpson to be a "Bastard coloured," (having had a slave mother and Khoi father), that is, "not white," was an element in their support for Damon Booysen. It also turned out to be a pillar upon which Judge Menzies was to rest his appeal for clemency. By designating the couple as coloured the petitioners in effect cast the first slur on the character of Anna Simpson. When black men raped white women they were not as likely to receive such a warm defense by white men. Willem Patience, a Khoi laborer in the service of Willem Basson, a farmer in Stellenbosch district, received the death sentence in 1838 for raping Huibregtje Johanna Elizabeth Croeze, the daughter of a farmer in the same district.[64] In contrast, when a white farmer, Cornelis Volschenk, was convicted of raping a farmer's daughter and sentenced to death on 13 March 1848, the governor commuted the sentence to ten years hard labor—the

---

63 CA, CO 615, SG to Governor, enclosing report of proceedings in case of Kobus Goliath for rape with intent to commit murder, 28 February 1852. I find myself falling into the same situation as the judge. Since racial designations were not written into trial proceedings very often, one has to make guesses according to the names. Goliath was a typical slave surname. As such I am presuming he was probably a member of the freed community. CA, CO 615, Memorial of Undersigned Inhabitants at George, undated. Signatories included names such as W. Elliot, Robert Mollison, J. C. Truter (a distinguished Cape settler family), J. M. Johnson, and J. W. Cooper. See also CA, CO 503, No. 118, Justice Menzies to Governor commenting on the case of Jacob Magerman for Rape, 15 November 1841.

64   CA, 1/STB 2/36, No. 15, Documents in the case of Regina vs. Adam, alias Willem Patience for rape, 5 January 1838.

jury and others having written a memorial in his support.[65] The rape of a white farmer's daughter involved all the elements which Menzies was to argue constituted a case of aggravated rape—loss of status, feelings of shame, and great "injury"—yet ultimately the race of the rapist helped determine sentencing.

One way of understanding the Booysen case is through attention to the narratives, or the "sexual stories" that white men told themselves in the aftermath of emancipation.[66] Hanna Rosen has suggested that during Reconstruction in the U.S. South, white men, both former slaveholders and poor white men, perceived relations of power operating through a complex racial and sexual economy premised upon the subordination and availability of black women. They sought to shape the understandings and social definitions of rape in a way which excluded any sexual activities on their part being defined as rape.[67] White male domination in the postemancipation Cape operated around a similar linkage of racial and sexual domination, which saw black women's bodies as the property of men, and more specifically the property of white men. Possibly white men in the rural areas perceived the negation of their sexual abuse of black women as particularly important in maintaining a representation of white sexual dominance of black women which had its formative roots in the sexual economy of slaveholding. While Roman Dutch law prohibited slave owners from "forcing a slave to obey any such commands which are contrary to law or morality," apparently the statute was never used to prosecute rape cases.[68]

It is unclear if white men regarded black women in particular, or working-class women in general, as particularly vulnerable to sexual exploitation. It is also unclear to what extent black men in the postemancipation Western Cape shared this sense of the right to have sexual relations with black and/or working-class women. Historians have pointed to widespread violence by slave men against slave women in the Cape Colony, citing the uneven sex ratio in which men competed for few women, or frustration of masculinity as reasons for this abuse.[69] Perhaps we might more fruitfully examine the silences which pertained to the sexual violence of white men against both white and black women and rather interrogate the constitution of the archives as productive of the historical subjects of the "violent slave man" and the "sexual slave woman." The criminal records produce and reproduce the "fact" of violence and degeneracy within freed families and the "fact" of harmony and support within settler families.

One can read the response of the petitioners in the Booysen case as a defensive reaction. These white men's sense of identity had in part derived from their power

---

65   CA, CO 578, Chief Justice to Governor, enclosing a report on the proceedings in the trial of Cornelis Volschenk for rape . . . , 20 March 1848.

66   See Hall, "The Mind that Burns in Each Body."

67   Hanna Rosen, "Sexual Violence in the Era of Reconstruction" (paper presented to Postemancipation Conference, University of Michigan, April 1990). For other observations on this definition of rape see Edwards, "Sexual Violence."

68   "Statement of the Laws of the Colony of the Cape Regarding Slavery," cited in Mason, "Fit for Freedom," 210. Some disagreement exists on the nature of sexual violence under Cape slavery. Patricia van der Spuy argues that "many slaveholders did not take the right of sexual possession for granted." John Mason suggests instead that for most slave women relationships with slave masters were premised not on consent, but abuse. The weight of power in Cape slave society as in many others in favor of the masters makes the latter interpretation most likely. Van der Spuy, "Collection," 18; Mason, "Fit for Freedom," 210.

69   For a critique of this historiography see Van der Spuy, "Collection," Ch. 2.

over others: with the ending of slavery the power over the bodies of black men was symbolically and, in some senses, actually curtailed. And if the bodies of black women were also no longer legally owned, the sexual economy which made all women subject to the power of men made black women a close and easy target for sexual abuse. One might say that the sexual story that these petitioners told themselves was that while one arena of domination had been foreclosed another still existed. The identity of the petitioners as white males in a colonial society in part depended upon a negation that their abuse of black women constituted a crime punishable by death. This view therefore depended also upon a negation of the possibility that black women had "honor" to lose.

The petitioners' "rescue" of Damon Booysen perhaps illustrates a tenuous bridge of masculinity thrown across class and racial identities in one particular juncture. Yet this bridge across race was itself a defense of a racially constructed sexual right to the bodies of black women. In the end the petition by respectable white men on behalf of a disreputable black man should not be read as a denial of the salience of race in Cape colonial life—that is, that white men and a black man could find commonality. Rather the petitioners thereby defended and legitimated a racial interpretation of female sexuality which ultimately overrode any claims black women might have to respectability. The "respectable" white men of George came to the rescue of Damon Booysen not so much to save him as to save themselves.

And what of Judge Menzies' switch in the Booysen case? In light of his statement of 1843, we can appreciate why Menzies sentenced Booysen to death for rape of a white woman seven years later. In his first reading of the case Menzies saw an instance in which a virtuous white woman was raped by a man of a class which Menzies had called "half-civilized . . . whose passions & appetites are under no restraint."[70] In addition, the woman had been left on her farm when her husband had to go to town, in precisely the kind of situation which Menzies saw as so dangerous to virtuous wives at the Cape. He had believed "that for the due protection of the chastity and honor of respectable married women in this colony, it was necessary that the sentence of Death should be pronounced on the Prisoner."[71] Yet, after his meeting with the deputation from George, Menzies came to revise the premises upon which he had evaluated the case. Now, the case seemed of another sort, in which a licentious woman of "mixed" race (being of Khoi and white descent) had seduced a young man of eighteen, a man whose passions were, after all, "under no restraint." Now Anna Simpson's lifestyle came under review and was found wanting. The fact that she was married did not serve as sufficient reason for maintaining the sentence of death since, by the accounts of the "respectable" men of George, she was not respectable, and neither was she white. While in 1843 Menzies had alluded to the fact that women of "mixed race" might have a sense of virtue, in 1850 he ultimately relied upon a racial determination in his assessment of the severity of the crime perpetrated against Anna Simpson.[72]

It is unclear what helped anchor her racial status as black, when the judge had been so sure she was white, but in part it seems it was fixed by the other claims

---

70   CA, CO 521, No. 16, Justice Menzies to Governor, 26 February 1843.

71   CA, CO 599, Justice Menzies to Governor, 27 September 1850.

72   CA, CO 521, No. 16, Justice Menzies to Governor, 26 February 1843. CA, CO 599, Declaration of Damon Booysen to CP, George, 4 April 1850, enclosure in letter from Justice Menzies to Governor, 27 September 1850.

relating to Anna Simpson's putative adulterous behavior. Damon Booysen's mother claimed that she had on a previous occasion seen Anna Simpson "lay hold of my son by his private parts," and Damon stated in a memorial drawn up after the initial sentence that he had previously had sex with Anna Simpson.[73] Thus Anna Simpson's race was explained with reference to sexuality—the one category helped explain and construct the other.

Yet by other accounts Anna Simpson was a respectable woman, and she was married in a period in which many of the rural poor were not. In addition, both she and her husband worked. Yet once defined as a "Bastard coloured," probably a synonym for "Bastard Hottentot," the illegitimate child of a slave father and Khoi mother, Anna Simpson received the first strike against her meriting the full protection of the law. The term "Bastard Hottentot" derived from the understanding that a slave man could not claim legal heirs, being a man without honor, outside of the natal circle, devoid of social standing.[74] A slave's "bastard" child implicitly inherited this marginal status: beyond the pale of family and, in one respect, beyond the law. In addition the ascribing of "Bastard coloured" or "Bastard Hottentot" status to Anna Simpson also made more feasible the innuendoes about her sexual behavior—the resident magistrate of George who argued that he could draw no conclusions from the depositions of numerous witnesses who testified to her morality since they were "all related by marriage to Anna Simpson."[75]

In a context in which he had to evaluate the sexuality of a black man and a black woman the judge fell back upon notions of black women's rampant sexuality which had a long history in Cape colonial discourse, dating from at least the late eighteenth century. By the 1820s Europeans increasingly fashioned knowledge about Khoi and slave women through a sexually delineated lens. It was after all a Khoi woman who was paraded through Europe in the early 1800s, shown off at balls, named the "Hottentot Venus," and made an object of elite and intellectual discussion.[76]

Menzies' interpretation of the punishment required for the rape of Anna Simpson reveals, at least in this instance, that when race, class, sexuality, and gender were put up against one another, a woman's sexuality was determined by her race: class and culture could not "rescue" her. The referential relationship between racial and sexual stereotypes served to categorize Anna Simpson in a situation where both her race, her status, and her sexual life were far from apparent.

---

73 Jan Botha, the man who Booysen claimed as a witness to his having had sex previously with Anna Simpson, denied this. CA, CO 599, Statement by Jan Botha, Statement by Maria Platjes, Statements in Inquiry into case of Damon Booysen, 16 October 1850; Petition of Damon Booysen, George, 21 September 1850, enclosures in letter from Justice Menzies to Governor, 27 September 1850.

74 Patterson, *Slavery and Social Death*, Ch. 1.

75 CA, CO 599, RM, George, to SG, 17 October 1850, enclosure in letter from Justice Menzies to Governor, 27 September 1850.

76 See Sander L. Gilman, *Difference and Pathology: Stereotypes of Sexuality, Race, and Madness* (Ithaca: Cornell University Press, 1985), Ch. 3.

Conclusion

Rape clearly marks one arena in which men and women's experience of liberty differed. Slave women had lived with sexual violence legitimated through an intersection of ideas about masculinity and slaveholder power which made slave women vulnerable to rape by slaveholders and by slave men. On emancipation freed women continued to live under the threat of sexual violence, which was now legitimated through claims to a specific form of masculinity and by older configurations of race, sexuality, and gender which targeted black women as immoral, sexual, and available to male sexual desires.

Male sexual violence clearly impinged on the freedom experienced by freed women. The rape cases suggest, however, that while freed women continued to live with the threat of rape, the process of amelioration and emancipation did mark a break from slavery by conferring on women the right to charge men with rape.[77] Freed women made liberty count for something by bringing men to court. Rape cases also demonstrate the ways in which the very struggle over the terms of freedom helped shape gender, class, and racial identification. The Booysen case, in particular, suggests how seemingly unambiguous categories and boundaries in Cape colonial life such as race unravel as discrete units of explanation on closer scrutiny and points to a number of paradoxes which solidified in colonial discourse in the latter half of the nineteenth century.

As racial categorization based on the inevitability of biology became increasingly hegemonic in the British Empire and elsewhere the very malleability of race—the cultural construction of race—continued to facilitate the successful deployment of racism in societies with discrete relations of power. Ironically while the race of Anna Simpson was invoked as the determining yardstick in ascertaining the appropriate punishment for rape, the judge's own remarks illustrate how malleable and subjective racial categories indeed were: Menzies changed his own interpretation of Anna Simpson's race to accord with the "common sense" racial knowledge of "respectable" inhabitants of George. The petitioners and the judge participated in a broader colonial discourse in which words like "virtuous" frequently were metonyms for "whiteness," and in which the relationship between and stability of categories such as respectability, race, and sexuality was far from self-evident.

An analysis of sexual violence at the Cape demonstrates the centrality of gender to the construction of racial and class identities. Judges' evaluations of men's guilt, and of the credibility of women's testimony were informed both by metropolitan discourses about the uncontrolled sexuality of working-class women, and by empire-wide representations of the hypersexuality of black women both under slavery and after. Their ultimate reliance upon intertwined racial and sexual discourses underscores the powerful appeal of racial explanations and the confusion in British colonialism, and its settler subjects in general, as to whether cultural practice alone could bring a person within the fold of European civilization.

---

77 Under the amelioration laws slaves were first allowed to testify in court.

Conclusion:
Family Histories, Slave Emancipation, and Gender History

The most recent narratives of the Cape in the 1840s and 1850s have concentrated for good reason on the ignominious triumph of settler capitalism and settlers' control of political power in the making of the inequitable rural worlds of the Cape Colony.[1] This book has demonstrated that slave emancipation is as much a story about culture and identity as it is a narrative of the emergence of free wage labor. In the Cape Colony the ending of slavery was integrally connected with discussions regarding the relations between men and women within marriage and between parents and children, the discrete roles of men and women, and the influence and role of the state. The struggles over definitions of freedom, family, and gender relations testifies to the ongoing debates and tensions which surrounded these issues in the mid-nineteenth century British colonial experience.

The conflicts over the meanings and significance of gender, family, and race following emancipation at the Cape echoed and constituted part of wider tensions within British imperialism in this period. The 1830s and 1840s represented a time of great optimism on the part of abolitionists and some key members of the Colonial Office as to the possibility of claiming freed people to "civilization." These years witnessed a "flowering" of metropolitan "organizations dedicated to the advancement or protection of the welfare of" Africans and freed people in the British Empire.[2] At the Cape, as in many areas of the West Indies which experienced emancipation concurrently with the Cape, the 1840s represented a liminal period between slavery and

---

1 See for example Crais, *White Supremacy and Black Resistance*, esp. Epilogue; Marincowitz, "Rural Production"; and Rayner, "Wine and Slaves," Conclusion. For an overview of transitions in economy and society in the nineteenth-century Cape see Ross, *Beyond the Pale*.

2 John Galbraith, *Reluctant Empire: British Policy on the South African Frontier, 1834–1854* (Berkeley: University of California Press, 1963), 76.

the "new" political economy which was dominated by white settlers. In the 1840s freed people attempted, and in many cases managed, to reframe the rural world of the Western Cape through withdrawal from permanent farm labor, through a reframing of gender relations, and through emphasis on family and community. In this decade settlers complained about labor shortage, and looked to labor legislation to get laborers to work.

Freed people's experience of slavery as a denial of familial relations shaped their attempts to create a freedom which disentangled the public sphere of contract from the internal organization of the family. They forced former slaveholders to confront the meanings of emancipation by questioning settlers' assumptions that the wife and children of a male worker would automatically work for his employer. Freed people seem to have adhered to the notion that in the public sphere the worker engaged his or her labor power as an individual. Yet freed people did waged work as part of a larger economic strategy. In so doing they exposed as fiction the notion that most women were free to stay within a domestic space isolated from the world of wages and production. Freed women now avoided permanent domestic labor for other households and, at least on the missions, took on the prime responsibility for looking after their households and children. But most freed women did engage in waged work.

Emancipation did not revolutionize former slaveholders' perceptions of the organization of labor. They attempted, in the era of contract, to resuscitate their fiction of the farm as family. They continued to generate labor through ties of violence and the language of familial obligation, this time on the part of the laborer's family to the laborer and the employer. Former slaveholders continued to assume that they had a right, through being head of the farm, to the labor of all the people living on it. With the introduction of representative rule in 1853 settlers were able conclusively to shape the political economy to their benefit.

The freedom inaugurated by the Abolition Act, and bolstered by the postemancipation labor laws that followed, gave slave men title to a masculinity based on patriarchal gender relations within a discrete nuclear family structure. Women and children, emancipated into a hierarchical world in which men enjoyed customary and legal authority, continued to be the most vulnerable members of the rural working class. Evidence suggests the continuation after emancipation of a pervasive masculine identity located in a notion of male entitlement to authority over women in the sexual realm.[3] As I have shown, husbands appear to have dominated wives by invoking their rights as spouses or lovers and as men. Some men, both black and white, also felt free to rape women, and particularly black women, on the assumption that they were available for men's sexual pleasure.

Yet some gaps existed between the theories of emancipation framed by law, and the lives that freed people forged after 1838. The very concept of slave emancipation as well as the postemancipation political economy of the Cape made freedom fraught with ambiguity and qualifications for all who experienced the ending of slavery. Both the structure of family and labor relations hindered the emergence of that mythic nuclear rural family so beloved by abolitionists and missionaries. Emancipators sought to replace slavery with wage labor founded in a gendered separation of spheres; As we have seen, for many freed people the private sphere of family and

---

3   Another book might be written of the makings of masculinity in the eras of slavery and emancipation.

household existed only as a chimera. Most freed people, like their peers in many other nineteenth-century rural societies founded on wage labor, shared living quarters with their fellow workers. If a worker had family members working alongside her she had very rare opportunities to see them alone, and many workers only saw their family members on weekends or once a month.

The ways in which race, gender, and class helped define one another inserted tension into people's experience of freedom. Freed men's masculine status was subverted by their place in a colonial world which was shaped as much by ascriptions of race and class as by gender identities. White judges and juries, for example, evaluated black men's behavior according to both their race, and the race and class of the victim. Black men constantly had to prove, through evidence of regular work, and/or by belonging to a Christian mission or congregation, and by being married, that they were worthy of their liberation into masculine title.

Women too experienced female identity, as well as these other central categories of South African history, as an ill-defined, shifting, but pervasive sensibility which circumscribed their experience of freedom. Slave emancipation laws did free slave women from ownership by others. Amelioration and abolition legislation liberated women into greater legal protection than they had enjoyed under slavery. Legally they could no longer be flogged and their personal relationships now had legal sanction. Freed women in the rural Western Cape also freed themselves. Where possible, they avoided work they did not like, they pursued their rights in court by charging men with abuse, they went to church, they learned to read, and they raised children on missions and sent them to school.

But individual liberty from being owned as slaves did not erase other forms of gender subordination. Women's experience of male sexual violence marked a continuity between the eras of slavery and free wage labor. Emancipation also ushered in new forms of subordination and weakened the previous associations between maternity and power. From 1838 women lost the authority over their children that they had exercised in the apprenticeship period. Maternal power to indenture children now passed into the hands of fathers. And those women who married in accordance with the 1839 marriage laws automatically became legal minors. Furthermore, postemancipation labor laws recognized all freed women who were part of a heterosexual couple, whether married or not, as being married for the purposes of labor contracts. This gave minor status to all women working under wage contracts, making them subject to the legal care and authority of their male partners.

A focus on gender as a category of analysis forces a reconsideration of the shaping of South African society. This study adds to others which highlight the importance of the first half of the nineteenth century in the history of South African racism.[4] However I also show that ethnic and racial categories cannot be understood without reference to conceptions of gender. By using gender as a category of analysis and paying attention to the relations between women and men, the book reveals new evidence about the nineteenth-century past. This study of the emancipation and postemancipation contexts at the Cape suggests how categories such as race and sexuality themselves were reconfigured and redeployed. An analysis which combines a discursive approach to the understanding of identities, attention to political economy, as

---

4   For example see Crais, *White Supremacy,* and Bank, "Liberals."

well as sensitivity to gender has wide application for the study of African history. For example, authors have shown that in societies as diverse as the Anlo-Ewe of Ghana in the precolonial and colonial eras as well as the Maasai in Tanzania up to the early 1990s, ethnic and gender identities helped shape one another.[5]

To the slaves who experienced emancipation in the nineteenth-century Cape, the conjoining of histories of race, ethnicity, and gender would come as no surprise. For freed people, as well as other colonial actors, sexuality, ideas and practices of gender, and definitions of family comprised the very fabric of emancipation. Ex-slaves and their descendants still celebrated the abolition of slavery well into the late nineteenth century. Freed people embraced emancipation even while acknowledging its limitations. Through the public recitation of memories of slavery, both in ex-slave communities and in the presence of former owners, freed people talked of emancipation as a crucial moment in their histories of the nineteenth century. Memory was never very far away from practice. Freed people reminded not just their peers, but also their former masters that freedom had come.

Nearly thirty years after the initial abolition of slavery, Rosina, of Caledon, formerly the slave of a Mr. Klein, would stand outside the windows of her former master's house and, to his great "misery," would "read the statute [of emancipation] in a loud voice on every anniversary of the day."[6] Rosina's commemoration speaks of slavery and emancipation not only as a grand transition in the productive basis of the economy of the Western Cape. Slavery also summoned up memories of family, of personal relationships framed in the shadow of violence. However circumscribed by the economic and political power enjoyed by former slaveholders in the rural Western Cape, freedom suggested possibilities of asserting to former owners truths which had been muted by slavery.

Each year, when Rosina stood in front of Klein's windows to recite the Abolition Act, she did so not just as his former slave, but also as the mother of two of his children. Rosina's experience of motherhood was forged in a relationship which contradicted slaveholding mythologies of family yet testified to the power of slaveholder sexual and political/economic domination. Her appearance at Klein's window on December 1 each year recalled their mutual history, but also ridiculed him and the slaveholding mythologies of family which had recognized some family members at the expense of others. Rosina's experiences of slavery as a gendered system of domination helped drive some of the meanings she attached to freedom those long years after the final abolition of Cape slavery in 1838.

---

5 Sandra Greene, *Gender, Ethnicity, and Social Change on the Upper Slave Coast: A History of the Anlo-Ewe* (Heinemann: Portsmouth, NH, 1996); also Dorothy Hodgson, "The Politics of Gender, Ethnicity, and Development: Images, Interventions and The Reconfiguration of Maasai Identities in Tanzania, 1916–1993" (Ph.D. diss., University of Michigan, 1995).

6 Lady Duff Gordon, *Letters from the Cape*, annotated by Dorothea Fairbridge, with an Introduction by Mrs. Janet Ross (London: Oxford University Press, 1927), 112. See also the account of a commemorative meeting of the "coloured people" at Uitenhage, in the Cape Colony in 1897, where Jacobus Felix, aged eighty-five, recalled his days as a slave. He talked of the sale of his mother, and of his father, of the brand mark on his right side. "The story of the floggings . . . and subsequent freedom, were told with much feeling, and although his tale was somewhat long, it lagged nothing of interest to those who were present." *Diamond Fields Advertiser* (7 December 1897), under "Local and General." I am grateful to Keletso Atkins for sharing this information with me.

SELECT BIBLIOGRAPHY

Archival Sources

CA Cape (Government Archives), Cape Town

Accessions
A 79	Diary of Petrus Johannes Truter
A 602	Diaries of Samuel E. Hudson

CCP Cape Colony Publications

Acts
6/2/1/1	1857
6/2/1/2	1859

Ordinances
6/3/1/2	1826–1832

Government Proclamations and Notices
6/5/2	1806–1825

AG Archives of the Department of the Attorney General

Letters Despatched
2161	1855–1857

Reports Despatched
2616–2623	1841–1863
2625	1866–1870

GH Government House

General Despatches Received by Governor from Secretary of State for Colonies (SSC), London
1/97	November–December 1833
1/99–100	January 1833–August 1834
1/103	January–February 1835
1/110	June–August 1836
1/114	August–June 1837
1/116–118	September 1837–December 1837
1/120–129	April 1838–August 1840
1/139	January–February 1841
1/142–145	April 1841–February 1842
1/148	June–July 1842
1/151	November–December 1842
1/153	February–March 1843
1/199–203	February 1849–October 1849

| 1/212–213 | October 1850–November 1850 |
| 1/223 | January–February 1852 |

Registers of Despatches from SSC
| 6/4 | September 1843–December 1852 |

Despatches from Governor to SSC
23/10–12	1832–1840
23/14–16	1843–1847
23/18–20	1847–1852

Index to Despatches to SSC
| 24/5–9 | 1832–1861 |

Duplicate Despatches to SSC
26/72	November 1835–April 1836
26/72	April 1836
26/77–78	September 1836–March 1837
26/88–89	January 1838–November 1838
26/96	June 1838
26/138	July 1844

Enclosures to Despatches
28/12/1	June 1835–November 1837
28/16–17	January 1840–December 1841
28/19–20	June 1842–December 1842
28/21	1842
28/24	1843
28/35	1847
28/42	1848
28/60	1851

LCA (Clerk of the Legislative Council)

Masters and Servants Committee 1848
| 33 | Replies to Questionaire, Resident Magistrates, Ministers of Religion, Justices of the Peace |
| 34 | Replies to Questionaire, Field Cornets, General, Meetings |

Varia
35	Replies to Questions re Wine and Spirit Ordinance October–November 1848
37	Varia 1835–53
38	Cape of Good Hope Blue Book and Statistical Register for 1837

Annexure A

Appendix Vol. 1
| 6 | Vagrancy Ordinance |

Appendix Vol. 2
No. 3	Juvenile Emigrants Bill
No. 31	Medical Practitioners Bill S 21, 27 September 1836
No. 37	Hottentot Apprentice Bill: Draft S 23, 2 November 1836

Appendix Vol. 3
| Nos.33–35 | Marriage Bill and 2 Memorials, 2 October 1837 |

Appendix Vol. 4
   Nos. 15–9   Apprentice Labourers Ordinance Amendment Bill

Appendix Vol. 5
   No. 17   Wagenmakers Valley Memorial M 28, 7 September 1839
   No. 18   Judges Opinion Masters and Servants Bill M 48, 13 January 1840

Appendix Vol. 7
   Nos. 25–35   Special Justices M 88, 4 October 1841

1/CAL Magistrate Records of Caledon District

Miscellaneous
9/1/1	Registry of Marriages at Caledon 1813–1839
21	Diary, Justice of the Peace 1832–1836
22	Land Reports, Justice of the Peace 1832–1836
1/1/1–4	Criminal Cases 1840–1864
1/2/1	Criminal Record Book 1841
5/1/1/1–4	Letters Despatched 1848–1865
7/1/1	Quitrent Register February 1844–January 1875
7/1/2	Quitrent Register May 1847–December 1907
7/7/1	Return of Places in Division of Caledon 1857
12/2	Voters List 1865

Records of Proceedings, Periodical Court, Genadendal, 1858–1863
   A1/1/1–3

CO Colonial Office (Cape Town)

Indexes to Letters Received
2469	1828–29
2471–81	1832–47
2484	1852
2486	1855

Letters Received from Heads of Departments, Various Committees, and Private Individuals
323	Agents and Missionaries in Interior 1827
337	Supreme Court 1828
346	Slaves 1828
360	Missionaries in Interior 1828
362	Churches 1829
378	Orphan Chamber, Protector of Slaves 1830
395	Slaves 1831
398	Missionaries 1831
407	Orphan Chamber, Protector 1832
411	Missionaries 1832
421	Churches and Missionaries 1833
441	Special Justices 1835
452	Special Justices 1836
465	Special Justices 1837
475	Churches 1838
476	Special Justices 1838
485	Clergymen 1839
492	Clergymen 1840
501	Clergymen 1841
503	AG, Supreme Court, CP, Cape Town 1841

511	Clergymen 1842
513	Supreme Court, CP, AG, 1842
519	Clergymen 1843
520	AG 1843
521	Supreme Court, Master and High Sheriff 1843.
537	Supreme Court, AG, CP, Cape Town 1844
545	High Sheriff, Superintendent of Police 1845
546	Supreme Court, AG, CP, Cape Town 1845
550	Clergymen 1846
561	Supreme Court 1846–1847
562	High Sheriff and Superintendent of Police 1846
565	Clergymen 1847
570	Superintendent of Police and High Sheriff 1847
574	Clergymen 1848
575	Superintendent of Police and High Sheriff 1848
584	High Sheriff and Superintendent of Police 1849
589	Supreme Court, Master and AG 1849
593	Churches 1850
594	Education 1850
611	Surveyor-General 1851–52
615	Supreme Court and Master's Office 1852
619	Colonial Office 1853–54
624	High Sheriff and AG 1853
629	Supreme Court and Registrar of Deeds 1853
631	AG, CP, and High Sheriff 1854

Letters Received from Civil Commissioners and Resident Magistrates

2732–4	STB, SWM, WOC 1832
2737	WOC 1832
2739–41	STB, SWM, George and Uitenhage 1833
2759–62	Cape District, STB, SWM, George and Uitenhage 1836
2765	WOC 1836
2767	Cape 1837
2769–70	SWM, George 1837
2773	WOC 1837
2776–7	SWM, George 1838
2779	WOC 1838
2783	STB 1839
2788	WOC and Clan William 1839
2792–3	STB, Paarl, SWM and CAL 1840
2796	WOC and Clan William 1840
2800–1	STB, Paarl, SWM and CAL 1841
2804	WOC and Clan William 1841
2807	STB, Paarl, SWM and CAL 1842
2812	STB, Paarl SWM and CAL 1843
2814	WOC and Clan William 1843
2817	STB, Paarl, WOC and Clan William 1844
2818	SWM and George 1844
2823	STB, Paarl, WOC and Clan William 1845
2824	SWM and George 1845
2830	STB, Paarl, WOC and Clan William 1846
2831	SWM, CAL, and George 1846
2838	SWM and CAL 1847

Memorials Received

3946	A–C 1830
3949–51	P–Z 1830
3980	L–M 1835
3982	R–S 1835
3992	A–E 1837
4000	A–E 1839
4024	A–E 1845
4029	F–K 1846
4035	S–Z 1847
4331	Index to Memorials Received 1837–1839

Miscellaneous

4911	Letter Book June–December 1838
4950	Index to Letters Despatched 1832–1835
5101	Letter Book Ecclesiastical and Schools 1836–41
5177	Judicial 1836
5178–9	Letter Books Judicial c. 1838–1842
5990	Letters Received 1848

CSC Cape Supreme Court

8/1/1	Marriages of Minors, Applications

Records of Proceedings in Criminal Cases, Cape Town

1/1/1/1	1828
1/1/1/12	1843–1845
1/1/1/14–22	1849–1870

Records of Proceedings in Criminal Cases, Circuit Court

1/2/1/1–2	1828
1/2/1/15 Vol 1	1835
1/2/1/34 Vol 2	1844
1/2/1/35	1845
1/2/1/43	1849

J Returns for Taxation Purpose (Opgaaf Rolle)

J302	Opgaaf lists of Field Cornets 1830–1838
J309	Opgaaf Rolle, STB 1838
J410	Opgaaf Rolle, WOC 1830–1831
J429	Opgaaf Rolle, WOC 1832
J437	June–December 1840
J442	Recapitulation of Opgaaf Rolls 1811–1882

Press Cuttings

14	*Die Banier*

1/STB Magisterial Records of Stellenbosch District

2/1–2/93	Records of Proceedings in Criminal Cases 1818–1909
2/26	May 1828
2/34–39	1834–62

Criminal Record Books

4/3/1	Index to Criminal Record Book 1828–1868

Civil Cases

5/56	Records of Proceedings in Civil Cases 1828–1868
6/94	Civil Record Book 1841–1858
6/98	Civil Cases tried in Circuit Court 1832–1837

Miscellaneous

8/17	Inquests, 1849–1862
9/23	Journal of the Civil Commissioner 1830
9/42	Journal of the Resident Magistrate 1834–1850
9/70	Annexures to the Journal of the Civil Commissioner 1851–1863
9/72	Index to Journal of Civil Commissioner 1828–1833
19/8–10	Ordinances 1828–1849
19/162	Election Papers 1834–1904
19/170	Memorials Register 1825–1839

Letters Received

10/79	Miscellaneous 1830
10/126	Miscellaneous 1829–1830
10/161	Field Cornets 1828–1844
10/170	Private Individuals 1827–1887
10/173–4	Register of Letters Received 1827–1882

Land Matters

11/29	Applications for Grants of Land 1812–1848
15/13	Attestations of Consent 1828–1837

Contracts

18/183	Wage Contracts 1843–1873
18/184	With "Native" Labourers 1858–1901
18/188–90	Khoi and Free Black Children 1836–1869
18/194	Returns and Observations 1842–1885
18/198	Register of Wage and Indenture Contracts 1828–1840

Letters Despatched by Resident Magistrate

20/94–96	Letters Despatched 1828–1865
20/103	Letters Despatched 1843–1907

Clerk of the Peace

22/31–32	Letters Received June 1833–1835
22/35–43	Letters Received 1838–1849
22/44–5	Letters Despatched 1828–1850
22/46	Rough Letter Book July 1834–November 1835

Marriage Court

22/56	Notes of the Matrimonial Court 1837–1880
22/83	Rough Notes December 1837
22/87	List of Marriages 1806–1826
22/93	Marriage Register 1805–39

Slave Issues

22/120	1835
22/122	Letters Despatched 1825–1834
22/153	Complaints Book 1826–1857
22/158–60	Letters Received by APS 1830–1835

22/161	Letters Despatched APS 1830–1834
22/162–5	Miscellaneous Papers of APS 1826–1834
22/167	Miscellaneous Documents 1823–1838

School Committee
| 22/180 | Letters Received 1832–1848 |

1/SWM Magisterial Records of Swellendam District

Criminal Proceedings
2/8	1828
2/26	1840–1842
2/29	1846–1847
2/31	1849–1853
2/36–7	1865–1869

Clerk to Justice of the Peace
| 3/30 | Note Book February 1845–October 1851 |

Civil Cases
| 6/5 | Civil Cases Records of Proceedings 1847–48 |

Miscellaneous Letters Received
11/25	Judges 1821–1844
11/27	AG 1854
11/29	Clerks of the Peace 1823–47
11/32	Miscellaneous 1796–1904
11/38	Deputy Magistrate, and JP, CAL 1813–1837
11/41	Missionaries 1810–1845
11/43	Field Cornets 1802–1846

Land Documents
| 12/8 | Quitrent |
| 12/22 | Miscellaneous Land Documents 1746–1892 |

School Papers
| 12/87 | 1814–1862 |

Notarial Deeds
| 13/7–9 | Register of Apprenticeship Contracts 1829–53 |

Assistant Registrar of Slaves
16/4–5	Letters Received 1830–35
16/6	Letters Despatched
16/20	General Register of Slaves 1825–1832
16/22	Diary of APS 1828–1831

Clerk of the Peace
| 16/24–31 | Letters Received 1831–1870 |
| 16/32–37 | Letters Despatched 1828–1869 |

1/WOC Magisterial Records of Worcester District

Records of Proceedings in Criminal Cases
2/15	1828, 1833, 1835
2/16	1851–1862
2/18	1867

Circuit Court

5/17–19	Miscellaneous Papers regarding Circuit Court Cases with registers of cases 1828–1842
6/14	Records of Proceedings in Civil Cases 1838
6/30	Records of Proceedings in Civil Cases 1863

Letters Received

11/12–18	Colonial Office 1832–1881
13/23–4	Field Cornets 1831–1834
13/28	Field Cornets 1844–1848
14/14	Private Persons 1836–1839
14/28	Memorial Book 1836–1847

Land Documents

15/7	Quitrent Register, 1809–1861

Opgaaf and Population

15/109	Register of Births and Deaths of Inhabitants 1834–1842
15/110	Register of Births and Deaths of Hottentots 1824–1841
15/114	Field Cornetcy Lists of Inhabs., Slaves, Hottentots 1827–1833

Apprenticeship Contracts

16/37	Hiring Contracts of "Hottentots and Free Blacks" 1828–1853
16/40–43	Apprenticeship Contracts 1835–1863

Letters Despatched

17/14	1834–1838

Slave Office

19/19	Incoming Letters 1829–1837
19/22	Outgoing Letters 1826–1832
19/24	Day Book of APS 1826–1831
19/27	Criminal Record Book 1836–1838
19/28	Drafts of Proceedings in Slave Cases
19/60–1	Incoming and Outgoing Letters to SM 1835–1838

Clerk of the Peace, Letters Received

19/64	From Civil Commissioner Worcester 1828–1841
19/66	From Clerks of the Peace 1836–1841
19/69	Miscellaneous 1828–1851

Matrimonial Court

19/88–90	Minutes of the Matrimonial Court 1828–1883
19/115	Miscellaneous Documents of Court 1801–1847
19/116	Letters Received from Colonial Office 1845–1868
19/120	Marriage Register 1826–1839

School Commission

19/122	Notes of Proceedings 1831–1854

DRC Dutch Reformed Church Archives

G2	Stellenbosch Gemeente
1/7–8	Notes of the Kerkraad 1828–38
2/5	Missionary "Sending" 1791–1857
2/6	Education 1814–1856
2/7	Letters Received 1816–1894

6/1–3	Membership Lists 1788–1843
7/2–4	Marriage Registers 1788–1887
11/1	Register of "Sit plekke" 1837–1845
17/1/3–4	Stellenbosse Medewerkend Sendinggenootskap Notule 1825–1875
17/2/1	Stellenbosse Mederwerkend Sendinggenootskap Letters Received 1799–1872
17/2/3	Stellenbosse Merderwerkend Sendinggenootskap Outgoing Letters 1836–1846

Personal Diaries
P1–P1a	Dominee A. Murray (Senior and Junior)
P1/1	Paul D. Luckhoff Dagboek 1829–1838
P1/2	Paul D. Luckhoff Dagboek 1839–1854
P42/1–2	Zahn Diary 1830–1882

Microfilm Collection of Cape Archives Depot

London Missionary Society Papers 1795–1923
ZL 1/3/12–20	Letters Received, South Africa 1834–1852

Colonial Office (Public Record Office, London): CO 48 series 1807–1910
ZP 1/1/81	PRO CO 48/152	Offices and Individuals 1833
	PRO CO 48/153	Chief Justice Wylde 1833
ZP 1/1/93	PRO CO 48/171–4	Despatches 1837
ZP 1/1/94	PRO CO 48/174	Despatches 1837
ZP 1/1/99	PRO CO 48/182–3	Despatches 1837
ZP 1/6/4–9	PRO CO 53/51–8	Reports of PS, and Despatches 1830–35

Entry Books of Correspondence, Letters from the Secretary of State
ZP 1/3/9	PRO CO 49/25	Despatches 1832–36
	PRO CO 49/26	Offices and Individual 1835–37
	PRO CO 49/27	Despatches 1836

CL Cory Library, Rhodes University, Grahamstown, South Africa
Methodist/Wesleyan Church Archives
MS 17 274/1	Register of Marriages in the Methodist/Wesleyan Church, STB County, 1840–1923

SOAS School of Oriental and African Studies, University of London
MMS Methodist Missionary Society Archives
FBN 7	South Africa, Cape

Published Primary Sources
Government Documents
ASL African Studies Library, University of Cape Town

CGH Cape of Good Hope
Blue Books, 1840–1860.
CA, *The Cape of Good Hope Annual Register, Directory, and Almanack for 1837.* Compiled by B. J. van de Sandt. Cape Town: Cornelius Moll, 1837.

CA, *The Cape of Good Hope Annual Register, Directory, and Almanack for 1839*. Cape Town: A. S Robertson, 1839.

CA, *The Cape of Good Hope Almanac and Annual Register for 1842*. Compiled by B. J. van de Sandt. Cape Town: Saul Solomon, 1842.

CA, *The Cape of Good Hope Almanac and Annual Register for 1845*. Compiled by B. J. van de Sandt. Cape Town: A. S. Robertson, 1845.

Cases Decided in the Supreme Court of the Cape of Good Hope, as Reported by the Late Hon. William Menzies, Esquire. Edited by James Buchanan, Advocate. 3 vols. Vol. 3. Cape Town: J. C. Juta and Co., 1903.

Census of the Colony of the Cape of Good Hope 1865. Cape Town: Saul Solomon and Co., 1866

CA, *South African Almanac and Directory for 1830*. Cape Town: George Greig, 1830.

CA, *South African Almanac and Directory for 1832*. Cape Town: George Greig, 1832.

CA, *South African Almanac and Directory for 1833*. Cape Town: George Greig, 1833.

Legislative Council. *The Cape of Good Hope Government Proclamations from 1806 to 1825, As In Force and Unrepealed; and, the Ordinances Passed in Council from 1825 to 1839, with Notes of Reference to Each, and a Copious Index*. Compiled by Walter Harding. v2 vols. Cape Town: A. S. Robertson, 1839.

Legislative Council. Master and Servant. *Documents on the Working of the Order in Council of the 21st July 1849*. Cape Town: Saul Solomon and Co., 1849.

Legislative Council. Master and Servant. *Addenda to the Documents of the Working of the Order in Council of 21st July 1849 . . .* Cape Town: Saul Solomon and Co., 1849.

Legislative Council. *Proceedings of and Evidence Given before the Committee of the Legislative Council Respecting the Proposed Ordinance to Prevent the Practice of Settling or Squatting upon Government Lands*. Cape Town: Saul Solomon and Co., 1852.

Parliament. *The Advertiser and Mail's Parliamentary Debates in the First Session of the First Parliament of the Cape of Good Hope, Appointed to Meet 30th June 1854*. State Library Reprints, 33, 1. Pretoria: State Library., 1968.

Select Committee on Granting Lands in Freehold to Hottentots. *Report of the Select Committee on Granting Lands in Freehold to Hottentots*. S.C. 11. Cape Town: Saul Solomon and Co., 1854.

Select Committee of the House of Assembly on Granting Lands in Freehold to Hottentots. *Minutes of Evidence Taken Before the Select Committee of the House of Assembly on Granting Lands in Freehold to Hottentots*. S.C 13. Cape Town: Saul Solomon and Co., 1856.

Statutes of the Cape of Good Hope, 1652–1895. 3 vols. Edited by Hercules Tennant and Edgar Michael Jackson. Cape Town: J. C. Juta and Co., 1895.

GB Great Britain

Parliament. House of Commons. *Appendices to the Votes and Proceedings 1817–1890. Reports of the Select Committee on Public Petitions 1833–1900*. Microfiche ed. Cambridge: Chadwyck-Healey Microform Publishing Services, 1982.

Parliament. House of Commons. *Report of the Select Committee on Negro Apprenticeship in the Colonies; Together with the Minutes of Evidence, Appendix, and Index. Ordered by the House of Commons to be Printed, 13 August 1836*. Microfiche ed. Cambridge: Chadwyck-Healey Microform Publishing Services, 1980–82.

Parliament. *Hansard Parliamentary Debates New Series, 1823–1838*, 1838.

Contemporary Accounts

Barrow, Sir John. *Travels into the Interior of Southern Africa in the Years 1797 and 1798*. 2 vols. London: T. Cadell Jr. and W. Davies, 1801–1804.

Barrow, John Henry Esq, ed. *The Mirror of Parliament for the Second Session of the Eighth Parliament of Great Britain and Ireland, Commencing 29 January 1828*. Vol. 1. London: Winchester and Varnham, 1828.

Bigge, John Thomas. "Report on the Slaves and State of Slavery at the Cape of Good Hope." In George McCall Theal, comp., *Records of the Cape Colony*, Vol. 35. London: William Clowes and Sons Printers, 1905.

Bird, William. *State of the Cape in 1822*. Fascimilie Reprint. Cape Town, Struik Ltd., 1966.

Birmingham Ladies Society. *Records Relating to The Birmingham Ladies Society for The Relief of Negro Slaves 1825–1919 in the Birmingham Reference Library*. Microfilm ed. East Ardsley, U.K.: Microform Academic Publishers, n.d.

Blumenbach, Johann F. *On the Natural Varieties of Mankind*. 1775. Reprint, New York: Berfman Publishers, 1969.

Burchell, W. J. *Travels in the Interior of South Africa*. 2 vols., 1822, 1824. Vol. 1, 1822; Vol. 2, 1824. London: Longman, Hurst, Rees, Orme,and Brown, 1824.

Camper, Petrus. *The Works of the Late Professor Camper, on the Connexion between the Science of Anatomy and the Arts of Drawing*. . . . London: Printed for C. Dilly, 1794.

Freeman, J. J. *A Tour in South Africa, with Notices of Natal, Mauritius, Madagascar, Ceylon, Egypt, and Palestine*. London: John Snow, 1851.

Godwin, Benjamin. *The Substance of a Course of Lecture on British Colonial Slavery*. . . . London: J. Hatchford and Son, 1830

Gordon, Lady Duff. *Letters from the Cape*. Annotated by Dorothea Fairbridge, with an introduction by Mrs. Janet Ross. London: Oxford University Press, 1927.

A Lady [pseud.]. *Life at the Cape a Hundred Years Ago*. Cape Town: C. Struik, 1963.

Lichtenstein, Henry. *Travels in Southern Africa, in the Years, 1803, 1804, 1805, and 1806*. 2 vols. Translated by Anne Plumptre. 1812. Reprint, Cape Town: Van Riebeeck Society, 1928.

Moseley, Sir Oswald. *Speech of Sir Oswald Moseley in Manchester Gazette March 25 1826*. . . . Birmingham: Richard Peart Bull, 1826.

Philip, Rev. John. *Researches in South Africa; Illustrating the Civil, Moral, and Religious Condition of the Native Tribes*. . . . 2 vols. London: James Duncan, 1828.

Porter, William. *The Porter Speeches. Speeches Delivered by The Hon. William Porter, During The Years 1839–1845 Inclusive*. Cape Town: Trustees Estate and Saul Solomon and Co., 1886.

Raven-Hart, R., trans. and ed. "Johan Schreyer's Description of the Hottentots, 1679." *Quarterly Bulletin of the South African Library* 19 (March), 1965.

Selby, H. C., comp. *Report of the Case of C. A. van der Merwe for the Murder of his Wife, Tried in the Supreme Court of the Colony of the Cape of Good Hope, at the Sessions Holden upon the 18th April, 1838*. Cape Town: The Victoria Press, 1838.

Sturge, Joseph. *Horrors of the Negro Apprenticeship System in the British Colonies as Detailed at the Public Breakfast Given by the Citizens of Birmingham to Mr. Joseph Sturge*. Glasgow: W. & W. Miller, 1837.

Tennant, H. *Laws Regulating the Relative Rights and Duties of Masters, Servants, and Apprentices in the Cape Colony, Including the Workmen's Compensation Act, 1905*. Cape Town: J.C. Juta and Co., 1906.

United Brethren. *Periodical Accounts Relating to the Missions of the Church of the United Brethren, Established among the Heathen* n.p., 1823–1853.

Ward, D. A. *Handbook to the Marriage Laws of the Cape Colony, the Bechuanaland Protectorate, and Rhodesia*. Cape Town: J.C. Juta, 1906.

Warner, Brian, ed. *Lady Herschel's Letters from the Cape 1834–1838*. New Series, No. 3. Cape Town: Friends of the South African Library, 1991.

Wesleyan Methodist Missionary Society. *Annual Reports*, 1830–1860.

Annual Report for 1830: London: Mills, Jowlett, and Mills, Boltcourt.

Annual Reports for 1835, 1837, 1838-41: London: P.P. Thomas.

Annual Reports for 1842-1860: London: Weslayan Missionary Society.

Newspapers

The Anti-Slavery Monthly Reporter 1825–1827
The Anti-Slavery Reporter 1827–1833

The Cape Monthly Magazine 1858–1862
The Cape Town Mail 1845
The Mirror of Parliament 1828
The Oriental Herald and Colonial Review. Vol. 1: January to April, 1824. London: J. M. Richardson, 1824.
The South African Commercial Advertiser 1837, 1838, 1840, 1843, 1846
De Zuid Afrikaan 1830, 1837–1840, 1859

Secondary Sources

Bibliographies and Guides

De Kock, W. J [until 1970], and D. W. Kruger [since 1971], eds. *Dictionary of South African Biography.* 4 vols. Vol. 2. Cape Town: Tafelberg-Uitgewers, for the Human Science Research Council, 1972.

Hinchliff, Patricia Shaen. "Domestic Life in South Africa in the Nineteenth Century." Bibliography compiled for School of Librarianship, University of Cape Town, 1960.

Lombard, R. T. J. *Handbook for Genealogical Research in South Africa.* Pretoria: Human Sciences Research Council, 1977.

Schrire, D. *The Cape of Good Hope 1782–1842 from De la Rochette to Arrowsmith.* Map Collectors' Circle, Map Collectors's Series. No. 17. London: Map Collectors' Circle, 1965.

Potgieter, D. J., editor in chief. *Standard Encyclopaedia of Southern Africa.* 12 vols. Vol. 7. Cape Town: Nasionale Opvoedkundige Uitgewery, 1972.

Articles

Adhikari, Mohammed. "The Sons of Ham: The Making of Coloured Identity." *South African Historical Journal* 27 (1992): 95–112.

Benenson, Harold. "Victorian Sexual Ideology and Marx's Theory of the Working Class." *International Labor and Working Class History* 25 (Spring 1984): 1–23.

Bickford Smith, Vivian. "Black Ethnicities, Communities, and Political Expression in Late Victorian Cape Town." *Journal of African History* 36, 3 (1995): 443–66.

Bozzoli, Belinda. "Marxism, Feminism, and Southern African Studies." *Journal of Southern African Studies* 9 (1983): 139–71.

Bradlow, Edna. "The Children's Friend Society at the Cape of Good Hope." *Victorian Studies* (Winter 1984): 155–77.

——. "Women at the Cape in the Mid-Nineteenth Century." *South African Historical Journal* 19 (1987): 51–75.

Brindley, Marianne. "Old Women in Zulu Culture: The Old Woman and Childbirth." *South African Journal of Ethnography* 8 (1985): 98–108.

Bundy, Colin. "The Abolition of the Masters and Servants Act." *South African Labour Bulletin* 2 (1975): 37–46.

Burman, Sandra, and Margaret Naude. "Bearing a Bastard: The Social Consequences of Illegitimacy in Cape Town, 1896–1939." *Journal of Southern African Studies* 17 (September 1991): 373–413.

Carby, Hazel V. "'On the Threshold of Woman's Era': Lynching, Empire, and Sexuality in Black Feminist Theory." *Critical Enquiry* 12 (Autumn 1985): 262–77.

Chanock, Martin. "Writing South African Legal History: A Prospectus." *Journal of African History* 30, (2)(1989): 265–88.

Charles, Persis. "The Name of the Father: Women, Paternity, and British Rule in Nineteenth-Century Jamaica." *International Labor and Working-Class History* 41 (Spring 1992): 4–22.

Cobbing, Julian. "The Mfecane as Alibi: Thoughts on the Dithakong and Mbolompo." *Journal of African History* 29 (1988): 487–519.

Comaroff, Jean, and John Comaroff. "Christianity and Colonialism in South Africa." *American Ethnologist* 13 (1986): 1–22.

Cooper, Frederick. "The Problem of Slavery in African Studies." *Journal of African History* 20 (1979): 103–125.

Crais, Clifton C. "The Vacant Land: The Mythology of British Expansion in the Eastern Cape, South Africa." *Journal of Social History* 25 (Winter 1991): 255–74.

Edholm, F., et al. "Conceptualizing Women." *Critique of Anthropology* 3, 9–10 (1977): 101–130.

Edwards, Laura F. "Sexual Violence, Gender, Reconstruction, and the Extension of Patriarchy in Granville County, North Carolina." *The North Carolina Historical Review* 68 (July 1991): 237–260.

Elbourne, Elizabeth. "Freedom at Issue: Vagrancy Legislation and the Meaning of Freedom in Britain and the Cape Colony 1799–1842." *Slavery and Abolition*, Special Issue on Unfree Labour in the Development of the Atlantic World, edited by Paul Lovejoy and Nicholas Rogers, 15, 2 (August 1994): 114–50.

Eldredge, Elizabeth A. "Women in Production: The Economic Role of Women in Nineteenth-Century Lesotho." *Signs* 16, 4 (1991): 707–731.

Etherington, Norman. "Natal's Black Rape Scare of the 1870s." *Journal of Southern African Studies* 15 (1998): 2–53.

Glassman, Jonathon. "The Bondsman's New Clothes: The Contradictory Consciousness of Slave Resistance on the Swahili Coast." *Journal of African History* 32, 2 (1991): 277–312.

Guelke, Leonard. "The Anatomy of a Colonial Settler Population: Cape Colony, 1657–1750." *International Journal of African Historical Studies* 21 (1988): 453–73.

Guelke, Leonard, and Robert Shell. "An Early Colonial Landed Gentry: Land and Wealth in the Cape Colony, 1682–1731." *Journal of Historical Geography* 9 (1983): 265–86.

Guyer, Jane. "Household and Community in African Studies." *African Studies Review* 24 (1981): 87–137.

Hadley, Elaine. "Natives in a Strange Land: The Philanthropic Discourse of Juvenile Emigration in Mid-Nineteenth-Century England." *Victorian Studies* 33 (1990): 411–37.

Hall, Catherine. "In the Name of Which Father?" *International Labor and Working-Class History* 41 (Spring 1992): 23–28.

———. "White Visions, Black Lives: The Free Villages of Jamaica." *History Workshop*, Special Issue: Colonial and Post-Colonial History, 36 (Autumn 1993): 100–132.

Hall, Jacqueline Dowd. "'The Mind that Burns Each Body': Women, Rape, and Racial Violence." *Southern Exposure* 12 (1984): 61–71.

Malherbe, V. C. "Indentured and Unfree Labour in South Africa: Towards an Understanding." *South African Historical Journal* 24 (1991): 3–30.

Mason, John Edwin. "Hendrik Albertus and his Ex-Slave Mey: A Drama in Three Acts." *Journal of African History* 31 (1990): 423–45.

———. "The Slaves and Their Protectors: Reforming Resistance in a Slave Society, 1826–1834." *Journal of Southern African Studies* 17 (March 1991): 104–128.

McSheffrey, Gerald M. "Slavery, Indentured Servitude, Legitimate Trade, and the Impact of Abolition in the Gold Coast, 1874–1901: A Reappraisal." *Journal of African History* 24, (3) (1983): 349–68.

Rafael, Vicente. "Confession, Conversion, and Reciprocity in Early Tagalog Colonial Society." *Comparative Studies in Society and History* 29, 2 April 1987: 320–39.

Razack, Sherene. "What Is to Be Gained by Looking White People in the Eye? Culture, Race, and Gender in Cases of Sexual Violence." *Signs* (Summer 1994): 894–923.

Rose, Sonya O. "Gender Antagonism and Class Conflict: Exclusionary Strategies of Male Trade Unionists in Nineteenth-Century Britain." *Social History* 13 (May 1988): 191–208.

Ross, Robert. "Oppression, Sexuality, and Slavery at the Cape of Good Hope." *Historical Reflections* 6 (1979): 421–43.

———. "Paternalism, Patriarchy, and Afrikaans." *South African Historical Journal* 32 (1995): 34–47.

———. "The Rule of Law at the Cape of Good Hope in the Eighteenth Century." *Journal of Imperial and Commonwealth History* 6 (1980): 5–16.

Saks, Eva. "Representing Miscegenation Law." *Raritan* VII (1988): 39–69.

Saunders, Christopher. "Between Slavery and Freedom: The Importation of Prize Negroes to the Cape in the Aftermath of Emancipation." *Kronos* 9 (1984): 36–43.

——. "Liberated Africans in the Cape Colony in the First Half of the Nineteenth Century." *International Journal of African Historical Studies* 18 (1985): 223–35.

Scheper-Hughes, Nancy. "Culture, Society, and Maternal Thinking: Maternal Detachment and Infant Survival in a Brazilian Shantytown." *Ethos* 13 (1985): 291–317.

Scott, Joan. "The Evidence of Experience." *Critical Enquiry* 17 (Summer 1991): 773–97.

Scott, Rebecca. "Exploring the Meaning of Freedom." *Hispanic American Historical Review* 68 (August 1988): 407–488.

——. "The Battle over the Child: Child Apprenticeship and the Freedman's Bureau in North Carolina." *Prologue* (Summer 1978): 101–113.

Scully, Pamela. "Criminality and Conflict in Rural Stellenbosch, South Africa, 1870–1900." *Journal of African History* 30 (1989): 289–300.

——. "Rape, Race, and Colonial Culture: The Sexual Politics of Identity in the Nineteenth-Century Cape Colony, South Africa." *American Historical Review* 100 (April 1995): 335–59.

——. "Narratives of Infanticide in the Aftermath of Slave Emancipation in the Nineteenth-Century Cape Colony, South Africa." *Canadian Journal of African Studies*, Special Issue on Wicked Women, Wayward Wives, and the Reconfiguration of Gender, 30, 1 (1996): 88–105.

Sharpe, Jenny. "The Unspeakable Limits of Rape: Colonial Violence and Counter-Insurgency." *Genders* 10 (Spring 1991): 25–46.

Shell, Robert. "A Family Matter: The Sale and Transfer of Human Beings at the Cape, 1658–1830." *International Journal of African Historical Studies* 25 (1992): 285–336.

Spivak, Gayatri Chakravorty. "Three Women's Texts and a Critique of Imperialism." *Critical Inquiry* 12 (Autumn 1985): 243–61.

Stanley, Amy Dru. "Conjugal Bonds and Wage Labor: Rights of Contract in the Age of Emancipation." *Journal of American History* 75, 2 (September 1988): 471–500.

Stoler, Ann. "Making Empire Respectable: The Politics of Race and Sexual Morality in Twentieth-Century Colonial Cultures." *American Ethnologist* 16 (1989): 634–60.

——. "Rethinking Colonial Categories: European Communities and the Boundaries of Rule." *Comparative Studies in Society and History* 13 (1989): 134–61.

——. "Sexual Affronts and Racial Frontiers: European Identities and the Cultural Politics of Exclusion in Colonial Southeast Asia." *Comparative Studies in Society and History* 34 (1992): 514–51.

Stoler, Ann, and Frederick Cooper. "Tensions of Empire: Colonial Control and Visions of Rule." *American Ethnologist* 16 (November 1989): 609–621.

Trapido, Stanley. "From Paternalism to Liberalism: The Cape Colony, 1800–1834." *International History Review* 13 (February 1990): 76–104.

Van der Spuy, Patricia. "Slave Women and the Family in Nineteenth-Century Cape Town." *South African Historical Journal* 27 (1992): 50–74.

Ward, Kerry. "The Road to Mamre: Migration and Community in Countryside and City in the Early Twentieth Century." *South African Historical Journal* 27 (1992): 198–224.

Women's History Review. Special Edition on Feminism and Empire. 3, 4 (1994): 483–500.

Women in South African History. 1 (January 1981): 1–24.

Books and Chapters in Books

Adepoju, Aderanti, and Christine Oppong, eds. *Gender, Work, and Population in Sub-Saharan Africa.* Portsmouth, NH: Heinemann, 1994.

Alloulah, Malek. *The Colonial Harem.* Translated by Myrna Godzich and Wlad Godzich, with an introduction by Barbara Harlow. Minneapolis: University of Minnesota Press, 1986.

Balie, Isaac. *Die Geskiedenis van Genadendal 1738–1988.* Cape Town: Perskor, 1988.

Ballhatchet, Kenneth. *Race, Sex, and Class Under the Raj: Imperial Attitudes and Policies and Their Critics 1793–1905.* New York: St. Martin's Press, 1980.

Bank, Andrew. *The Decline of Urban Slavery at the Cape, 1806–1843.* Communications No 22. Cape Town: University of Cape Town, Center for African Studies, 1991.

Barrett, Michele. *Women's Oppression Today: Problems in Marxist Feminist Analysis.* London: New Left Books, 1980.

Beinart, William, Peter Delius, and Stanley Trapido, eds. *Putting a Plough to the Ground: Accumulation and Dispossession in Rural South Africa 1850–1930.* Johannesburg: Ravan Press, 1986.

Blackburn, Robin. *The Overthrow of Colonial Slavery.* London: Verso, 1988.

Boserup, Ester. *Women in Economic Development.* London: Allen and Unwin, 1970.

Boswell, John. *The Kindness of Strangers: The Abandonment of Children in Western Europe from Late Antiquity to the Renaissance.* New York: Pantheon Books, 1988.

Botha, Graham. *Collected Works: General History and Social Life at the Cape of Good Hope.* Vol. 1: Cape History and Social Life. Cape Town: Struik, 1962.

Bourdieu, Pierre. *Outline of a Theory of Practice.* New York: Cambridge University Press, 1977.

Bush, Barbara. *Slave Women in Caribbean Society, 1650–1838.* Bloomington: Indiana University Press, 1990.

Clark, Anna. *Women's Silence, Men's Violence: Sexual Assault in England, 1770–1845.* London: Pandora Press, 1987.

Comaroff, Jean, and John Comaroff. *Of Revelation and Revolution: Christianity, Colonialism, and Consciousness in South Africa.* Vol. 1. Chicago: University of Chicago Press, 1991.

Coontz, Stephanie. *The Social Origins of Private Life: A History of American Families 1600–1900.* London: Verso, 1988.

Cooper, Frederick. *From Slaves to Squatters: Plantation Labor and Agriculture in Zanzibar and Coastal Kenya, 1890–1925.* New Haven: Yale University Press, 1980.

Crais, Clifton C. *White Supremacy and Black Resistance in Pre-Industrial South Africa: The Making of the Colonial Order in the Eastern Cape.* Cambridge: Cambridge University Press, 1992.

Davidoff, Leonore, and Catherine Hall. *Family Fortunes: Men and Women of the English Middle Class, 1780–1850.* London: Hutchinson, 1987.

Davis, David Brion. *The Problem of Slavery in the Age of Revolution 1770–1823.* Ithaca: Cornell University Press, 1975.

——. *Slavery and Human Progress.* New York: Oxford University Press, 1984.

De Kock, Victor. *Those in Bondage: An Account of the Life of a Slave at the Cape in the Days of the Dutch East India Company.* London: George Allen and Unwin, 1950.

Dooling, Wayne. *Law and Community in a Slave Society, Stellenbosch District, South Africa, c.1760–1820.* Cape Town: University of Cape Town, Center for African Studies, 1992.

Du Toit, Andre, and Hermann Giliomee, eds. *Afrikaner Political Thought: Analysis and Documents.* Vol. 1: 1780–1850. Cape Town: David Philip, 1983.

Edwards, Isobel Eirlys. *Towards Emancipation: A Study in South African Slavery.* Cardiff: Gomerian Press, 1942.

Eisenstein, Zillah. *Capitalist Patriarchy and the Case for Socialist Feminism.* New York: Monthly Review Press, 1979.

Eldredge, Elizabeth, and Fred Morton, eds., *Slavery in South Africa: Captive Labour on the Dutch Frontier.* Boulder, Colorado: Westview Press, 1994.

Elphick, Richard. *Khoikhoi and the Founding of White South Africa.* Johannesburg: Ravan Press, 1985.

Elphick, Richard, and Hermann Giliomee, eds. *The Shaping of South African Society: 1652–1840.* 2d ed. Cape Town: Maskew Miller Longman, 1989.

Ferguson, Moira. *Subject to Others: British Women Writers and Colonial Slavery, 1670–1834.* New York: Routledge, 1992.

Flandrin, Jean-Louis. *Families in Former Times: Kinship, Household, and Sexuality in Early Modern France.* Translated by Richard Southern. Librairie Hachette 1976; Cambridge: Cambridge University Press, 1979.

Foucault, Michel. *Discipline and Punish: The Birth of the Prison*. Translated by Alan Sheridan. New York: Vintage Books, 1982.
——. *History of Sexuality: An Introduction*. Vol. 1. New York: Vintage Books, 1990.
Fraser, Nancy. *Unruly Practices: Power, Discourse, and Gender in Contemporary Social Theory*. Minneapolis: University of Minnesota Press, 1988.
Giddens, Anthony. *Central Problems in Social Theory*. Berkeley: University of California Press, 1979.
Gilman, Sander L. *Difference and Pathology: Stereotypes of Sexuality, Race, and Madness*. Ithaca: Cornell University Press, 1985.
Glassman, Jonathon. *Feasts and Riot: Revelry, Rebellion, and Popular Consciousness on the Swahili Coast, 1856–1888*. Portsmouth, NH: Heinemann, 1995.
Green, William A. *British Slave Emancipation: The Sugar Colonies and the Great Experiment, 1830–1865*. 1976; Reprint, Oxford: Clarendon Press, 1987.
Greene, Sandra. *Gender, Ethnicity, and Social Change on the Upper Slave Coast: A History of the Anlo-Ewe*. Portsmouth, NH: Heinemann, 1996.
Grossberg, Lawrence, et al., eds. *Cultural Studies*. New York: Routledge, 1992.
Gutman, Herbert G. *The Black Family in Slavery and Freedom 1750–1925*. New York: Vintage Books, 1977.
Hafkin, Nancy J., and Edna G. Bay. *Women in Africa: Studies in Social and Economic Change*. Stanford: Stanford University Press, 1976.
Halbersleben, Karen. *Women's Participation in the British Antislavery Movement 1824–1865*. Lewiston, ME: Edwin Mellen Press, 1993.
Hall, Catherine. *White, Male, and Middle Class: Explorations in Feminism and History*. New York: Routledge, 1992.
Harlow, Vincent, and F. Madden. *British Colonial Developments, 1774–1834*. Oxford: Oxford University Press, 1953.
Hay, Douglas, et al. *Albion's Fatal Tree: Crime and Society in Eighteenth-Century England*. New York: Pantheon Books, 1975.
Heese, J. A. *Nederduitse Gereformeerde Kerk: Gedenkboek Worcester*. Worcester: Nederduitse Gereformeerde Kerk, 1970.
Holt, Thomas C. *The Problem of Freedom: Race, Labor, and Politics in Jamaica and Britain, 1832–1938*. Baltimore: The Johns Hopkins University Press, 1992.
Hunt, Lynn, ed. *The New Cultural History*. Berkeley and Los Angeles: University of California Press, 1989.
Hurwitz, Edith F. *Politics and the Public Conscience*. London: George Allen and Unwin, 1973.
Inglis, Amirah. *The White Women's Protection Ordinance: Sexual Anxiety and Politics in Papua*. London. Sussex University Press, 1975.
James, Wilmot G., and Mary Simons, eds. *The Angry Divide: Social and Economic History of the Western Cape*. Cape Town: David Philip, 1989.
Jones, Jacqueline. *Labor of Love, Labor of Sorrow: Black Women, Work and the Family from Slavery to the Present*. New York: Basic Books, 1985.
Klein, Martin, ed. *Breaking the Chains: Slavery, Bondage, and Emancipation in Modern Africa and Asia*. Madison: University of Wisconsin Press, 1993.
Kruger, Bernhard. *The Pear Tree Blossoms: The History of the Moravian Church in South Africa, 1737–1869*. Genadendal: Genadendal Printing Works, 1966.
Landes, Joan. *Women and the Public Sphere in the Age of the French Revolution*. Ithaca: Cornell University Press, 1988.
Litwack, Leon F. *Been in the Storm So Long: The Aftermath of Slavery*. New York: Alfred A. Knopf, 1979.
Lovejoy, Paul. *Transformations in Slavery: A History of Slavery in Africa*. Cambridge: Cambridge University Press, 1983.
Lovett, Richard. *The History of the London Missionary Society 1795–1895*. 2 vols. London: Oxford University Press, 1899.

Mandala, Elias. *Work and Control in a Peasant Economy: A History of the Lower Tchiri Valley in Malawi, 1859–1960.* Madison: University of Wisconsin Press, 1990.

Marais, Johannes Stephanus. *The Cape Coloured People, 1652–1937.* New York: AMS Press; Longmans, Green and Co, 1939.

Marks, Shula, and Anthony Atmore, eds. *Economy and Society in Pre-Industrial South Africa.* Harlow, UK: Longman, 1980.

Marks, Shula, and Stanley Trapido, eds. *The Politics of Race, Class and Nationalism in Twentieth-Century South Africa.* London: Longman, 1987.

Martinez-Alier, Verena. *Marriage, Class and Colour in Nineteenth-Century Cuba: A Study of Racial Attitudes and Sexual Values in a Slave Society.* Cambridge: Cambridge University Press, 1974; Ann Arbor: University of Michigan Press, 1989.

Medick, Hans, and David Warren Sabean, eds. *Interest and Emotion: Essays on the Study of Family and Kinship.* Cambridge: Cambridge University Press, 1977.

Midgley, Clare. *Women Against Slavery: The British Campaigns, 1780–1870.* London: Routledge, 1991.

Miers, Suzanne, and Igor Kopytoff, eds. *Slavery in Africa: Historiographical and Anthropological Perspectives.* Madison: University of Wisconsin Press, 1977.

Miers, Suzanne, and Richard Roberts, eds. *The Ending of Slavery in Africa.* Madison: University of Wisconsin Press, 1988.

Nicholson, Linda J. *Gender and History: The Limits of Social Theory in the Age of the Family.* New York: Columbia University Press, 1986.

Oakes, James. *Slavery and Freedom: An Interpretation of the Old South.* New York: Knopf, 1990.

Painter, Nell Irvin. "Soul Murder and Slavery: Toward a Fully-Loaded Cost Accounting." In Linda Kerber et al., eds., *U.S History as Women's History: New Feminist Essays.* Chapel Hill: University of North Carolina Press, 1995.

Pateman, Carole. *The Sexual Contract.* Stanford: Stanford University Press, 1988.

Patterson, Orlando. *Slavery and Social Death: A Comparative Study.* Cambridge: Harvard University Press, 1982.

Poovey, Mary. "Domesticity and Class Formation: Chadwick's '1842 Sanitary Report.'" In David Simpson, ed., *Subject to History: Ideology, Class, Gender.* Ithaca: Cornell University Press, 1991.

——. *Uneven Developments: The Ideological Work of Gender in Mid-Victorian England.* Chicago: University of Chicago Press, 1988.

Riley, Denise. *"Am I That Name?" Feminism and the Category of 'Women' in History.* Minneapolis: University of Minnesota Press, 1988.

Robertson, Claire, and Martin Klein, eds. *Women and Slavery in Africa.* Madison: University of Wisconsin Press, 1983.

Rose, Lionel. *The Massacre of the Innocents: Infanticide in Britain 1800–1939.* London: Routledge and Keegan Paul, 1986.

Ross, Andrew. *John Philip (1775–1851): Missions, Race, and Politics in South Africa.* Aberdeen: Aberdeen University Press, 1986.

Ross, Robert. *Beyond the Pale: Essays on the History of Colonial South Africa.* Hanover: Wesleyan University Press, University of New England Press, 1993.

——.*Cape of Torments: Slavery and Resistance in South Africa.* London: Routledge and Keegan Paul, 1983.

Sachs, Albie. *Justice in South Africa.* Berkeley: University of California Press, 1973.

Sacks, Karen. *Sisters and Wives: The Past and Future of Sexual Inequality.* Urbana: University of Illinois Press, 1979.

Sayles, Jane. *Mission Stations and the Coloured Communities of the Eastern Cape, 1800–1852.* Cape Town: A. A.Balkema, 1975.

Schapera, Isaac. *The Khoisan Peoples of South Africa.* Reprint. London: Routledge and Keegan Paul, 1960.

Schmidt, Elizabeth. *Peasants, Traders, and Wives: Shona Women in the History of Zimbabwe 1870–1939*. Portsmouth, NH: Heinemann, 1992.

Scott, Joan. *Gender and the Politics of History.* New York: Columbia University Press, 1988.

Scott, Rebecca. *Slave Emancipation in Cuba: The Transition to Free Labor, 1860–1899*. Princeton: Princeton University Press, 1985.

Scully, Pamela. *The Bouquet of Freedom: Social and Economic Relations in the Stellenbosch District, c. 1870–1900*. Communications No. 17. Cape Town: Center for African Studies, University of Cape Town., 1990

———."Liquor and Labor in the Western Cape." In Jonathan Crush and Charles Ambler, eds., *Liquor and Labor in Southern Africa*. Athens, OH: Ohio University Press, 1993.

Shanley, Mary Lyndon. *Feminism, Marriage, and the Law in Victorian England, 1850–1895*. Princeton: Princeton University Press, 1989.

Shell, Robert C.-H. *Children of Bondage: A Social History of the Slave Society at the Cape of Good Hope, 1652–1838*. Hanover: Wesleyan University Press; University Press of New England, 1994.

Spivak, Gayatri Chakravorty. "Can the Subaltern Speak?" In Cary Nelson and Lawrence Grossberg, eds., *Marxism and the Interpretation of Culture*. Urbana: University of Illinois Press, 1988.

Snitow, Ann, Christine Stansell, and Sharon Thompson, eds. *Powers of Desire: The Politics of Sexuality*. New York: Monthly Review Press, 1983.

Steedman, Carolyn. *Landscape for a Good Woman: A Story of Two Lives*. New Brunswick, NJ: Rutgers University Press, 1986.

Stoler, Ann Laura. *Carnal Knowledge and Imperial Power: Bourgeois Civilities and the Cultures of Whiteness*. Berkeley: University of California Press, forthcoming.

———.*Race and the Education of Desire: Foucault's History of Sexuality and the Colonial Order of Things*. Durham, NC: Duke University Press, 1995.

Strassberger, Elfriede. *The Rhenish Mission Society in South Africa, 1830–1950*. Cape Town: Struik, 1969.

Strobel, Margaret. *Muslim Women in Mombasa, 1890–1975*. New Haven: Yale University Press, 1979.

Taylor, Barbara. *Eve and the New Jerusalem*. New York. Pantheon, 1983.

Taylor, Jean. *The Social World of Batavia*. Madison: University of Wisconsin Press, 1983.

Temperley, Howard. *British Antislavery 1833–1870*. London: Longman, 1972.

Thompson, F. M. L. *The Rise of Respectable Society: A Social History of Victorian Britain, 1830–1900*. Cambridge: Harvard University Press, 1988.

Tilly, Louise, and Joan Scott. *Women, Work, and Family.* 2d ed. New York: Routledge, 1989.

Turley, David. *The Culture of Antislavery, 1780–1860*. London: Routledge, 1991.

Van der Linden, Johannes. *Institutes of Holland, or Manual of Law, Practice, and Mercantile Law, for the Use of Judges, Lawyers, Merchants and All Who Wish to Have a General View of the Law*. Cape Town, 1806; 5th ed., Cape Town: J. C. Juta and Co., 1906.

Van der Merwe, P. J. *The Migrant Farmer in the History of the Cape Colony, 1657–1842*. Translated by Roger B. Beck. Athens, OH: Ohio University Press, 1995.

Walkowitz, Judith. *City of Dreadful Delight: Narratives of Sexual Danger in Late-Victorian London*. Chicago: University of Chicago Press, 1992.

———.*Prostitution and Victorian Society: Women, Class, and the State*. Cambridge: Cambridge University Press, 1980.

Walvin, James, ed. *Slavery and British Society, 1776–1846*. Baton Rouge: Louisiana State University Press, 1982.

Ware, Vron. *Beyond the Pale: White Women, Racism, and History.* London: Verso, 1992.

Watson, Robert L. *The Slave Question*. Hanover: University Press of New England, 1990.

Weeks, Jeffrey. *Sex, Politics, and Society: The Regulation of Sexuality Since 1800*. London: Longman, 1981.

White, Deborah Gray. *Ar'n't I a Woman?: Female Slaves in the Plantation South*. New York: W. W. Norton and Co., 1985.

Worden, Nigel. *Slavery in Dutch South Africa*. Cambridge: Cambridge University Press, 1985.

Worden, Nigel, and Clifton C. Crais, eds. *Breaking the Chains: Slavery and its Legacy in the Nineteenth-Century Cape Colony.* Johannesburg: University of the Witwatersrand Press, 1994.

Wright, Marcia. *Strategies of Slaves and Women: Life Stories from East/Central Africa*. New York: Lilian Barber Press, 1993.

Unpublished Papers and Dissertations

Bank, Andrew. "Crime in Cape Town, 1890 to 1900." B.A. Hons. diss., History Department, University of Cape Town, 1989.

——."Liberals and Their Enemies: Racial Ideology at the Cape of Good Hope, 1820–1850." Ph.D. thesis, Cambridge University, 1995.

Boddington, Erica. "Domestic Service: Changing Relations of Class Domination 1841–1948: A Focus on Cape Town." M.Soc.Sci. diss., University of Cape Town, 1983.

Buffington, Sean. "After the Riot: Social Relations and Ideologies in Metcalfe Parish, Jamaica, 1866–1871." Paper presented to the Conference on Postemancipation Societies and Race, University of Michigan, April 1993.

Crais, Clifton C. "Race, the State, and the Silence of History in the Making of Modern South Africa." Paper presented at the African Studies Association Meeting, Seattle, November 1992.

Dooling, Wayne. "Slaves, Slaveholders, and Amelioration in Graaff-Reinet, 1823–1830." B.A.Hons. diss., Department of History, University of Cape Town, 1989.

Edwards, Laura F. "Sexual Violence and Political Struggle: Finding Women in Reconstruction Politics." Paper presented at the Ninth Berkshire Conference on the History of Women, New York, June 1993.

Elbourne, Elizabeth. "'To Colonize the Mind': Evangelicals in Britain and the Eastern Cape, 1790–1836." Ph.D. diss., Oxford University, 1992.

Hengherr, E. "Emancipation and After: A Study of Cape Slavery and the Issues Arising from It, 1830–1843." M.A. diss., University of Cape Town, 1953.

Hodgson, Dorothy. "The Politics of Gender, Ethnicity, and Development: Images, Interventions and The Reconfiguration of Maasai Identities in Tanzania, 1916–1993." Ph.D. diss., University of Michigan, 1995.

Ludlow, Elizabeth Helen. "Missions and Emancipation in the South Western Cape: A Case Study of Groenekloof (Mamre), 1838–1852." M.A. diss., University of Cape Town, 1992.

Marincowitz, John Carel. "Proletarians, Privatisers, and Public Property Rights: Mission Land Regulations in the Western Cape." Paper presented to the African History Seminar of the Institute for Commonwealth Studies, SOAS, University of London, 23 January 1985.

——."Rural Production and Labour in the Western Cape, with Special Reference to the Wheat Growing Districts, 1838–1888." Ph.D. diss., University of London, 1985.

Mason, John Edwin. "'Fit for Freedom': The Slaves, Slavery, and Emancipation in the Cape Colony, South Africa, 1806–1842." 2 vols. Ph.D. diss., Yale University, 1992.

Midgley, Clare. "The Gender of Politics and the Gender Politics of History: Interpreting the Involvement of Women in the Anti-slavery Movement in Nineteenth-Century Britain." Paper presented at University of California, Berkeley, April 1990.

Pierce, Steven. "Unseemly Habits: Slavery, Indirect Rule, Islamic Law, and Emancipation in the Sokoto Caliphate." Paper presented to the Postemancipation Societies Conference, University of Michigan, April 30–May 1 1993.

Raum, Johannes. "The Development of the Coloured Community at Genadendal Under the Influence of the Missionaries of the Unitas Fratum 1792–1892." M.A. diss., University of Cape Town, 1952.

Rayner, Mary Isabel. "Wine and Slaves: The Failure of an Export Economy and the Ending of Slavery in the Cape Colony, South Africa, 1806–1834." Ph.D. diss., Duke University.

Rosen, Hanna. 1990. "Sexual Violence in the Era of Reconstruction." Paper presented at the Postemancipation Workshop, University of Michigan, April 1986.

Ross, Robert. "The Roman Dutch Law of Inheritance, Landed Property, and the Afrikaner Family Structure." Paper presented at the Conference on the History of the Family in Africa, London, September 1981.

Scully, Pamela. "Liberating the Family?: Some Thoughts on Emancipation in the Rural Western Cape, 1830–1870." Paper presented at the Cape Slavery and After Conference, Department of History, University of Cape Town, August 1989.

——."Gender, Emancipation, and Free Wage Labor Ideology: The Cape Colony, 1830–1860." Paper presented at the Graduate Women's Studies Conference, University of Michigan, March 1991.

Thorne, Susan. "Protestant Ethics and the Spirit of Imperialism: British Congregationalists and the London Missionary Society, 1795–1925." Ph.D. diss., University of Michigan, 1990.

Van der Spuy, Patricia. "A Collection of Discrete Essays with the Common Theme of Gender and Slavery at the Cape of Good Hope with a Focus on the 1820s." M.A. diss., University of Cape Town, 1993.

——."The Involvement of Women in Violent Crime as Processed by the Institutions of Justice in Cape Town 1860–1879." B.A. Hons. diss., History Department, University of Cape Town 1989.

Van Ryneveld, T. A. "Merchants and Missions: Developments in the Caledon District, 1838–1850." B.A.Hons. diss., Department of History, University of Cape Town, 1983.

Ward, Kerry. "The Road to Mamre: Migration, Memory, and the Meaning of Community c. 1900–1992." M.A. diss., University of Cape Town, 1992.

Worden, Nigel. "Cape Slave Emancipation and Rural Labour in a Comparative Context." Paper presented at the Africa Seminar, Center for African Studies, University of Cape Town, 1983.

INDEX

abolition of slavery, 111, 113,
  celebration of, 181
  See also Abolition Act; abolitionists;
    British antislavery movement;
    emancipation
Abolition Act (1833), 14, 46, 49, 179
  and indenture of apprentices' children,
    49–50, 52, 53, 54, 55, 58
  and affirmation of motherhood, 56
abolitionists, 3, 49, 87,
  gender ideologies of, 1, 5–9, 34–38, 45, 82,
    179
  and promotion of morality, 109,
  views of women's sexuality, 57
  women, 49
  See also immorality; family; marriage;
    wage labor
adoption, 66, 99–100,
African history
  relationship of Western Cape to, 9–11, 26
agriculture, 20, 41, 59, 74, 88–92, 97–98,
  158
Alexander, David Fredricks, 73–74, 123
amelioration, 14, 34–46,
  Cape government resistance to, 40
  See also protector of slaves; assistant
    protectors of slaves
antiliberalism, 35
Anti-Slavery Monthly Reporter, 36, 39
Anti-Slavery Reporter, 42, 45
Anti-Slavery Society, 34, 38, 49
apprentices, 24, 48–51, 64, 118
  as parents, 49, 53, 68
  labor of, 51
  See also apprenticeship period; family
apprenticeship, 9, 87–89
  changing meanings of, 98–99
apprenticeship period, 2, 7, 15, 23, 34, 46, 47,
  49–51, 53, 67, 82, 83, 167, 180
  mothers and, 48–49
  See also family; indentureship; neoslavery
architecture, 127–132

archives,
  construction of, 12–13, 125, 126, 130–131,
    137, 165, 169, 174
artistans, 31, 95, 96, 98, 99, 148
  marriage of, 123, 124, 126
assistant protector of slaves, 29, 32, 39, 43–45,
  50
attorney general, 54, 57, 65, 71, 115, 127, 163
  and apprenticeship of children, 54, 65,
    102–104,
  and infanticide, 143, 144, 149, 151–153
  law and, 84, 111, 132–133
  views of women, 57
  See also Porter, William.
August, Elizabeth, 137, 143–144, 145, 148,
  150–152
  See also infanticide

Bank, Andrew, 5
baptism, 38, 73, 76n, 77,
  marriage and, 111, 113, 115, 123,
  women and, 141
Bastards, 13, 19, 27, 157
  land and, 70, 71
  See also coloured
Bastard Hottentots, 13, 19, 27, 70, 157, 159,
  173, 176
  See also coloured
Barrow, Sir John, 24, 26
body, 138
  gendered, 3
  power and the, 149, 153, 169
boundaries,
  and production of colonial culture, 19,
    24–30, 93–94, 131, 171–172, 177
  mobility across farm and district 33, 51,
    76, 124, 139
  race and, 8, 125, 171, 172
Britain, 4–7, 35, 42, 49, 86, 112, 161, 163, 173
British Antislavery movement, 116
  Cape Colony and, 5, 6, 173
  history of, 34